KOH - I - NOOR

One fabulous diamond whose value could feed the entire world for two-and-a-half days. Four races: Indian, Afghan, Persian and English, whose destinies were inextricably involved with this gem. A Persian oilman's son who went on to virtually rule Golconda and its vast diamond mines. A Mughal prince, hated by history, who was sinned against as much as sinning. Only an Indian or a Persian could tell this great story with all its nuances.

IRADJ AMINI was born in 1935 in Iran and studied in Teheran, Oxford and the U.S.A. He was the Shah of Iran's last ambassador to Tunisia and has authored a book on Napoleon and Persia for the Napoleon Foundation. Iradj Amini lives in exile in Paris and overcomes his nostalgia for Persia by visiting India frequently and by writing on Indian history. He is particularly fascinated by Maharaja Ranjit Singh.

THE KOH-I-NOOR DIAMOND

OTHER LOTUS TITLES

ANIL K. JAGGIA & SAURABH SHUKLA	*IC 814: Hijacked! The Inside Story*
ARJAN SINGH	*Arjan Singh's Tiger Book*
CLAUDIA PRECKEL	*Begums of Bhopal*
DHANANJAYA SINGH	*The House of Marwar*
E. JAIWANT PAUL	*'By My Sword and Shield'*
E. JAIWANT PAUL	*Baji Rao – The Warrior Peshwa*
GERALDINE FORBES (ed.)	*The Memoirs of Dr. Haimabati Sen*
INDIRA MENON	*The Madras Quartet*
J.C. WADHAWAN	*Manto Naama*
JOHN LALL	*Begam Samru*
JYOTI JAFA	*Really, Your Highness!*
KHUSHWANT SINGH	*Kipling's India*
KANWALBIR PUSHPENDRA SINGH	*The Ruse*
K.M. GEORGE	*The Best of Thakazhi Sivasankara Pillai*
LAKSHMI SUBRAMANIAN	*Medieval Seafarers*
MANOHAR MALGONKAR	*Dropping Names*
MAURA MOYNIHAN	*Masterji and Other Stories*
MUSHIRUL HASAN	*India Partitioned*. 2 vols
MUSHIRUL HASAN	*John Company to the Republic*
NAMITA GOKHALE	*Mountain Echoes*
NINA EPTON	*Mumtaz Mahal: Beloved Empress*
P. LAL	*The Bhagavad Gita*
RALPH RUSSELL	*The Famous Ghalib*
ROMESH BHANDARI	*Goa*
RUSKIN BOND	*Ruskin Bond's Green Book*
SHOVANA NARAYAN	*Rhythmic Echoes and Reflections: Kathak*
SUDHIR KAKAR (ed.)	*Indian Love Stories*
V.S. NARAVANE (ed.)	*Devdas and Other Stories by Sarat Chandra*

FORTHCOMING TITLES

E. JAIWANT PAUL	*The Tea Story*
SUMATI MUTATKAR	*Shri Krishna Narayan Ratanjankar*
DHANALAKSHMI FORDYCE	*Purna Ghata*
SUJATA S. SABNIS	*A Twist in Destiny*

The Koh-i-noor Diamond

IRADJ AMINI

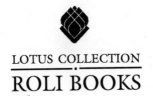

LOTUS COLLECTION
ROLI BOOKS

Lotus Collection

First English edition published 1994
Reprinted 2001
The Lotus Collection
An imprint of
Roli Books Pvt Ltd
M-75, G.K. II Market
New Delhi 110 048
Phones: 6442271, 6462782, 6460886
Fax: 6467185, 6213978
E-mail: roli@vsnl.com, Website: rolibooks.com
Also at
Varanasi, Agra, Jaipur and the Netherlands

ISBN: 81-7436-027-1
Rs. 175.00

Cover: *Maharaja Dalip Singh. "I was but a child, an infant, when forced to surrender the Koh-i-noor but now I am a man . . ."*

Typeset in Galliard by Roli Books Pvt Ltd and
printed at Pritha Offsets Pvt Ltd, New Delhi-110 028

THE KOH-I-NOOR'S TRAVELS: Who acquired it, when, how?

	INDIA	PERSIA	AFGHANISTAN	ENGLAND
BABUR'S DIAMOND	Arjuna's Samantik Mani?			
	Raja Bikramajit of Gwalior			
	Humayun (May 1526, gift, Bikramajit's family)			
		Shah Tahmasp (July 1544, gift, Humayun)		
	Mahtar Jamal (envoy, from Shah Tahmasp to Sultan of Ahmadnagar, 1547, sold?)			
KOH-I-NOOR	Mir Jumla (*c.* 1650, bought?)			
	Shah Jahan (gift, Mir Jumla, 8 July 1656)			
	Mohammed Shah 'Rangila' (1719, Mughal legacy)			
		Nadir Shah Afshar (1 May 1739, stratagem, Mohammed Shah)		
			Ahmed Shah Adbali (17 June 1747, Nadir Shah's deathbed?)	
			Timur Shah (October 1777, legacy, father Ahmed Shah)	
			Shah Shuja (July 1803, conquest)	
	Ranjit Singh (1 June 1813, ransom, Shah Shuja)			
	The East India Company (April 1849, conquest)			
				Queen Victoria (3 July 1850, gift, Lord Dalhousie)

'John Lawrence hated the conventionalities of life and had no use for jewels . . . he stuffed the box containing the Koh-i-noor into his waistcoat pocket and went about his business.

About six weeks afterwards, when Lord Dalhousie asked for the diamond to send to Queen Victoria, Lawrence was horrified.

He went to his room, his heart pounding wildly, and asked his old Indian bearer if he had found a small box in his waistcoat pocket.

"Yes Sahib, I found it and put it in one of your boxes."

"Bring it here."

The bearer did so, and he held it out for John Lawrence who heard a huge sigh of relief.

The bearer observed with astonishment: "There is nothing here, Sahib, but a bit of glass!" '

CONTENTS

Babur, the first of the Timurids who conquered India. His name will always be linked to the Koh-i-noor for it is in his memoirs that the stone first finds mention.

PREFACE

On 29 June 1850, HMS *Medea,* a warship flying the British flag, docked at a deserted quay in Portsmouth, ending a long journey that had begun in Bombay on 6 April, the previous year. Apart from the crew, there were only two passengers on board: Captain Ramsay, aide-de-camp to the Marquis of Dalhousie, Governor General of India, and Lieutenant Colonel Mackeson, Dalhousie's liaison officer with the British expeditionary corps in the Punjab.

All the *Medea* carried was a packet so tiny, it could easily be slipped into a pocket. Only Captain Ramsay and Colonel Mackeson knew what it contained. Several days later the press at last lifted the veil of secrecy: the ship's "cargo" was none other than the Koh-i-noor, a fabulous diamond due to be presented to Queen Victoria by the Directors of the East India Company. The ceremony was to take place at four o'clock on the afternoon of 3 July at Buckingham Palace.

On 29 March 1849, Dalip Singh, the young Maharaja of the Punjab, had ratified the instrument surrendering his state to the British. Article Three of this document provided for the Koh-i-noor ("Mountain of Light"), one of the most famous diamonds in the world, to be handed to Queen Victoria.

Dalhousie wrote to his sovereign: "Formerly placed in the throne of the Emperors of Delhi; captured there in his invasion by Nader Shah—thence transferred to the Kings of Kabul and extorted from Shah Shuja by the Maharaja Ranjit Singh, the Koh-i-noor may be regarded as a historical symbol of conquest in India, and the Governor General rejoices that it has found its fitting rest in Your Majesty's Crown."

But in fact, the Koh-i-noor has never adorned the crown of a ruling British monarch, perhaps because it was reputed to bring ill luck, though legend has it that only men were affected. After the stone was displayed at the Great Exhibition in London in 1851, it was re-cut and set in one of Queen Victoria's tiaras, the crown of Queen Mary, and finally in 1937, the crown of Elizabeth, the present Queen Mother.

Today the Koh-i-noor is neither the biggest nor the most beautiful diamond known. Several stones—the Cullinan (the "Great Star of Africa", now in the British sceptre), the Regent (on view at the Louvre) and the Orlov (at the Kremlin), to mention only the most famous—are bigger and brighter. But the Koh-i-noor is the most romantic of them all, for each one of its glittering facets reflects a colourful and often violent episode in Indian, Persian, Afghan, and British history and evokes the life of the people who took part in those stirring events.

Ever since the Koh-i-noor found its way to England, countless writers have speculated about its origin. Some said it went back to the beginning of time; others dated it from the appearance of the Mughal dynasty in India, or believed it first emerged at the time of Shah Jahan. Was it the same as the Samantik Mani, the diamond that adorned the bracelet of Karna and Arjuna, legendary heroes of the *Mahabharata*? Or was it "Babur's diamond", as most historians and mineralogists seem to think? It might even be the "Great Mughal", the enormous stone that the French traveller and jeweller Jean-Baptiste Tavernier saw in the court of the Emperor Aurangzeb in 1665.

Much still remains unknown. We can speak of the Koh-i-noor's history with certainty only after it became known by that name in 1739, though there is no doubt that its origins go back much further, to the coming of the Timurid dynasty in India, better known as the Mughal.

To behold the first flash of the Koh-i-noor in recorded history, the reader must accordingly go back to the early sixteenth century, when Zahir-ud-din Mohammed Babur, King of Kabul, was preparing to conquer the fabled land of Hindustan . . .

BABUR'S DIAMOND

CHAPTER ONE

The Koh-i-noor never really belonged to Zahir-ud-din Mohammed Babur: a fleeting touch is all he can ever have had of it. But his name will always be linked to this legendary diamond because it is his memoirs that first mention the stone, and long before it was immortalised as the Koh-i-noor, it was already known as Babur's diamond. Who then was this man?

Babur—derived from "babr", or "tiger" in Persian—was born in Andijan, capital of the small kingdom of Farghana, on 14 February 1483. His father, Umar Sheikh Mirza, the reigning sovereign, was the great-great-grandson of Timur or Tamerlane, who himself belonged to the Barlas clan of Turkish origin from Transoxiana. Babur's mother, Qutluq Nigar Khanum, the daughter of the Khan of Mongolistan, was of Mongol stock and a descendant of Chagatai, the second son of Chengiz Khan. Of all his ancestors, Babur favoured Timur. Therefore, he would have been furious had he guessed that posterity would regard him as the founder of the Mughal, not the Timurid dynasty.

The kingdom of Farghana occupied a valley within the lofty mountain range of the Tian-Shan, watered by the Syr Darya, (the Jaxartes of antiquity), bordering on Uzbekistan, Kirghizistan and Tajikistan, and linked by a winding road to Samarkand. Farghana was once part of Timur's empire, which stretched in its heyday from Anatolia to Chinese Turkistan and from the Himalayas to the lower reaches of the Indus. But the empire could not survive the death of its founder on 19 January 1405, and by the time Babur was born all that remained of Timur's heritage was a mosaic of independent states, plagued by the jealous rivalries of his successors.

To the south-west of Farghana lay Transoxiana, the region situated between the Amu-Darya (Oxus) and the Syr-Darya, with the incomparable city of Samarkand as its capital. Three of Babur's uncles ruled over Samarkand, Badakshan and Kabul, but it was Sultan Hussain-i-Baikara, the Badshah of Herat and Babur's third cousin, who was *primus inter pares* and most powerful of all the Timurid princes. A man of great culture and a talented poet, he made Herat the centre of Timurid renaissance. It was there that men of letters, poets, historians, painters, musicians and architects flocked to seek inspiration and patronage.

In the north-west, to the east of Farghana, lived Babur's maternal relations, chiefs of Mongol tribes descending from Chengiz Khan through his son Chagatai. One of his uncles, Mahmud Khan, who had given up his nomadic ways, ruled over the city of Tashkent, while another, Ahmad Khan, "trained to the rude existence of prairies and tents, lacking in refinement, coarse of language, a redoubtable swordsman", camped on the vast steppes near China.

Finally, the Uzbeks dominated the territories situated to the north of Tashkent; their chief, Mohammed Shaibani Khan, also a descendant of Chengiz Khan from his grandson Shaiban, was to become Babur's bête noire.

It was in this environment that the future founder of the Mughal dynasty grew up. His training—both physical and intellectual—was evidently of a very high standard. This is amply borne out by his exploits on the battlefield and his literary works. Among the latter are his memoirs, the elegantly written *Babur Nama* or *Vakiats*, an acknowledged masterpiece that is frank in its disclosures and rich in imagery.

In June 1494, when he was barely eleven years old, Babur was called upon to succeed his father, who had died in an accident. A thorny inheritance indeed! Hardly was he seated on the throne than his Mongolian and Timurid relatives began to dispute his claim, on the principle that might is right.

In the years that followed Babur fought, one by one, his uncles and cousins, both paternal and maternal, as well as his own brothers. Finally, he had to fight Shaibani Khan, the fearsome Uzbek chief, not only to preserve Farghana but also to conquer Samarkand, which he was to occupy on three occasions—in 1497, 1500 and 1512.

Samarkand was once the fabulous capital of Timur and its conquest was the dream that bewitched the young Babur. Sadly, it was a prize that would elude him time and again.

Those early years were a time of swiftly changing fortunes. He was a prince one day and a nomadic pauper the next, even reaching a point once when he and his ragtag band of fighters had to seek refuge in the mountains and survive by raiding neighbouring villages.

During this year of distress and privation, he had plenty of time to reflect on the inconstancy of supporters and the treachery of friends: "Those who still believed in me and had come with me into exile", Babur wrote later, "numbered between two and three hundred in all, young and old; most had to travel on foot, with the aid of a staff, and protected from the elements only by long cloaks and shoes of untanned leather. We were so poor we had but two tents between us. My own I gave up to my mother, and at every halt my companions rigged up an alatchuk for me." This last was a light felt tent.

In August 1504, however, Babur almost miraculously obtained the army of a Herati vassal, Khusro Shah, whom he described as a "fat, old midget" who had run out of energy and courage and was glad enough to flee to

Khorasan after handing over his army to Babur.

Babur, who had once contemplated seeking refuge himself in Herat, now turned his sights on Kabul. Though small, Kabul was strategically located on a high mountain plateau at the crossroads linking India to Persia through the Khyber Pass. Babur wrested Kabul from its ruler Mukhim Arghun who had usurped it from Babur's uncle Ulug Beg. With his suzerainty established he assumed the title of Padshah in 1507. He now had a kingdom again, at the age of twenty-two. He was to flee it once under threat of invasion by the Uzbeks which, however, passed and he re-entrenched himself in Kabul.

"His portraits", says Fernand Grenard, a latter-day French historian, "show him with a fine, long face, a well-shaped nose, a thin pointed beard under his chin and a small moustache highlighting the ironical quirk of his smile. A trace of his ancestors is to be seen in his narrow slanting eyes. But the desert has handed down to him something of much greater consequence, virtues of prime importance for his political career: independence and a spirit of opposition. When the winds of misfortune blew, he knew how to bide his time, keep his own counsel and remain firm against all odds, not in vain protest, but in order to size up the situation and take the tide of fortune at the flood."

It was therefore, as king, that Babur celebrated the birth of his first son, Humayun ("the fortunate"), born in the citadel of Kabul on 6 March 1508. The event was marked by a magnificent banquet to which all the courtiers brought gold and silver coins, according to tradition.

The child's mother—whom Babur had married in Herat in 1506—was to remain his favourite wife. Curiously enough, neither he nor anyone else speaks of her origins.

Only Abul Fazl, the friend and the panegyrist of Emperor Akbar, has vaguely recorded that she belonged to a noble family from Khorasan. Even her real name is not known. Her husband used to call her by the affectionate nickname of Maham, which means "my moon".

Humayun was to become the first Mughal owner of the Koh-i-noor. But at his birth, Babur's final conquest of India was still a long way off and he was more concerned with the dramatic arrival on the Asian political scene of a man four years younger than he: Ismail I, the founder of the Persian Safavid dynasty. Although of Turkish origin, this dynasty was to preside over the renaissance of Persian nationalism which had lain dormant for over eight-hundred-and-fifty-years.

The Venetian travellers Caterino Zeno and Angiolello have left a very vivid portrait of Ismail: "He was a handsome boy of noble bearing, as graceful as a girl, as lively as a young fawn, blond, broad-shouldered, a skilful archer, with the look of a born leader; he was quick of perception, with friendly manners and a ferocious temper. His soldiers worshipped him."

After assuming both spiritual and temporal power and brandishing the banner of Shiism, the declared state religion, Shah Ismail restored Persia to her old borders, within less than ten years. Such an enterprise made him enemies: two groups deeply attached to Sunnism, the Turks in the west and the Uzbeks in the north-west, considered him to be not just an enemy but also a heretic.

The conflict with the Uzbeks had been simmering ever since they had become masters of Khorasan and started carrying raids into Persian territory. Shaibani Khan, Babur's old enemy, having turned a deaf ear to all the Shah's protests, a showdown between the two leaders became inevitable. It took place on 2 December 1510, near Merv. Shaibani Khan, awaiting his troops, was caught off-guard by the forty-thousand-strong Persian army and was killed after a bloody battle. Shah Ismail made a drinking cup of his skull and had it mounted in gold. Then, in an act of defiance, he sent the skin of his head, stuffed with straw, to Sultan Bayazid II of Turkey, and his limbs to various Sunni rulers, including the Mameluk Sultan of Egypt.

Babur was overjoyed by the news of Shaibani Khan's defeat. He heard of it in the second half of December 1510 through a letter from his cousin and vassal Mirza Khan, the Governor of Badakshan: "I myself," wrote Mirza Khan, "went to Kunduz. Should you desire turning forthwith the reins of power in that direction, I shall join you in the firm hope that we will soon be able to recover your ancestral kingdom."

Babur didn't hesitate a second. After all, Kabul was not a choice, but a necessity. His sights were still set on Samarkand, the unfulfilled dream. Braving the rigours of the cold Afghan winter, he crossed the snow-capped Hindu Kush mountains with a small army, and reached Kunduz on 31 January 1511. An ambassador of Shah Ismail was waiting for him with an offer of friendship. Babur immediately dispatched his cousin to thank the Persian ruler and suggest an alliance against the Uzbeks, whose forces were still intact beyond the Amu-Darya, in spite of their chief's defeat. The Shah welcomed this suggestion for he wanted to safeguard his eastern border before going off on a campaign against the Ottoman Turks, at the other end of his country. He decreed that Babur would have the right to all the territories he could conquer in Transoxiana.

At this juncture, Babur had taken over Hissar Chadman, an advanced fortress on the road linking Badakshan to Transoxiana: a success which opened the prospect of a rapid recovery of the throne of Samarkand. But he still needed the support of Persian auxiliary forces. Shah Ismail granted him the troops he required.

In the early days of October 1511, having sent his allies away with abundant praise and rewards, Babur made a triumphant entry into Samarkand. It would have been hardly acceptable to the local population if their emperor, a fervent Sunni, had returned to the capital of his ancestors on the heels of a heretic army. However, the inhabitants of Samarkand were no fools. According to the historian Mirza Haydar Dughlat, a cousin of Babur, they knew perfectly well that Babur had embraced Shiism in order to achieve his ends. But they hoped that once he had mounted "the throne of the Law of the Prophet" he would go back on his apostasy. They were soon disappointed. Babur did not feel secure enough to dispense with Shah Ismail's support. This was his undoing. Eight months after having given him a hero's welcome, the people of Samarkand decided to sacrifice Babur to Ubaidullah Khan, the nephew and successor of Shaibani Khan, concluding that between a beloved apostate and a fervent, though hated Sunni, the latter was a lesser evil. Babur had to leave Samarkand for the third time.

After this loss, Babur set his sights on India, a country coveted by almost all the rulers of Kabul. Several Muslim conquerors before him had marched on India: some to plunder it, others to settle there, unable to resist the lure of India's wealth and fertility.

Babur's first three expeditions to that country across the Khyber Pass were mere forays. It was during the fourth raid in 1523 that he took Lahore, which in any case he considered as part of the Timurid legacy. He was not entirely wrong. Before leaving the Punjab, Timur had left there a governor by the name of Khizr Khan, who founded the Sayyid dynasty which ruled over Delhi and north India from 1414 to 1451. It was subsequently replaced by the Lodhis, an Afghan dynasty which was on its last legs when Babur decided to seek his fortune in India.

The reigning Sultan, Ibrahim Lodhi, had come to the throne in 1517 at the death of his father Sikander. Little did he realise that he had inherited a confederation rather than an empire. His sovereignty extended in the south-west to the borders of Bengal; near Agra he held Dholpur and Chanderi; his supremacy was recognised in the Punjab, and in the south, his influence stretched to Bundelkhand in Central India. However, his authority was merely symbolic. The reins of power were in fact held by powerful Afghan chieftains, very often relatives of the emperor, who looked upon Ibrahim as *primus inter pares* rather than as an overlord.

The first two Lodhi Sultans, Bahlol and Sikander, who were courteous and unpretentious, abided by this principle and treated their courtiers more as friends than as subjects.

But Ibrahim humiliated them, forcing them to remain standing in his presence, cross-armed, in a gesture of servility. Distrustful and cruel, at the least suspicion Ibrahim would have them locked up in a dungeon where they languished, chained to the walls of their cells. It is hardly surprising that the chief supporters of his regime, amongst whom was Daulat Khan Lodhi, the Governor of the Punjab, began to challenge his rule. Ibrahim called the latter to Agra, but fearing for his life, he excused himself and sent instead his son Dilawar Khan. As soon as the young man reached the capital, he was threatened with the famous dungeon, unless his father came in person to court with the tribute of his province. Dilawar managed to escape and warned his father that if he did not take immediate action, he would be lost. Without a moment's delay, Daulat Khan asked Babur, the King of Kabul, for help.

Babur, who had recaptured Kandahar in 1522 to protect his western borders, gladly agreed, all the more so since Daulat Khan's request echoed the displeasure of Ibrahim's own uncle, Alam Khan. After three brief expeditions, Babur undertook a fourth one in 1523, supposedly to help the Afghan dissidents, but in reality to pave the way for his own conquest.

Meanwhile, his family had grown with the birth of three boys and a girl: Kamran (1509), Askari (1516), Hindal (1519) and Gulbadan Begum (1523). In 1520, Humayun, who was then a mere twelve years old, had been appointed Governor of Badakshan. There he remained till his father called him to Kabul to participate in his Indian expedition.

On 25 November 1525, Babur reached the Garden of Fidelity, one of the numerous gardens he had laid out in and around Kabul. His eldest son was to join him there with the Badakshan contingent. While waiting for Humayun, the Emperor relaxed in the company of his officers, alternating between bouts of wine and opium. But his patience began to wear thin. Humayun seemed to be in no hurry. God alone knew what kept him in his fiefdom. Was he unwilling to give up his state of semi-independence? Or did he hesitate to associate himself with his father's venture? The fact is that he only arrived on Sunday, 3 December. "I spoke very severely to him at once", confided Babur in his memoirs. At last they could set off on their expedition.

On Thursday, 12 April 1526, the Mughal army reached the outskirts of Panipat and set up camp on a vast plain. In the deathly stillness of that arid landscape there was nothing but an occasional blade of grass and a few thorny bushes—the only signs of life that a mean trickle of water could sustain.

As soon as he arrived, Babur fortified the area surrounding his camp. To the right lay the city of Panipat; to the left and facing the camp were seven hundred carts joined together with ropes of raw hide. Between every two carts stood five or six mantelets to protect the matchlock men and the infantry men, while spaces were provided at intervals "of an arrow's flight" to allow the movement of a hundred to a hundred-and-fifty horsemen.

It was the first time Babur was leading such a large army, of twelve thousand men. However, it was insignificant compared to Ibrahim Lodhi's forces which consisted of a hundred thousand men and a thousand combat elephants. Babur's artillery, though, was considerable and included Turkish gunners, who were considered the best in all Asia, especially after the Ottomans had defeated the formidable Shah Ismail Safavi at the battle of Chaldiran in 1514.

On Friday, 20 April, the Indian troops attacked at dawn. It took several days for the Mughal cavalrymen to draw them out of their trenches. Meanwhile, Babur's troops took up conventional battle positions: right and left wing, centre, vanguard, reserves and two cavalry squadrons, one to the right and the other to the left, aimed at encircling the enemy.

The right wing, led by Humayun, had to bear the brunt of the enemy's assault. A reserve force went immediately to its rescue while Babur's cavalrymen rained arrows on the Indian army from behind the lines. At this juncture the matchlock men and the falconers of the Turks sprang into action, the noise of their attack causing panic among men and elephants alike. The Indian army was paralysed; it could neither advance nor retreat. "When the incitement to battle had come, the Sun was spear-high; till midday fighting had been in full force; noon passed, the foe was crushed in defeat, our friends rejoicing and gay. By God's mercy and kindness, this difficult affair was made easy for us!" wrote Babur fervently.

According to him, there were about fifteen to sixteen thousand corpses strewn over the battlefield; Indian chronicles however put the estimate at forty to fifty thousand men. Among the dead was Ibrahim Lodhi. His head, and that of his ally Bikramajit, the Maharaja of Gwalior, were brought to Babur.

Strange indeed was the fate of this Bikramajit whose birth even more than his death was shrouded in an aura of tragedy.

It was said that Raja Maan Singh, the most illustrious ruler of the Tomar dynasty of Gwalior, was once hunting in a forest nearby when he came across a young peasant girl struggling with an elephant and promptly fell besottedly in love with her.

"Will you marry me?" he asked the bewildered girl. Recovering her senses, she replied: "On three conditions." "What are they?" asked the King. "First, you must spare me from being veiled in purdah. Second, you must always keep me at your side, even in times of adversity. Third, you must change the course of the waters irrigating my garden towards Gwalior, as they are the source of my beauty."

In this way, the beautiful, intrepid peasant girl became the ninth wife of the Raja of Gwalior. She bore him two sons; none of his earlier wives had been able to do so. Maan Singh had a magnificent residence built for her in the citadel, at the foot of his palace. This favouritism excited the jealousy of his other wives who had been relegated to the basement of Man Mandir, the king's palace in Gwalior Fort. Soon however, one of them gave birth to a son, whom she called Bikramajit. In order to ensure his succession to the throne of Gwalior, she had the peasant-girl and her two sons poisoned, to the great chagrin of Maan Singh, who unable to bear this grief, died shortly afterwards in 1517.

It is said that the fort of Gwalior housed an immense treasure which included a diamond whose size, colour and water were beyond comparison. The Tomar dynasty had received it as a reward for services rendered to Ala-ud-din

Khilji. The latter, after treacherously assassinating his uncle, the ruling Sultan of Delhi, and usurping his throne, had launched upon a series of conquests. These led him to Malwa, the Deccan and south India. It was at Malwa, in 1306, that he must have laid his hands on the famous diamond.

According to the great Indian poet Amir Khusro, who was also the historiographer of the Khilji dynasty, Rai Mahlak Deo, the sovereign of the Hindu dynasty which ruled over Malwa, locked himself in the fort of his capital Ujjain and consulted his ministers. Having lost all hope of victory, he sent a message to one of Ala-ud-din's lieutenants: "If it is my jewels you covet, they are considerable. I am ready, once the siege is raised, to shower them on the road on which the Sultan's officers tread."

The king's proposal was accepted and an ambassador was sent to hand over the fort's treasure to the enemy commander, who after examining it, enquired whether the most beautiful pieces were among them. "I swear in the name of God who created man", replied the emissary, "that each one of these jewels is priceless. One of them is a stone whose counterpart cannot be found in the Universe, even though philosophers would have us believe that such a substance does not exist."

Ibrahim Lodhi conquered Gwalior in 1518, eight years before the battle of Panipat. He gave Bikramajit another fief and made him his vassal and ally. There is no doubt that he left Bikramajit some of the treasure of his ancestors, for just after the battle of Panipat a large number of precious stones including the great diamond were with Bikramajit's relatives, who lived in the Agra Fort with the family of the fallen Sultan. Some claim that they had taken refuge there after the Mughal invasion of India. Others assert that Ibrahim had entrusted his treasure to the Raja.

Be that as it may, after the Battle of Panipat, Babur sent

his son Humayun with a detachment to Agra to seize Ibrahim Lodhi's treasure. He himself lifted camp the next day to march to Delhi where, on the first Friday after his arrival, he had the khutba, the Friday midday sermon, recited in his name, thereby consecrating his sovereignty over Hindustan or northern India. Once this was done, he took the road to Agra, where he arrived on 10 May 1526.

In the meantime, Humayun had been welcomed by a delegation of nobles who begged him to spare the citadel. Always reluctant to resort to violence, the young prince set up his camp on the banks of the Yamuna opposite the fortress and merely ordered that the doors of the latter be sealed so that no one could make off with the treasure.

One evening, a sentinel came and informed him that the wife, children and servants of the Maharaja of Gwalior had been caught while trying to escape from the fort; they had been placed under house arrest till such time as the Prince took a decision. After some thought, Humayun ordered that they be allowed to leave. "They expressed their gratitude", Babur was to recount, "by making him a voluntary offering of a mass of jewels and valuables amongst which was the famous diamond which Ala-ud-din must have brought. Its reputation is that every appraiser has estimated its value at two-and-half days' food for the whole world. Apparently it weighs eight misqals (*approximately 186 carats*). Humayun offered it to me when I arrived at Agra; I just gave it back to him."

Another account, contained in the manuscript of Khor Shah, the Ambassador of Golconda to the court of the Shah of Persia, claims that the diamond belonged not to Bikramajit but to Sultan Ibrahim Lodhi himself, who must have seized it when he conquered Gwalior. According to Khor Shah, Ibrahim's mother handed it over to Humayun when he came to Agra to take possession of the fallen Sultan's treasure.

"As Humayun entered the Sultan's palace", writes Khor Shah, "the women of Ibrahim's family began to wail. The prince consoled them, promising them that their honour would be safe in his hands and that he would treat them with the respect due to their rank. Upon hearing this, Ibrahim's mother went to another room and came back a few minutes later with a golden box which she gave to the young prince with trembling hands. As soon as he lifted the lid Humayun saw the diamond."

This account does not seem very plausible. We know that Ibrahim's mother, far from adopting a conciliatory attitude towards her son's successor, tried to poison Babur. She would have succeeded had the cook assigned the deed poured the poison into the cauldron in which the Emperor's meal was being cooked, instead of sprinkling it over the fine slices of bread accompanying it. "Our unfortunate tasters", wrote Babur, "were not on their guard when the food was placed on the dish. The cook, while placing the fine slices of bread on a porcelain plate, sprinkled a little more than half the poison and covered the whole lot with a layer of fried stuff. Had he powdered the fried stuff with poison or put it in the cauldron, mine would have been a sorry plight indeed."

CHAPTER TWO

After the occupation of Agra, Babur distributed the Lodhi treasure amongst his men, each receiving what was due to his rank. He rewarded even those who did not take part in the campaign: his sons, Kamran, Askari and Hindal, as well as his relatives, "adults and children alike", the holy men of Samarkand and Khorasan as well as those of Mecca and Medina. "In the land of Kabul and the Varsak valley each man and woman, slave and free man, child and adult received a shahrukhi (gold coin)."

As a reward for his courage at the Battle of Panipat—his valour had wiped out the shame of being late for his appointment at the Garden of Fidelity—Humayun received seventy lakh rupees and "a house containing so much treasure it had never been counted". This wealth was in addition to the famous diamond and jewels he had received from the family of the Raja of Gwalior. As for Babur, it seems that he kept nothing for himself. His scorn for things material won him the epithet of "kalandar"—the godly mendicant.

The euphoria of victory and the glitter of newly-acquired wealth paled as soon as the realities of victory began to set in. Babur's first impressions of India were not at all favourable. He felt that town and country in Hindustan were both greatly wanting in charm: "Except their large rivers and their standing-waters which flow in ravines or hollows, there are no running waters in their gardens or residences." He noticed the absence of good horses, good dogs, good fruit—in particular grapes and melons—public baths, schools, candles, torches and candlesticks. The intense heat of May, preceding the monsoon, made him dislike

India's weather. He found the people ugly, without character or talent, discourteous and uncharitable, lacking in virile qualities. "In handicrafts and work, there is no form or symmetry, method or quality", he noted crossly in his memoirs.

He nevertheless wanted to found an empire, and as his predecessors had, was willing to bear with hardship to appropriate India's wealth, just as the British would in later centuries. "Pleasant things of Hindustan are that it is a large country and has masses of gold and silver. Its air in the Rains is very fine. Sometimes it rains, ten, fifteen or twenty times a day; torrents pour down all at once and rivers flow where no waters had been", he wrote, rationalizing his invasion. Or else he would say to himself: "Another good thing in Hindustan is that it has unnumbered and endless workmen of every kind. There is a fixed caste for every sort of work and for every thing, which has done that work or that thing from father to son till now."

Alas! neither his lieutenants nor his soldiers shared his clear-sightedness or his ambition. "The year", recounts Babur, of 1526, "was a very hot one; violent pestilential winds struck people down in heaps together; masses began to die off. On these accounts the greater part of the *begs* and best braves became unwilling to stay in Hindustan."

Humayun, besides the Lodhi wealth, had just received the fief of the district of Sambhal to the east of Delhi, on the left bank of the Ganga, with an annual income estimated at around one crore, thirty-eight lakh rupees (thirteen million, eight hundred thousand). Even he could not wait to return to Badakshan. All the more so as his contingent, made up for the most part of conscripts, was used to fighting for two or three months of the year and had been on the campaign trail for over fourteen months. But despite his anxiety to return, the young prince was to add another feather to his cap before leaving his father.

To the east of Agra some Afghan lords, former vassals of the Lodhis, had occupied the city of Kanauj situated north-west of Lucknow. They were threatening to take the Doab, the fertile riparian region between the Ganga and the Yamuna. But Humayun offered to put a stop to their advance and succeeded in pushing them back beyond the Ganga.

In the meantime, while the morale of the Mughal army was at its lowest ebb, an even greater danger loomed large over the invaders' nascent empire: the Rajputs, the original Hindu rulers of the land. These were the legendary warriors who donned robes of saffron (the sacred Hindu colour) when defeat was certain and rode out to fight and die. Their womenfolk preferred to commit the terrible rite of *jauhar*, self-immolation by fire, rather than suffer dishonour at enemy hands.

Babur accordingly assembled his chief lieutenants and with his characteristic frankness, exhorted them to fight: "There is no supremacy and grip on the world without means and resources; without lands and retainers, sovereignty and command are impossible. By the labours of several years, by encountering hardship, by long travel, by flinging myself and the army into battle, and by deadly slaughter, we, through God's grace, beat these masses of enemies in order that we might take their broad lands. And now what force compels us, what necessity has arisen that we should, without cause, abandon countries taken at such risk of life? Was it for us to remain in Kabul, the sport of harsh poverty? Henceforth, let no well-wisher of mine speak of such things! But let not those turn back from going who, weak in strong persistence, have set their faces to depart!"

His appeal was heard. Humayun and most of the chieftains were won over by the arguments of their master. The only one who left was Khaja Kalan, Babur's faithful companion and friend in need. Babur was unhappy to see him go, but did not hold it against him. In fact, he gave him the command of some troops stationed in Kabul and Ghazni and a fiefdom in India whose incomes he could collect.

During this time, the Rajputs had reached the outskirts of Bayana, a stronghold to the south-west of Agra, near Sikri. They were led by Sangram Singh, better known as Rana Sanga, a veteran of many battles in which he had suffered numerous injuries. At first he thought that Babur would support him against Ibrahim Lodhi. Then he changed his mind. The new conqueror, he surmised, was not like his ancestor Timur. He would not be content with a large booty alone. Having come to India to stay, he was unlikely to help the Rajputs regain Delhi, their lost capital, nor their empire in Hindustan.

After acceding to the throne of Mewar in 1509, Rana Sanga had become the most powerful chief of Rajputana or Rajasthan as we know it today. This westerly Indian state is located between the plains of Hindustan and the Thar desert and crossed by the ancient Aravalli range of hills. It is famed for its cyclopean forts at Chittorgarh, Amber, Jodhpur, Jaisalmer, Bikaner, and many others, their brooding majesty dominating the rugged landscape of the province.

On 16 March 1527, Rana Sanga advanced to meet Babur, followed by a hundred-and-twenty chieftains, eighty thousand horsemen and five hundred combat elephants. Although this army belonged to the Rajput confederation, it included several Afghan chieftains whom Babur had been unable to win over.

The decisive battle took place at Khanua, sixteen kilometres from Sikri, where Akbar was later to build his city, Fatehpur. As the two armies approached each other, a feeling of despondency swept through the Mughal forces. They realised that they were badly outnumbered, despite their artillery, of which the Rajputs had none, preferring their horses, lances and swords and shortsightedly disdaining guns. And then there were gloomy predictions by that accursed trader Mohammed Sharif who had come from Kabul the day before, with three rows of camels carrying wine from Ghazni, who went around, insisting to all he met that "Mars is in the west these days; who comes into fight from this (east) side will be defeated!" Who could hope to conquer these warriors who drew their spiritual strength from the east, whose chief, it was said, was a descendant of the Sun God himself?

Drawing inspiration from the fervour of the Rajputs, Babur exhorted his men to win or die for the glory of Islam. He announced a veritable jihad or holy war. To counter the fears and hesitations of his men, he said that there was no greater joy than dying for one's faith. In the bargain, he smashed his precious drinking vessels and issued a royal decree against the imbibing of wine.

Victory was his. The Rajputs' reckless cavalry charges were mowed down by Babur's cannons. Rana Sanga was carried off the field, severely wounded, but many other chieftains fell on the battlefield. To celebrate the defeat of the "infidels", Babur assumed the title of Ghazi, "Victorious in Holy War".

While Babur was consolidating his conquest and laying the foundations of a powerful empire, his son Humayun returned to his fief of Badakshan where, for the first time, he took to the pleasures of opium. This prompted the historian Mirza Haydar Dughlat to say: "The relations between Humayun and his sensuous and corrupt servants, in particular with Maulana Mohammed Parghali, caused him to get into bad habits. One of these was his addiction to opium. This vice has given rise to much gossip and is the root cause of all his misfortunes." However, his decision-making power had not yet been affected. Babur informed Humayun of the recent victories of Shah Tahmasp, who had succeeded Shah Ismail, over the Uzbeks, and ordered him to seize this opportunity to recover the Timurid heritage in Transoxiana. Humayun forthwith sent his troops in three directions: Hissar, Tirmiz and Samarkand. Had it not been for the Uzbeks' tenacity and their superior numbers, he would perhaps have achieved a brilliant success. Thereafter, having heard that his father was ill, he decided to go to Agra. Without verifying the information, which proved to be groundless, or requesting the Emperor's permission, he left Badakshan in the early autumn of 1529 after having entrusted its government to his brother Hindal.

His parents were happy to see him again. "I was talking about him to his mother", Babur relates, "when he appeared before us. Our hearts blossomed like flowers and our eyes shone like flames." Responding to his desire to stay in India, Babur allowed him to take residence in Sambhal, the fief granted to him just after the victory of Panipat.

After spending six months in the pursuit of his favourite pastimes—astrology, opium and women—Humayun fell gravely ill. Struck by an unknown disease, he hung for several days between life and death. Thereupon his father ordered that he be moved to Delhi from where he was to be taken to Agra by boat.

It was a sad sight to see the ailing prince arrive in the capital. When the boat anchored, Babur went on board accompanied by his wife Maham, Humayun's mother. Their son was stretched out on a litter, his face emaciated, his eyes burning with fever. The Emperor's distress was movingly obvious. "Do not be sad", Maham told him, "you have other sons. I am crying because he is my only one." To which Babur replied: "Even though I have other sons, none do I cherish more than Humayun. I desire with all my heart that this beloved child fulfill all his wishes and enjoy a long life. I want the kingdom for him and not for the others, as he is without equal."

Every conceivable treatment was tried but to no avail. It was then that one of Babur's closest relatives suggested that the remedy for such ailments was to sacrifice something of great value, that God grant health in return.

"It came to my mind", recounts Babur, "that nothing was dearer to Humayun than myself and that I had to make the sacrifice of my own person in the hope that God would accept it."

Others suggested that it would be enough to sacrifice the large diamond which had fallen into Humayun's hands. Wasn't it priceless?

The Emperor would have none of it. "May I myself be his ransom", he replied, "because his condition is serious and the time has come for me to exchange my strength for his weakness."

Having said this, he entered the sickroom, went thrice around Humayun's bed and said: "Whatever be your disease, may I take it upon myself." At that moment, he began to grow heavy whereas Humayun slowly began to come out of his coma.

Babur summoned the notables and dignitaries of the empire, enjoined them to hold out their hands to Humayun as a sign of allegiance and proclaimed him heir to the throne.

Babur died on 26 December 1530 at the age of forty-eight, after having implored his successor never to harm his brothers even if they deserved such treatment. His body was taken to Kabul and he was buried next to his favourite wife, in one of the ten gardens he had laid out.

When he came to the throne, Humayun was a handsome man of average height. He had the typically slanted eyes of the Mughals, a fine beard, and a drooping moustache that fell on both sides of his mouth. He was said to be gallant, courteous, intelligent, as accomplished as his father, warm and sensitive, almost visionary in his conception of honour and magnanimity, as we have already seen in his conduct towards the family of the Raja of Gwalior. The very stuff kings were made of, except that in Humayun's case these qualities had been diluted by his indecisiveness and propensity for indolence and hedonism, which probably stemmed from his predilection for opium. Moreover, he was never able to galvanise his men as his father could. In brief, he was, like most crown princes, born to rule over an established empire, rather than to consolidate a new conquest.

His love for his brothers was boundless. He gave them rights over the richest lands of the empire. To Askari, he gave his own fief of Sambhal; to Hindal, the youngest brother, a portion of Rajputana. Kamran, a debauched, selfish, ungrateful man, was made almost an equal: Humayun granted him not only Kabul and Kandahar but also acquiesced to his seizure, without prior approval, of Lahore and the Punjab.

This proved to be a fatal error. In a society where the rule of primogeniture had yet to be firmly established, successors to the throne would take recourse to the most sordid machinations in order to reach supreme power. It was, as the old Persian dictum says, "the throne or the coffin". In order to survive and impose his writ, Humayun should have eliminated all his rivals, or at least blinded them, thus excluding them from succession, as was the custom of his clan. He did neither.

In the meantime, a formidable enemy was emerging beyond the Ganga. His name was Farid Suri, and he was called Sher Khan for having killed a lion with a single blow of his sword, during a hunt, when it attacked his master, the King of Bihar. Born in 1486, Sher Khan had served formerly under Babur who, deeply impressed by his talents, is believed to have told his ministers: "Keep an eye on Sher Khan. He is cunning and bears the mark of royalty on his forehead. I have seen many Afghan noblemen more important than him but none have made such an impression on me. The minute I saw this man, I felt that his ambitions had to be checked, for I see in him the qualities of greatness and the attributes of power."

Sher Khan was fifty years old when he tried to rally his Afghan compatriots scattered over Bihar and Bengal and to offer them the opportunity of dominating India once again. A remarkable administrator, a born soldier, a leader of men, he used every mean to drive away the Mughals from Hindustan.

Humayun played into his hands. Instead of tracking down and eliminating the enemy when he had the chance, the Emperor came to terms with him in return for an oath of allegiance and returned to Agra to enjoy for a whole year the inebriating fumes of opium and the delights of his harem.

Sher Shah used this breathing space to gather together the Afghan clans, invade Bengal, take away fabulous treasures and establish his supremacy east of the Ganga. He also conferred upon himself the title of Emperor and became known as Sher Shah. Humayun might have overcome the threat to his throne had he received timely support from his brothers and in particular from the twelve thousand men of the Kabul contingent commanded by Kamran. This precious help having been denied him, he had to face two crushing defeats, first at Chausa in 1539 and then at Kanauj, in the summer of 1540.

Hounded by Sher Shah, Humayun sought refuge in Lahore, where his family had already retreated. Some of his officers advised him to get rid of his brother Kamran, whom they suspected rightly of being in secret league with the enemy. It was said that the young prince was willing to come to terms with Sher Shah, provided the latter left him the Punjab. "No", replied the Emperor, outraged. "Never shall I stain my hands with the blood of my brother. On the contrary, I shall never forget the words of our respected father, who on his death-bed implored me never to quarrel with my brothers nor to harbour any ill-will against them. These words are forever engraved in my heart."

For five long months Humayun, Kamran, Askari and Hindal, assembled in Lahore, discussed in vain ways and means of saving what remained of the Timurid empire. Every time a plan was suggested, it was rejected by Kamran under some pretext or other.

It turned out that he wanted to buy time before coming to some kind of understanding with Sher Shah, whose troops were just a few days' march from Lahore. Brother, dynasty and independence mattered little to Kamran, who was ready to sacrifice them all for the rich plains of the Punjab. If he could not have the Land of Five Rivers, then he would cling to Kabul and prevent his elder brother from entering the city. Was it not Humayun who, as king, had granted him this fief, and could not Humayun, should he wish to do so, take it away? Consequently, when the beleaguered Humayun proposed to go back to Badakshan, Kamran refused him access to that city. Kabul being on the road to Badakshan, he feared that Humayun would settle there for good.

In the early autumn of 1540, it was learnt that Sher Shah and his army had crossed the Beas, one of the five tributaries of the Indus, and were likely to appear at any moment. It was imperative to leave Lahore at all costs.

Of all the setbacks, and there were many in Humayun's life, none was more tragic than this flight from the Punjab. A little to the west of the Jhelum, another tributary of the Indus, at Khuchab, the road crosses a ravine flanked by rocky spurs, making a narrow pass. Beyond, it bifurcates to the north-west towards Kabul and to the south-west towards Sind. Kamran indicated his intention of going through the pass first, fearing that his elder brother might seize the opportunity to reach Kabul ahead of him. Offended by such arrogance, the Emperor asserted his right of precedence, which nearly led the two brothers to an armed confrontation. An old companion of Babur, respected for his wisdom and his age, was compelled to mediate. He convinced Humayun of the superiority of Kamran's forces and persuaded the latter of the validity of the fallen sovereign's prerogative. The Emperor finally opted for Sind as a haven.

At the crossroads, the refugee caravan split into two, the great majority, including Askari, preferring to follow Kamran. Hindal, the youngest brother, had already taken the road to Sind, hoping to find a base of operations for conquering Gujarat. Only a few faithful followers gathered around Emperor Humayun . . .

Four fugitive years slipped by after the Emperor and his companions left Lahore. During this time they wandered across the deserts of Sind and Rajasthan, hoping to find a haven either at the court of Shah Hussain Arghun, the King of Sind, or in the territory of Rao Maldeo, the ruler of Jodhpur. Fearing Sher Shah's wrath, both men deluded Humayun for some time with vague promises of help.

Rao Maldeo meanwhile tried by ruse to obtain Babur's diamond. One afternoon, as Humayun's small group was getting ready to leave the territory of Marwar for the south-west, a caravan appeared in the distance. A horseman broke away from it and galloped towards the Mughal camp. When he arrived at the entrance of the bivouac, he dismounted, and pretending to be a rich merchant, asked for an audience with their leader.

Humayun, sitting on a stone, was counting his amber beads while waiting for the camp to be lifted. He was exultant. A few hours earlier he had fallen asleep in an open space, exposed to the intense rays of the sun. An eagle had miraculously spread its wings and protected him from the scorching heat. Such a good omen gave him fresh hope and courage.

Received by the Mughal, the merchant pretended to sympathise with his financial problems and offered to buy Babur's diamond at any price. Humayun, suspecting the merchant to be one of Maldeo's courtiers, eyed him scornfully and replied: "Such a jewel cannot be bought. It is acquired either by the arbitration of the flashing sword, or through the munificence of great monarchs."

He dismissed the imposter, mounted his horse, and gave the signal for departure.

A short while after this incident, Humayun arrived at Amarkot, whose ruler, a Rajput of great distinction, welcomed him and his companions with open arms. Although unable to put more than two thousand, five hundred soldiers at the Emperor's disposal, he estimated that they would be sufficient for capturing the Jun district, a base of strategic importance for the conquest of Lower Sind. On 11 October 1542, the newly-formed Mughal army set off.

Four days later, a messenger caught up with Humayun and announced that his wife Hamida had given birth to a son. Hamida Banu Begum was the daughter of Hindal's Persian teacher. Humayun had met her a year earlier at his younger brother's camp. The virginal freshness and grace of the fourteen-year-old maiden so captivated him that he asked for her hand. To his great surprise, Hamida refused because of her age and her desire to stay with her parents. It is said that she was in fact in love with Hindal whom she had known since childhood and who, at twenty-two, was eight years older than her, whereas the Emperor, at thirty-three, could have been her father. At last, it was at the behest of Hindal's mother that the marriage took place.

Overwhelmed with joy, at the news of his son's birth, Humayun decreed that the infant be named Akbar, "the

Great", as astrologers in Lahore had predicted that his future son would achieve a great destiny. In better times Humayun would have, according to tradition, showered his officers and servants with fabulous gifts to celebrate such an event. But he had nothing at hand save his unique diamond and several rubies from Badakshan that were his nest-egg. Hence, he broke a fragment of musk against a porcelain plate and distributed the pieces among his followers, saying: "This is all I can offer you at the birth of my son, whose fame shall spread, I hope, across the world just as the perfume of this musk is today filling the air."

He stayed nine months at Jun, during which he subordinated a large number of local chiefs and gained control over almost all the territories bordering the lower reaches of the Indus. In the meantime, Hamida Banu Begum and Akbar had joined him. The Sultan of Sind, fearing that Humayun's presence in the region might become a threat to his kingdom, did his utmost to break the alliance between the Emperor and the Rana of Amarkot. But to no avail. The loyalty of the Rajput chieftain would have remained unshakeable had it not been for the thoughtlessness of a Mughal officer who called him an infidel. The Emperor having refused to reprove the culprit, the Rana and his men packed up and returned home, offended at the discourtesy.

At this critical juncture, Bairam Beg reached the camp. He and Jauhar Aftabchy, of all Humayun's followers, shared a staunch unswerving loyalty to the Emperor. Bairam, a remarkable officer born in a Persian tribe, had left his birth-place some years before to seek his fortune in India. While fighting in Humayun's army, he distinguished himself by his courage, sagacity and loyalty. No wonder that Humayun entrusted him with the task of covering his retreat when he set forth in exile. Bairam Beg's return to camp was nothing short of a miracle for no one imagined that he would ever manage to escape from the Afghans. As for Jauhar Aftabchy, he had been the Emperor's ewer-bearer since a long time. He authored *Tezkereh al Vakiat*, (Private Memoirs of the Emperor Humayun), an account of the life of the second of the Great Mughals.

The departure of the Rana of Amarkot who, in addition to military support, had provided the exiles with fresh supplies, dealt a severe blow to the Mughal morale, all the more so since the spectre of famine had begun to float over the camp.

It was then that the Sultan of Sind offered to supply them with ships, money and provisions provided that they left his lands. The Emperor accepted. Overcome by the ingratitude of his relatives and his past vassals, he even contemplated retreating to a solitary spot where he would live as a hermit, away from the troubles of the world. However, the will to recover his ancestral possessions prevailed over his longing for seclusion.

On 10 July 1543, Humayun decided to leave Sind, without knowing where to go next. He could not, however, seek refuge with his brother Hindal who had captured Kandahar, for Kamran had just thrown Hindal out of the city and had him imprisoned in the Kabul citadel.

Bairam Beg suggested going to Persia, where he was sure Shah Tahmasp would welcome them warmly. At first, Humayun was reluctant. He feared that the Shah would not have forgotten his father's misunderstanding with Babur, who had clashed with Shah Ismail's lieutenant during a campaign against Samarkand.

"Have no fear, Sire", assured Bairam Beg. "The presence of Your Highness in the states of the Shah shall be welcome, for it will boost his sagging fortune, especially after the loss of Tabriz and Baghdad to the Ottomans."

Towards the end of the autumn of 1543, Humayun and his men traversed the Bolan Pass, a narrow gorge clamped between sombre and steep mountains linking the plains of Sind to the mountainous borders of Afghanistan. So silent was the landscape that they could hear nothing but the echo of their horses' hooves. They were nonetheless being watched. It was as if each rock, each bush hid a spy.

Once they had crossed the Bolan Pass, they camped in a valley situated at the edge of a forest. The sun had set. The Emperor, having finished his evening prayer, was relaxing in his tent with Bairam Beg and some other officers. All of a sudden, the sentinel's torch spotted a strange silhouette.

It happened to be a young Uzbek soldier from Askari's army who, having fought formerly beside Humayun had remained faithful to him. Casting his sword on the ground to prove his peaceful intentions, he warned the sentinel of the threat which was hanging over the imperial camp. "Askari", he said, "now Kamran's representative in Kandahar, has received orders to arrest the Emperor and his retinue. That is why a close watch has been kept over all their movements ever since they entered the Bolan Pass. Askari's men are only waiting for nightfall tc encircle the camp."

Humayun did not have enough time to lift camp or take charge of his retinue, which in spite of all the defections, remained very large. Even though it was a painful decision, the Emperor resolved to part with most of his companions in exile, including his son Akbar. Assuming that an uncle would not shed his nephew's blood, he left the boy in the care of his wet-nurse and a few servants. And indeed he learnt later that Askari had taken Akbar to Kandahar and entrusted him to his wife's care.

After bidding farewell to his companions, Humayun mounted his horse and galloped away from the camp. Forty-two people followed him: his wife, her servant, and forty men, including Bairam Beg and Jauhar Aftabchy. With just a few morsels of bread and some dates for food, they crossed the high valleys separating Afghanistan from Persia. Winter had set in. Deep snow covered the ground, hampering the movement of the horses. Several, including Hamida's mount, succumbed to the cold, forcing her to ride pillion behind her husband. Humayun had abandoned much, but he still carried "Babur's diamond" with him, little imagining he was about to lose it.

Humayun and his followers had just reached the outskirts of a village where they hoped to recover from their hunger and thirst when they found themselves surrounded by a band of sinister-looking Baluchis armed to the teeth. Realising that any resistance would be futile, they allowed themselves to be taken to the latter's camp where, contrary to all expectations, they were treated with utmost generosity. The chief of the band, one Malik Khatti, had received orders from Kamran to arrest them. However, moved by the plight of the refugees, he did no such thing.

Refreshed, and supplied with fresh mounts and provisions by their host, Humayun and his suite resumed their journey. A month later, they saw on the horizon an isolated hill with a flat summit. Spurring their horses, they galloped towards it, hoping it would be the Kouhe-Khadje, a hill beyond which stretch the Helmand river and Persia. They were not disappointed. Having reached the top, they saw on the other side the Hamoun, a succession of lakes into which flow the waters of the Helmand. They eventually crossed it on tutins, a kind of reed raft, while flocks of wild duck flew overhead. At last, they were in the fair haven of Persia.

And haven it proved, straightaway, for further on they found a hamlet whose inhabitants gave them a rousing welcome. They were installed in a garden, enclosed by vine, pomegranate and mulberry trees, while a courier was dispatched to inform the governor of the province of their arrival.

On 4 January 1544, the caravan reached the outskirts of Farah, a town located a few days' march downstream from Herat. Humayun and his entourage set up camp at the entrance of the town, while royal arrangements were made for their journey. Shah Tahmasp had sent messages to the Governors of Sistan, Farah and Herat instructing them to treat the Emperor of India not as a fallen monarch but as a full-fledged sovereign. Humayun's march to Herat, Mashad and Qazvin, the capital of the Safavids, was to take place amidst unusual splendour. At all times he was to be escorted by five hundred cavalrymen with richly harnessed mounts. Silk and velvet lined tents were to replace the ragged ones which had sheltered his sufferings; a kitchen had to be set up to cater to his every culinary whim; his food had to be served in vessels of gold and silver, and musicians and dancing-girls were to be in constant attendance to fill his moments of leisure.

The Shah had also sent him magnificent presents: "a dagger with an amber handle in a sheath inlaid with precious stones, which had belonged to Shah Ismail; a sword and a belt embellished with magnificent gems; four hundred measures of satin and velvet from Europe and Yezd, with which to make garments for himself and his companions; golden brocade; goat's fur blankets with satin lining; fine silk carpets and twelve crimson, green and white tents."

Such a display of wealth, the kind he had not seen since his flight from India, filled Humayun with wonder. He was relieved to learn that the dagger he had been offered by the Shah belonged to his father. Did that not mean that Tahmasp had forgotten the misunderstanding that had soured relations between Babur and Shah Ismail?

The advance of the imperial cortege to Herat resembled a triumphal procession. Men, women, young and old, lined the streets by the thousands to applaud the Emperor. On the outskirts of the city, hills and plains, trees and rooftops swarmed with enthusiastic spectators. At the other end of the bridge that crossed the Malan river, provincial dignitaries led by the young prince Mohammed Mirza, the eldest son of the Shah, were waiting for their guest and took him to the Jahanara garden, where a magnificent camp site had been set up in welcome.

Humayun stayed for forty days at Herat. He visited mosques, palaces and gardens during the day. When night fell, he attended the numerous feasts given in his honour, where musicians and dancing-girls vied with each other to attract his attention. He loved poetry and was deeply moved when a singer dedicated to him the following verse of Amir Shahi, a Persian poet of the early fifteenth century:

Blest the abode to which such a moon hath come,
August the world where there is such a king,
Be not grieved nor glad at terrestrial pain or pleasure,
For the world is sometimes this, sometimes that.

In the meantime, the faithful Jauhar had been given an additional charge. "It was customary with his Majesty always to carry his valuable diamonds and rubies in a purse in his pocket; but when he was performing his ablutions he generally laid them on one side; he had done so this day, and forgot them: it so happened that when the king was gone, and the humble servant Jauhar was about to remount his horse, he saw a green-flowered purse lying on the ground, and a pen-case by the side of it: he immediately took them up, and as soon as he had overtaken the King, presented them. When his Majesty saw these articles he was amazed and astonished, and said, 'Oh, my boy, you have done me the greatest favour possible; if these had been lost, I should have ever been subject to the meanness of this Persian monarch: do you in future take care of them'."

On 10 March 1544, the golden dome of a mausoleum

appeared on the horizon. It was that of Imam Reza, the eighth of the twelve Shiite Imams. They had reached Mashad. The Governor and the provincial dignitaries received Humayun at the entrance of the town and escorted him to the palace that had been prepared for his visit.

During the forty days he spent in the holy city, the Emperor, a Sunni, never once missed an opportunity to pay his respects to the eighth Shiite Imam, thereby showing his tolerance of all religious faiths—a quality that was to leave its imprint on his son and successor Akbar.

At last came a message from Tahmasp inviting his guest to join him at Qazvin.

Humayun and his retinue had almost reached Qazvin when a messenger from the court came to announce that the Shah wanted to speak with one of the Emperor's ambassadors before receiving him in person. Humayun immediately set up camp and entrusted Bairam Beg with this mission.

The Shah received the officer in one of the rooms of his palace, in the presence of his brothers and counsellors.

After the interview, Bairam Beg was about to leave when Tahmasp called him back. In the meantime, he had signalled to a servant to bring him a taj. Holding out the red headgear favoured by the Shias, to Humayun's envoy, he ordered him to wear it, thus proving his fidelity to Shiism. Bairam Beg, though himself a Shia, refused to do so, insisting that he was a servant of the Emperor of India and as such it was to him that he owed obedience.

One can imagine the reaction of Tahmasp who, though not as cruel as his father, could fly into a tremendous rage when thwarted on religious matters. His bigotry was such that he could tolerate neither heresy nor apostasy, both of which were punishable by death. "You are a servant of yourself", he retorted furiously, and would have executed Bairam Beg had he not feared the consequence of such an act. Nevertheless, in a bid to intimidate Bairam Beg and to appease his own anger, he had twelve wretched men accused of heresy dragged across the room and ordered that their throats be slit without further ado.

On 15 July 1544, just before sunset, an impressive procession left Qazvin to greet Humayun. It included the Shah's brothers, his ministers, religious dignitaries and generals, accompanied by an escort of five hundred cavalrymen in their finest attire. As soon as the Emperor's camp came in sight, Bairam Beg galloped towards his master's tent to announce the imminent arrival of the Persian entourage.

Humayun immediately bathed, dressed, mounted a magnificent white steed—a present from Prince Bahram Mirza, the Shah's brother—and rode towards Tahmasp's envoys, followed by an escort.

When they got to an "arrow's throw" from Humayun, the Shah's brothers dismounted and walked to meet him. The Emperor also dismounted, took a few steps and embraced the envoys effusively. Bahram Mirza presented him on the Shah's behalf with a robe of honour decorated with clips of precious stones, and a taj. Thereafter, the procession set off for Qazvin where a royal apartment awaited Emperor Humayun.

The next day, at the hour appointed by the court astrologers, exactly two hours after the evening prayer, the two sovereigns met in the large hall of public audience. A little while before, Humayun, dressed in the robe of honour offered by Tahmasp, but wearing a turban instead of the taj, had covered the short distance separating his residence from the palace in a gilded palanquin inlaid with precious stones, carried by eight liveried servants.

The Shah, propped up by a profusion of colourful cushions, sat cross-legged on a podium on which was laid a magnificent silk carpet. He wore a scarlet caftan tied at the waist with a belt of twisted gold string across which hung a dagger with stone inlay work. He had a swarthy complexion, perfectly slanted eyes, thick lips, an aquiline nose, chestnut brown beard and moustache. He was then thirty years old, six years younger than Humayun.

His brothers and ministers stood on both sides of the podium, their hands crossed on their chest as a mark of deference. Tahmasp received Humayun with all the honour due to his rank, seating him on his right hand. Since the Mughal spoke fluent Persian, conversation between the two monarchs flowed smoothly.

However, it did not take long for Tahmasp to betray his religious designs. Noticing that his guest did not wear the taj he had offered him, he somehow managed to hold back his anger. Then, having enquired after Humayun's health and the events of his journey, he asked him point blank to exchange his turban for the taj. Humayun knew perfectly well that in the Persian language taj also meant crown. "The taj is a sign of greatness", he replied brilliantly, "I shall wear it." The Shah, bursting with satisfaction, placed this symbol of Shiite faith on his guest's head, while princes, ministers and religious dignitaries loudly expressed their approval with shouts of "Allah-o-Akbar", "God is great".

Humayun asked the Shah to help him recover his empire. Tahmasp agreed and promised to provide him with an army of twelve thousand men, provided he embraced the Shiite faith. History was repeating itself. Had not Shah Ismail imposed the same conditions for assisting Babur to recover Samarkand? The son, remembering the consequences of his father's apostasy among his subjects, Sunnis for the most part, hesitated and asked for some time to think about it.

Vacillating again, Humayun thought anew of retiring from the world rather than renounce his faith, when Ghazi Jahan Qazvini came by on a visit. This renowned theologian, who was one of Tahmasp's closest advisers, persuaded the

Emperor to accept the Shah's proposal, arguing that his obstinacy could endanger the life of his companions who, with the exception of Bairam Beg, were all Sunnis.

Humayun was a great lover of poetry and composed verse in his moments of leisure. Having learnt that the Shah shared his passion, he took a pen and confirmed his adhesion to Shiism with a quatrain dedicated to the glory of Ali ibn Abu Talib, son-in-law of the Prophet Mohammed and, according to Shiites, his legitimate heir.

Tahmasp, delighted with Humayun's decision, invited him to a hunt in the neighbourhood of Qazvin. A splendid camp had been set up in a glade covered with the most luxuriant vegetation. The weather could not have been better. Thousands of wild flowers filled the air with their scent. Several days before the arrival of the sovereign, the inhabitants of the neighbouring villages had, with the help of some detachments of the Persian army, rounded up game into an enclosure. The animals so assembled made an impressive sight. Everything was therefore ready when the Shah and the Emperor entered the enclosed area and had their pick of the choicest animals. Afterwards, it was the turn of princes, ministers and nobles to test their skill at what was left.

On returning to his tent, Humayun ordered Jauhar to bring him his jewels. He placed Babur's diamond and the Badakshan rubies in a mother-of-pearl box and asked Bairam Beg to hand them over to the Shah, with the message, "They were brought from Hindustan purposely for his Majesty." Noticing Bairam Beg's surprise, Humayun said: "I do not wish to be beholden to the Shah of Persia. These jewels will make up for the help he provides me."

Bairam Beg had not seen Tahmasp in private since the terrible scene which had taken place before Humayun's arrival at Qazvin. Having heard, however, of the Shah's meanness, he was certain that his new mission would dissipate all misunderstanding. All the more so since he too, like his master, now sported a taj.

Shah Tahmasp's reaction to the contents of the jewel box defies description. Never in his royal life had he seen a diamond of such size and lustre. He immediately ordered his jewellers to value it. All having agreed that it was priceless, Tahmasp signified his acceptance by putting the box in his tunic pocket. Then, smiling broadly the while at Bairam Beg, he conferred upon him the title of Khan with the privilege of having drums beaten in his honour, and his own standards.

In this way, Humayun sacrificed to Tahmasp his cherished diamond. The clouds that threatened their relationship disappeared. Shooting parties and banquets followed in rapid succession. One such banquet has been immortalised in a large fresco which decorates the main hall of the Forty Column Palace in Ispahan. Humayun and Tahmasp sit cross-legged on a podium covered with green cloth. Behind each monarch, their servants sit or stand, depending on their rank. At their feet, two young Persian girls are dancing to the accompaniment of Persian and Indian musicians, the latter, including the Emperor, standing out because of the darker colour of their skin.

The mobilisation of forces to reconquer India was duly decreed and the Emperor's exile was about to come to an end.

One fine day, however, everything was called in question: friendship, entertainment, promised troops. What had gone wrong?

Men in the pay of Kamran had come to the Persian court to undermine the relationship between the two sovereigns. They told the Shah a story which hurt his vanity and poisoned his mind against Humayun.

Several years ago, they claimed, Humayun used to fire divinatory arrows to measure his future greatness against the destiny of Persia. For this purpose, he used twelve first class arrows which bore his own name and twelve inferior arrows bearing Tahmasp's name.

Two months now went by since the Shah's last meeting with Humayun. In the meantime, Prince Bahram Mirza, his sister and Ghazi Jahan Qazvini used all their influence with the Shah to iron out the misunderstanding.

When the two monarchs finally met again, the Shah could no longer resist pouring out his heart. He rebuked Humayun for having offended him. The latter acknowledged his action, but justified himself by arguing that he had taken into account the relative size of their respective territories, India being at that time larger than Persia.

"Yes", replied Tahmasp in a fit of anger. "And one of the consequences of this senseless vanity is that you have not been able to govern your vast estates. You have been chased away from them by a band of puppets, and you have left your children and family prisoners behind you."

"We are all in the hands of God. May His will be accomplished", retorted Humayun bitterly.

Having recovered his calm, the Shah clasped his guest in his arms: "Now Humayun," he told him, "you can go. May divine protection be with you." He gave him two apples and a knife and bid him farewell after having asked Bahram Mirza to escort him up to a certain distance from the capital.

Once he reached the spot where the brothers of the Shah had welcomed him for the first time, Humayun cut one of the apples in two and offered one half to the prince while he ate the other. Then he took out a ring from his pocket and placed it on the finger of Bahram Mirza.

"This ring has been left to me by my mother. Keep it as a souvenir. My friendship for you is such that I would have stayed with you for the rest of my life. However, my reputation being at stake, I must leave you."

"Rest assured that I shall keep this ring as a token of your friendship," replied the Mirza. "Go in peace. May success be yours in all your undertakings."

Humayun left Persia towards the end of 1544. An army of twelve thousand Persian auxiliaries was to join him in Sistan.

Victory was not easy. He had to reconquer Kandahar, then Kabul, where he was reunited with his son Akbar. Further conflicts alienated him from his brother Kamran, and he finally had him blinded. Only then was he able to reconquer India where the genius of Sher Shah had given away to the incompetence of his successors. But Humayun had no more than a few months to rule over his recovered empire and had already forfeited his gem of fortune, Babur's diamond. It was to elude his dynasty for two generations.

CHAPTER THREE

In 1547, barely three years after Humayun's departure, Babur's diamond left Persia for the Deccan. Did Shah Tahmasp really present it to Burhan Nizam Shah, the King of Ahmadnagar, one of the five Deccan kingdoms? The others were Bidar, Berar, Bijapur and Golconda, which had come into being after the disintegration of the great Bahmani Kingdom (1347-1518).

It is hard to believe that a skinflint like Tahmasp would easily hand over such a precious jewel to a petty king whose lands moreover were far away from Persia. Perhaps proselytism outweighed financial interests.

Following the example of his counterparts from Bijapur and Golconda, Burhan Nizam Shah had actually embraced Shiism and ordered that the names of the twelve Imams as well as that of the Shah of Persia be henceforth recited at the Friday sermon. Furthermore, the colour of the canopy surmounting his throne had been changed from black, the colour of the caliphs of Baghdad, to the green tint of the Shiite Imams. Did not such a complete conversion deserve an exceptional reward?

The transfer of the diamond to the Deccan is confirmed by Khor Shah, the ambassador of the King of Golconda to the Persian court, in a manuscript preserved at the India Office Library in London. After referring to the famous diamond whose value was reckoned by experts to be "the expenditure of the whole universe for two days and a half", he adds: "But in the eyes of His Majesty the Shah, it was not of such great value. At last he sent that diamond along with Agha Islam, commonly known as Mahtar Jamal, as a present to Nizam Shah, the ruler of the Deccan, as will be recorded hereafter, if God wills."

Alas! Khor Shah did not live long enough to finish his story. Fortunately, another manuscript of the same period, whose author remains unknown, sheds some light on the outcome of Mahtar Jamal's mission, even though no mention is made of the fate of the diamond. According to this text, the Persian emissary was sent by Tahmasp to Burhan Nizam Shah with a message and numerous presents. Once he arrived at Ahmadnagar, he delivered the letter, but he afterwards fell under Tahmasp's displeasure on account of some improper acts.

It has been said that instead of handing over the diamond to Burhan Nizam Shah, Mahtar Jamal sold it in Vijayanagar and kept the proceeds for himself. This misdemeanour led Tahmasp to order his arrest. However, Mahtar Jamal was warned in time and managed to escape his pursuers.

This could well have happened, as Ahmadnagar is not very far from Vijayanagar which, at the time, was the capital of a vast Hindu kingdom of the same name, whose borders stretched from the banks of the river Krishna to Cape Comorin. Founded in 1336, this kingdom served the Hindus as a rampart against Muslim conquerors until 1565, when it crumbled before the onslaught of the combined armies of Bijapur, Golconda and Ahmadnagar at the Battle of Talikota. Vijayanagar possessed the richest diamond mines in the world and was a famous mart for those stones.

The principal mines were located on the north bank of the Krishna river, in the districts of Kurnool and Anantapur. They were leased out with the provision that all stones weighing more than 20 mangelin, that is 25 carats, had to be given to the king for his personal use. Apparently their number was so considerable that even after the Battle of Talikota, the King of Vijayanagar managed to keep a chest full of them.

There was one stone in particular that was fixed to the

ceremonial feather on his horse's head. This diamond fell into the hands of the King of Bijapur after the sack of Vijayanagar. Its exceptional size and lustre attracted the attention of Portuguese chroniclers like the historian Diogo do Couto, the author of the *Decades,* and his compatriot, Doctor Garcia de Orta, whose *Portuguese Colloquies concerning Simples and Drugs,* published in Goa in 1563, is believed to be the earliest book printed in India. Garcia de Orta relates that a man worthy of trust had told him many years ago that he had seen in Vijayanagar a diamond as big as a small hen's egg ("ovo pequeno de galinha"). Unfortunately, he does not mention the weight of this particular diamond, even though he reveals the weights of three other stones he had supposedly admired with his own eyes: they weighed respectively 120, 140 and 250 mangelin, that is 150, 175 and 312.5 carats. Given the varying criteria used to weigh precious stones in different regions of India, it may well be that the diamond shaped like a hen's egg, or perhaps the 175 carat stone, was Babur's diamond whose weight was around 186 carats.

However, all traces of Babur's diamond were lost in a maze of conjectures for more than a century. We must wait until the middle of the seventeenth century before suddenly rediscovering it at the court of Shah Jahan, Humayun's great-grandson, on the eve of a bloody fratricidal war which was to tear apart the Mughal empire. Meanwhile, the stage on which the stone's drama was to unfurl—north India—underwent a profound transformation.

Humayun's second reign over India was even more ephemeral than the first. On Friday, 24 January 1556, barely six months after having recovered the throne, this unfortunate monarch who had braved all the hazards of fortune, died in the most absurd of circumstances. On that day, he was in his library located, it is said, in the Sher Mandal, the octagonal building in red sandstone, surmounted by a small pavilion, which still stands in the Purana Qila complex in Delhi.

After a long conversation with some of his officers as well as with the Turkish admiral Sidi Ali Reis who had arrived from Gujarat, Humayun climbed up to the roof for some fresh air and received the homage of his subjects who had gathered at the entrance of the neighbouring mosque.

At nightfall, he was returning to the library to perform his prayers, when the call of a muezzin caught him unawares in the middle of the steep stairway. As he was kneeling in reverence, his foot got caught in his long robe and his cane slipped on the step, making him lose his balance. He fell headlong down the stairs and was seriously wounded. Two days later, he succumbed to his injuries.

His thirteen-year-old son Akbar was then in the Punjab, along with Bairam Khan who had been appointed by the Emperor as his ataliq or tutor-guardian, with the title of Khan-i-Khanan (the Khan of Khans). They were then in conflict with Sikander Shah Suri, a descendant of Sher Shah.

At the suggestion of Sidi Ali Reis, the Turkish admiral, it was decided to keep Humayun's death a secret until Akbar was officially enthroned. To allay popular suspicion, one Mulla Bekasi, the Emperor's double, was made to wear his clothes and appear every morning before the inhabitants of Delhi. Finally, on 12 February 1556, after the security of the capital had been ensured, the khutba (Friday sermon) was recited in the name of the new sovereign, Jalal-ud-din Mohammed Akbar.

The teenager who had been crowned Emperor of India a few days after the death of his father Humayun was to become the greatest of the Great Mughals. In 1560, at the age of eighteen, he freed himself from Bairam Khan's growing control and ordered him to go on pilgrimage to Mecca. Such a journey was indeed the wish of every pious Muslim, but the way in which it was suggested to Bairam

Khan meant clearly that his services were no longer needed. The friends of the "Protector" begged him to challenge this order, inspired in fact by his enemies at court. Their pleas fell on deaf ears. Bairam Khan refused to do anything that might compromise his unswerving loyalty to the Mughal dynasty.

However, he was mysteriously assassinated in Gujarat before sailing for the Holy Land. His son Abd-ur-Rahim, who was barely four years old then, was brought up by Akbar. He became not only a great general, but also a scholar and one of the Nava Ratna or "nine jewels" of the court, as Akbar's closest friends were called. Among these were Maan Singh, later the Maharaja of Amber (Jaipur), Abul Fazl, Akbar's private secretary and the author of the *Akbar Nama,* and Mian Tansen, the legendary singer from Gwalior.

Unlike his predecessors and successors, Akbar was illiterate. The circumstances of his nomadic childhood were such that he was unable to avail himself of the education normally imparted to Mughal princes. Nevertheless, thanks to a prodigious memory, he managed to acquire a wealth of knowledge. He possessed a large library composed of the priceless manuscripts left to him by his father. He had them read to him, and was particularly fond of listening to and learning by heart the mystic verse of Sufi poets like Hafiz and Jalal-ud-din Rumi.

The new Emperor also showed remarkable finesse in his political dealings, and was an outstanding administrator. These qualities enabled him to transform the kingdom he had inherited into a great empire. To achieve this object, he took steps to win over the loyalty of the Hindus, who constituted the majority of his subjects and filled numerous posts in the administration and the army.

First, he married a Rajput princess, the daughter of Bhagwan Das, the Raja of Amber (Jaipur), and promoted some Hindus like Raja Todar Mal, to key positions. Raja Todar Mal, one of the greatest finance ministers India ever knew, was given the task of reforming agricultural taxation. This reform, followed by the abolition of the jaziya (the poll tax imposed on non-Muslims) and the tax on pilgrimages, considerably reduced the Hindu tax payer's burden.

He also instituted a series of land reforms, measures and records based on Sher Shah's administration, which is today remembered as "Todar Mal's Bandobast" or arrangement.

Todar Mal also ordered that the accounts of the empire be kept in Persian. He thereby forced Hindus to learn the court language, thus giving them a chance to compete with Muslims for the greatest honours.

Akbar's open-mindedness was first and foremost reflected in his religious tolerance. Imbued with the doctrines of Persian mysticism which he had learnt in his youth and later through his friend Abul Fazl, he rejected the dogmas of Islam for the Din-i-llahi, or "Divine faith", a syncretism of the various religious and philosophical doctrines of the empire.

For some of his subjects Akbar's tolerance seemed to be far from being uniform. His critics felt he favoured Hindus, to the detriment of Muslims, going so far as forbidding the latter to call their children Mohammed. He also discouraged the study of Arabic and replaced the lunar calendar based on the Hegira (622 AD, the date Prophet Mohammed left Mecca for Medina), by the solar calendar based on the spring equinox. On this occasion, the festival of Navroz (New Year) was celebrated as in Persia, the only difference being that in India its highlight became the Meena Bazaar. This was a kind of garden-party held on the lawns of the palace, where the ladies of the court and the wives of high dignitaries, for the duration of an evening, turned into genuine merchant women, sat behind stalls with their faces uncovered and bargained for charms and fairings to the great delight of the select male audience.

The Din-i-llahi, which numbered few adepts, did not outlive its founder. But the fact remains that in a country torn by religious and ethnic conflicts, Akbar's syncretic vision succeeded in building for a period, however brief it may have been, a nation, in place of the factions of the time.

By the time of his death in 1605, Akbar had stretched the borders of his empire from Kandahar in the west to the Bay of Bengal in the east, from Kashmir in the north to the banks of the river Narmada in central India. But he was too wise to get involved in the politics of the Deccan (a name derived from Dakshin, the Sanskrit word for "south"). He contented himself with the annexation of Khandesh, a wild country situated in the valley of the Tapti river, between north India and the Deccan, mainly in order to protect his empire from southern invasions. He also took over Berar and the Ahmadnagar fort. The Shiite kings of Bijapur and Golconda, overawed by his boldness, assured him of their good will and agreed to pay tribute.

And it is entirely possible that Akbar was unaware of the fact that the diamond that his father had once possessed was somewhere in the very Deccan that he steered clear of. . . .

Although Akbar had many wives, none of his children managed to survive. Being more superstitious than religious, he turned for help to Sheikh Salim, a venerable old man who lived as a hermit in the small village of Sikri, thirty five kilometres to the west of Agra. The saintly man, a member of the mystical Chishti order of Sufis, promised him that his wishes would be fulfilled and that he would soon have not one, but three sons. In August 1569, the prophecy came true. The princess of Jaipur, Jodh Bai, bore Akbar a son whom he named Salim in honour of the Sikri hermit. In the following years, he had two other sons, Murad and Daniyal.

To celebrate the birth of Prince Salim, the future Emperor Jahangir, and to attest his gratitude towards his son's namesake, Akbar had a splendid town built at Sikri on top of a hill which he called Fatehpur Sikri, "the city of victory". Its construction took nearly fourteen years. It remained the capital of the empire until 1585, when it was abandoned for Agra. Akbar's successors never resided there, and it remains today the same as it must have been at the outset. Its most famous monument is the Buland Darwaza or "high gate", the magnificent entrance to the esplanade of the great mosque, where stands the white marbled mausoleum of Sheikh Salim Chishti.

In the twilight of his life, Akbar had to suffer the revolt of his son Salim, who was insolent enough to order the assassination of Abul Fazl, whom he hated. The Emperor nonetheless forgave him, no doubt for reasons of state, and named him his successor before dying in October 1605, of acute dysentery. However, the example set by Salim triggered off an inexorable cycle of fratricidal struggles that would bathe the Mughal empire in blood until its decline and fall.

Jahangir—which means "conqueror of the universe"—ascended the throne at his father's death, aged thirty-six. According to Vincent Smith, one of Akbar's modern biographers, "His character was a strange mixture of tenderness and cruelty, justice and capriciousness, refinement and coarseness, good sense and childishness"

His reign began with the rebellion of his eldest son Khusro, and ended with the revolt of his third son, Khurram, who eventually became Emperor Shah Jahan. Thus, Jahangir was hoist with his own petard.

Khusro, whose mother, like Jahangir's, was a Rajput princess of Amber, had been his father's rival even before the latter came to the throne. He had a very charming personality and his many supporters at court would have preferred him as master to the capricious Jahangir. This was particularly true of Abul Fazl, Akbar's most trusted advisor, whose open support of the young prince led to his tragic end.

Upon coming to the throne, Jahangir tried to win the favour of his son's friends by granting amnesty to all those who had somehow or the other plotted his overthrow. This did not stop the young prince from rising anew against his father. From the Punjab, where he had taken refuge, he raised an army and marched on Lahore, the first step in his conquest of the throne. His efforts proved futile. In a few days' time, the imperial army stifled his ambitions.

The emperor's vengeance was terrible. Before dealing with the rest of his son's supporters, Jahangir took it out on Hussein Beg and Abd-ur-Rahim, two of Khusro's most trusted lieutenants. He "ordered these two villains to be put in the skins of an ox and an ass, and that they should be mounted on asses with their faces to the tail and thus taken round the city. As the ox-hide dried more quickly than that of the ass, Hussain Beg remained alive for four watches and died from suffocation. Abd-ur-Rahim, who was in the ass's skin and to whom they gave some refreshment from outside, remained alive", Jahangir's memoirs relate.

Thereupon, Jahangir had the other rebels hung on gallows set up along both sides of the road leading from the palace to the gates of the city. After which, he inspected this gruesome guard of honour, followed by his miserable son. A year later Khusro made yet another attempt against his father who, this time, ordered that he be blinded. It is said that the executioner, filled with compassion, executed the sentence in such a way that the prince was able to recover his sight partially.

The Emperor also took on Guru Arjun, the fifth Guru of the Sikhs and the compiler of their sacred book, the *Granth Sahib*. Sikhism, a religion founded between 1460 and 1538 by Guru Nanak, the son of a trader from the Punjab, prescribed a symbiosis between Hinduism and Islam. By condemning idol worship, Nanak won the sympathy of the most enlightened Muslims and by proclaiming fraternity among men, a principle which ran counter to the Hindu system of castes, he gained numerous converts from among the provincial Hindu peasantry.

Guru Arjun had been imprudent enough to give Khusro financial help. However, in deference to his religious status, he was only required to pay a heavy fine. When he refused to obey, he was tortured to death.

Jahangir's life and reign were deeply affected by his marriage, in 1611, to Mehr-un-nissa, the daughter of a Persian nobleman who had come to seek his fortune at the court of Akbar.

The popular belief that Jahangir fell madly in love with her after having seen her in the *zenana* (women's apartments) for the first time, is, alas, mere fantasy. In fact, Mehr-un-nissa was first married to one of her compatriots, one Ali Quli Beg, better known as Sher Afkan, to whom Akbar had granted a jagir (fief) in Bengal.

Not long after he had left, Sher Afkan fell into disgrace and the Emperor sent his foster brother to arrest him and bring him back to Agra. The impetuous Persian resisted and in the scuffle that ensued lost his life. His widow and daughter, Ladli Begum, were brought back to the court and placed under the charge of one of Akbar's widows.

For some time Mehr-un-nissa stayed there unnoticed. However, as one chronicler of the time has so aptly said, "Fate having decreed that she become the queen of the world, her beauty caught the attention of the Emperor and captivated him so much that he chose her as one of the most privileged members of his harem."

Her influence and stature grew with each passing day. First, her name was changed to Nur Mahal, "light of the harem", then to Nur Jahan or "light of the universe". Her parents and relations were enriched with honours. Coins were struck bearing her name with the inscription: "By order of the King Jahangir, gold has a hundred splendours added to it by receiving the impression of Nur Jahan, the Queen Begum". Her name also appeared next to that of her husband on all firmans (royal decrees).

Except for Aurangzeb, hedonism was one of the main characteristics of all the Mughal rulers. Jahangir made it into almost a cult. He gradually relinquished all his responsibilities to give himself up to the pleasures of wine and opium, leaving the administration of his empire to his wife. He never tired of saying that he had handed over sovereignty to Nur Jahan Begum, for he himself needed nothing more than "a seer (*almost a kilo*) of wine and half a seer of meat."

In 1608, Captain William Hawkins arrived in Surat. He brought to Jahangir a letter from the King of England, James I, aimed at obtaining trading concessions for the East India Company, which had been founded some years earlier through a charter signed by Queen Elizabeth I. This mission did not please the Portuguese who, still very influential at the Mughal court, spared no effort to hinder it. Hawkins nevertheless managed to foil their intrigues and gained access to the Emperor. Jahangir was so taken up with him that he showered him with favours and gave him an official title at the court. Hawkins became one of his favourite drinking partners and partook in his nightly orgies. He remained in Agra for three years, after which he was replaced in 1615 by William Edwards, the bearer of a second letter from James I to the Great Mughal. A year later, Edwards was succeeded by a more official envoy, Sir Thomas Roe.

One evening Roe was called to the private apartments of the Emperor on the pretext of showing him a portrait.

"At ten o'clock at night, the King sent for me at my lodgings while I was in bed. It transpired that the Emperor had learnt of a painting in my possession which I had not shown him. He wished me to find it and bring it to him; that even if I did not wish to gift it to him, he should at least be able to see it and make copies for his wives. I rose and went to him with this painting. He was sitting cross-legged on a small throne covered with diamonds, pearls and rubies. In front of him was a table in pure gold on which were fifty golden plates, all decorated with stone work; some were very large and ornate, some were less precious but all of them were covered with beautiful stones. The Emperor was surrounded by the lords of the court, each one attired in all his finery. The Emperor ordered that they drink merrily the various wines contained in big flasks. When I approached him, he asked me about the painting. I showed him two portraits; he looked at one of them and asked me with astonishment who it was . . . He then threw to those sitting below him two bowlfuls of rubies and to the rest of us two huge bowlfuls of gold and silver almonds mixed together but hollow within. I did not feel the need to jump on them in the manner of the principals of his court, as I noticed that his son did not take any. He then gave the musicians and other courtesans very rich cloth so that they may make their turbans and belts, drinking all the while and ordering that the others do likewise. So much that His Majesty and the main noblemen of his court were in various stages of admirable humour except for his brother-in-law, Asaf Khan and two old men. When the king could support himself no longer, he fell asleep. We all retired."

Whilst Jahangir continued his frenetic quest for pleasure and ruined the robust constitution he had inherited from his ancestors, the ambitious Nur Jahan assumed imperial powers with the support of her father Mirza Ghyas Beg (Itimad-ud-daula), the prime minister, and her brother Asaf Khan, the grand chamberlain.

Asaf Khan's daughter Arjumand Banu had been married since 1612 to Prince Khurram who, having distinguished himself on the battlefields of Rajasthan and the Deccan, had received from his father the title of Shah Jahan. Like all Mughal princes, Khurram aspired to the throne. Nur Jahan supported the claims of her nephew by marriage for as long as the latter espoused her interests. But as soon as their ambitions began to diverge, she placed her hopes on Shahriyar, Jahangir's younger son, who was born to Khurram's mother, Rani Jagat Gossain of Marwar. Nur Jahan eventually made Shahriyar her son-in-law.

It was necessary for Khurram, given the precarious state of his father's health, to stay as close as possible to the court, so that he could capture the throne in case of the Emperor's sudden demise. Of his brothers, Parviz, a drunkard, was in Allahabad from where he governed Bihar; Shahriyar was considered a good-for-nothing: that left Khusro, who had still many supporters at the court, even though his semi-blindness excluded him in theory from succeeding his father.

In 1620, Khurram was called upon to re-establish order in the Deccan. He accepted after having obtained the charge of his half-blind elder brother. Two years later, it was officially learnt that Khusro had died of diarrhoe'a. This was the version to which Jahangir subscribed, as is shown in his memoirs. In reality, the unfortunate prince had been strangled in his cell in the Burhanpur citadel by Khurram's henchmen.

Khurram, rid of a potential rival and basking in the glory

of a new victory, was preparing to join the Emperor in Lahore, when he was ordered to relieve Kandahar, once again besieged by Persian troops. He hesitated for several weeks, rightly suspecting that the paternal injunction was but one of Nur Jahan's schemes to keep him away from court. The queen had just married her daughter Ladli Begum to Shahriyar. In favouring the latter's claim to the succession, she hoped to make him the instrument of her own designs. But first she needed to remove Khurram from her path.

At this juncture, the relationship between the Emperor and Khurram was further strained on account of a misunderstanding. The latter had asked his father to add Dholpur to his jagirs. After some time, presuming that his request had been granted, he sent one of his officers with a small force to take possession of it. Having reached Dholpur, the officer discovered to his great surprise that the city had been given to Shahriyar, whose men were guarding the gates. A bloody quarrel ensued in which a large number of soldiers from both sides were killed and Shahriyar's representative seriously wounded.

As soon as the news of this incident reached the court, Jahangir decreed that Khurram be stripped of all his jagirs, including Hissar Feroz, the traditional fief of the Crown Prince. All his jagirs were to go to Shahriyar. At the same time, he appointed the latter as commander-in-chief of the expeditionary force to Kandahar, unaware that the city had already fallen into the hands of the Persian army.

But Jahangir did not accept defeat. He ordered his son Parviz, the governor of Bihar, to gather as many soldiers as possible to reinforce the expeditionary corps to Kandahar. Khurram, in the meantime, rebelled against his father and marched on Agra at the head of a powerful army, with the blessings of the Muslim generals of the Deccan, Gujarat and Malwa among whom were Abd-ur-Rahim Khan-i-

Khanan, the son of Bairam Khan, one of the last figures of Akbar's time.

Nur Jahan found herself in a predicament. Jahangir had just had an acute attack of asthma which had impaired his already delicate health and would soon cause his death. Her father, Itimad-ud-Daula, had passed away a year earlier, depriving her of a faithful ally and advisor. As for her brother Asaf Khan, didn't his apparent display of brotherly loyalty hide a partiality for his own son-in-law Khurram? Forced to act alone against the rebel prince, she appealed to Mahabat Khan, the Governor of Kabul, for assistance. Though a Muslim, Mahabat Khan, a soldier and general in the heroic mould, was the idol of the Rajputs, five thousand of whom composed his personal guard. Promoted for the occasion to the mansab, or exceptional rank, of seven thousand sawar (horse), in January 1623, he assumed, effective control over the imperial army, under Parviz's titular leadership.

When the two armies clashed south of Delhi, Khurram's forces suffered a crushing defeat. The prince fled with Mahabat Khan on his heels. For three years, the two men played a game of hide-and-seek, criss-crossing several thousand kilometres across Rajasthan, the Deccan, Orissa and Bengal. At last the future Emperor took refuge in the Deccan with his wife and children. He stayed there until the death of his father with whom he had become reconciled after having sent his sons Dara Shikoh and Aurangzeb to court as proof of his good faith.

Hardly had Shah Jahan's rebellion been crushed than a new danger threatened the Mughal court. Mahabat Khan's success had excited the jealousy of Nur Jahan and her brother Asaf Khan. Hence, under the pretext that the general had failed to hand over to the Emperor the elephants captured in Bengal while pursuing Khurram, they persuaded Jahangir to call him back to court. Guessing rightly that this was a plot against him, Mahabat Khan refused to comply and decided to take action against its instigators.

After an unsuccessful coup d'état against the Emperor, aimed presumably at curtailing the growing influence of Nur Jahan and her brother, Mahabat Khan was pardoned. His services were once more needed to deal with Khurram, who was now suspected of fomenting new troubles. This time, however, Mahabat Khan chose to side with the prince rather than to oppose him, hoping thus to take a spectacular revenge on his detractors.

In the meantime, Prince Parviz died of cirrhosis of the liver, due to excessive drinking, though it was rumoured that Khurram had him poisoned. Years later, Aurangzeb was to justify his behaviour towards his father in these words: "How do you still regard the memory of Khusro and Parviz, whom you did to death before your accession and who had threatened no injury to you?"

In the early spring of 1627, Jahangir left Lahore for Kashmir to spend the summer there, as was his habit. That year however, the salubrious climate of his favourite province was of no benefit to his health. On the contrary, the rarefied mountain air seriously aggravated his asthmatic condition. He grew weaker by the day, lost appetite and even refused wine and opium.

In the autumn of the same year, as the imperial procession slowly came down the steep slopes separating Kashmir from the Punjab, Jahangir had a sudden urge to hunt deer. While driving the animals towards him, one of his gamekeepers slipped on a rock and fell into a precipice. The fate of the poor man greatly affected the Emperor who went into a decline . It seemed as though he had seen in this misfortune an omen of his own death, which came on 28 October 1627 at Bhimbar in the Kashmir valley after a severe fall while hunting. His body was buried in a magnificent park at Shahdara, on the banks of the Ravi, a few kilometres to the west of Lahore.

Jahangir's greatest contribution to India was his patronage of the arts. Under his reign, miniature painting reached sublime heights. Like his great-grandfather Babur, he too left us his memoirs, the *Tuzuk-i-Jahangiri* which although not of the same literary quality, are just as startlingly candid. For instance, he admits to having instigated the assassination of Abul Fazl, his father's friend and counsellor. He also shared with Babur a deep love for the beauties of nature.

His rule coincided with the decline of Portuguese influence and the beginning of a rapprochement between the Mughal empire and England. Since 1497, when Vasco de Gama crossed the Cape of Good Hope and planted the Portuguese flag in Calicut, on the Malabar coast, Portugal held the monopoly over Asian trade, to the detriment of other European powers. It was only towards the end of the 16th century that the situation began to change, first in favour of Holland and then of England, mainly because of the temporary annexation of Portugal by Spain between 1580 and 1640, the religious intolerance of the Portuguese, and finally their expulsion in 1622 from the island of Hormuz, in the Persian Gulf, by the Persian king, Shah Abbas the Great.

Meanwhile, after Jahangir's death, Nur Jahan sent a secret message to her son-in-law Shahriyar, who was then in Lahore, urging him to seize the crown. The latter immediately took over the treasures locked up in the citadel, distributed generous sums of money to the local nobility, and after having secured their allegiance, proclaimed himself Emperor.

But Shahriyar had reckoned without Asaf Khan, who henceforth openly espoused the cause of his own son-in-law Khurram. He moved swiftly while his sister Nur Jahan was revelling in Shahriyar's decision, and had her placed under house arrest. He next sent a courier with his signet ring to the Deccan to inform Khurram about the events that had taken place, urging him to return to Agra immediately. Meanwhile, anxious to fill the power vacuum and to neutralise Shahriyar's initiative, Asaf Khan chose as Emperor, Dawar Baksh, the late Prince Khusro's son and rightful heir by the Indian (if not Timurid) law of primogeniture.

In spite of Shahriyar's resistance, his troops were decimated by Asaf Khan's army, and he himself was forced to take refuge in the zenana of the Lahore fort. It was there that he was discovered by a eunuch in the pay of Asaf Khan, handed over to him, imprisoned, and finally blinded.

Meanwhile when Khurram got Asaf Khan's message he promptly headed towards Agra, advising his father-in-law "to send out from this world Dawar Baksh, the son, and Shahriyar, the useless brother of Khusro, as well as the offspring of Prince Daniyal".

On Thursday, 28 January 1628, Khurram arrived at the gates of the capital. He was welcomed by his father-in-law, who must have apprised him of his arrangements: Khurram's brother, nephews and cousins were to be executed the next day at dawn in their cells in Agra Fort.

Khurram waited for a few days before making his official entry into the citadel, so as to give the astrologers enough time to fix a propitious day for his coronation as Shah Jahan, "king of the world". It took place on 4 February 1628, one month after he had celebrated his thirty-sixth birthday, amidst a display of exceptional splendour.

Nur Jahan remained in Lahore where the new sovereign, forgetting their enmity, granted her a comfortable pension. She died in 1645 at the age of seventy-two and was buried near her husband's and her brother's tombs at Shahdara, in a baradari or pavilion she had had built during her lifetime. Ladli Begum, her only daughter, widow of the hapless Shahriyar, was to be buried later in the same mausoleum.

If Akbar was the greatest of the great Mughals, Shah Jahan is certainly the most famous. In spite of his rebellion against his father, the treatment he meted to his family and the excesses of his old age, he remains for most people the inspired creator of the Taj Mahal, the white marble monument to his wife Arjumand Banu, known as Mumtaz Mahal after her husband's accession to the throne.

Shah Jahan had fallen in love with her at a Meena Bazaar, when they were respectively sixteen and fourteen years old. Their betrothal was sealed by Emperor Jahangir with a magnificent ring he placed on the finger of his future daughter-in-law. The couple were married five years later, on 12 April 1612.

From that time on, Arjumand Banu became Shah Jahan's inseparable companion following him in all his military campaigns, sharing his exile and savouring his glory. Had she lived longer, she would have probably lightened, if not prevented, the trials of his old age. However, fate had other plans in store. On 7 June 1631, barely four years after her husband had mounted the throne, she died while giving birth to their fourteenth child. Of those children seven survived: four sons—Dara Shikoh (1615), Shuja (1616), Aurangzeb (1618), Murad Baksh (1624)—and three daughters—Jahanara (1614), Raushanara (1624), and Gauharara (1631). With the exception of Gauharara, forgotten by history, all the others were to partake in the tragic drama that was to unfurl itself around the future "Koh-i-noor".

CHAPTER FOUR

While Shah Jahan began his reign—one of the most magnificent, yet tragic, India ever witnessed—a young Persian boy of modest condition, named Mohammed Said, went about his daily chores in Ispahan. Little did they both know that Babur's diamond would one day unite their destinies.

The origins of Mohammed Said are rather obscure. It is said that he was born in 1591 in Ispahan, where his father, a native of the neighbouring city of Ardistan, was an oil merchant. One would have expected that the son would follow in his father's footsteps, as was the oriental custom. But the young man, who was of exceptional intelligence, had other ideas. Showing great enterprise, he acquired all by himself, an education which the few Koranic schools usually reserved for the privileged classes.

At the age of sixteen, he joined the services of an Ispahan diamond merchant who traded Persian steeds for Golconda diamonds. Ever since the foundation of the Bahmani kingdom of the Deccan and the Mughal Empire, the Indian sub-continent had caught the imagination of many Persians, who flocked there in search of fame and fortune. Their chances of success were considerably enhanced after the kingdoms of Ahmadnagar, Bijapur and Golconda became independent and embraced Shiite Islam.

The first few years of Mohammed Said's life are lost to history. In 1630, he was living in Golconda. He was thirty-nine years old and probably came there with his master who, having bartered his horses for precious stones, returned to Persia.

In spite of his advanced age, Mohammed Said became

an apprentice in the employ of a jeweller in Golconda, who kept shop on the famous diamond merchants' street. Today it is a dusty road bordered by a few dilapidated houses.

A few years later he was farming some diamond mines in his own name and had become a famous merchant. Thereafter he did not rest until he got an important position at court.

In 1634, Mohammed Said was appointed curator of the royal archives, a function which although not very prestigious, gave him access to court secrets and allowed him to insinuate himself into the good graces of the minister of finance, Sheikh Mohammed Ibn Khatun, the Amir Jumla or Mir Jumla. The latter, also a native of Persia, had lately been the ambassador of Golconda to the court of the Safavids.

Two years later, Mohammed Said was made Havildar (governor) of the port of Machilipatnam. This port, on the northern branch of the river Krishna, near the Bay of Bengal, was then Golconda's most important outlet to the sea. It was famous for its trade in chintz, calico and cotton. Enormous quantities were exported to Bantam, the first trading post of the Dutch East India Company, on the west coast of Java, as well as to other South Asian markets.

Mohammed Said's service record at Machilipatnam and subsequently as governor of the fortress of Mohammednagar in Telingana, a post he held concurrently, won him the approval of his superiors. Summoned to the court in the spring of 1637, he arrived in Golconda on 21 June, laden with lavish presents for Sultan Abdullah Qutb Shah, among which were beautifully caparisoned elephants from Sri Lanka and objets d'art from China and Europe. The sultan received him with kindness, and having heard of his talents, he appointed him Sar-i-Khail. This title, which literally means chief of a tribe, entailed considerable civil and military responsibilities, and made its holder a high dignitary of state.

Mohammed Said's first task in the capital was to construct the Hayat Mahal, a four-storied residence for the Queen Mother, Hayat Bakshi Begum. It was built in less than a year, much to the delight of its owner, who held the contractor in considerable esteem. If Nicolo Manucci, the gossipy Venetian traveller who lived for a long time in India, is to be believed, the Queen Mother, "a Princess who had preserved her beauty till quite an advanced age", was carrying on an affair with the ambitious Persian.

Mohammed Said thus became extremely powerful at the court. According to Andrew Cogan, an envoy of the British East India company to Golconda, "The Sar-i-Khail commanded in fact the entire Kingdom." Perhaps he had already succeeded Sheikh Mohammed Ibn Khatun as finance minister when the latter was promoted to the rank of Peshwa or prime minister. A modern historian of the Deccan claims that this transfer of power occurred on 18 June 1643.

Mohammed Said, henceforth known as Mir Jumla, next conquered Karnataka (Mysore) of which he was appointed governor. From then on, his power and fortunes knew no bounds. Besides four thousand men from the Golconda army whose officers he had won over through his liberality, he also commanded a personal army of five thousand horsemen, twenty thousand infantrymen, an excellent artillery served by English, French and Italian gunners, three hundred combat elephants, and four to five hundred camels.

Jean-Baptiste Tavernier, the French traveller and jeweller, on his fourth voyage to India, met Mir Jumla in September 1652 at Gandikota, the impressive fortress he had just conquered in the Cuddapah district, south of Hyderabad.

This fortress, which now stands in ruins, is located on a rocky spur, surrounded on all sides by plains. It can only be reached by a narrow winding path between the mountainside and a daunting precipice at the base of which flows the river Penner.

On 3 September, Tavernier and his companion, one Du Jardin, were received by the minister, whom they called "Nawab", as did all European residents of Machilipatnam. He gave them a warm welcome, asked them if they were comfortably housed, and whether they had been supplied with the food intended for them and their mounts. Then, without any further ado, they got down to business.

Tavernier knew that all dealings in precious stones had to have the backing of Mir Jumla. "We told him that we had some rare merchandise for the King, but that we had not gone to His Majesty before showing them to him (Mir Jumla), knowing well that the King bought nothing of value without his advice; and that in any case, we considered such deference to be due to him. The Nawab expressed his satisfaction, and presented us with betel leaves, whereupon we took our leave of him and returned to the city."

The next day, Tavernier went back to show Mir Jumla the goods he wished to sell the King of Golconda. They consisted of some pear-shaped pearls, whose weight, beauty and size were truly extraordinary, the smallest weighing 24 carats. Mohammed Said examined them with an expert eye, showed them to his subordinates, inquired about their price and returned them to their owner.

A week later, the jeweller, who had been waiting impatiently for the outcome of his meetings, was summoned again to Mir Jumla's tent. The Nawab rose to greet him and asked him to sit by his side, on the soft cushions scattered around. Afterwards, he had five small bags filled with diamonds brought to him, which he opened in front of his guest. "They were all lasques" (flat and oval stones) recalls Tavernier, "but of very dark water and very small. Most of them were barely one carat or half a carat in weight, but otherwise very clear. There were very few of them which weighed two carats."

Mir Jumla asked him if such goods were saleable in his country. Tavernier replied that they might, provided the water was white, for in Europe diamonds had value only if they were clear and white.

On 15 September, at seven o'clock in the morning, the two men met again and Tavernier saw Mir Jumla at work. The Nawab sat cross-legged on a magnificent Persian carpet, barefoot, with two scribes kneeling by his side. He had a pile of letters stuffed between his toes and the fingers of his left hand. He would pull some from his feet, some from his hand, and dictate the answers to the scribes. Once the letters were written, he had them read to him, after which he affixed his seal and had them dispatched to the four corners of his kingdom.

Tavernier also witnessed the summary justice dispensed by Mir Jumla. The latter was immersed in his correspondence when he was informed that four prisoners were awaiting judgement at the door of his tent. He did not react for half an hour, continuing to write and dictate to his scribes. All of a sudden he ordered that the criminals be brought before him. After forcing a confession from them, he fell silent again, absorbed in his correspondence for another half hour. In the meantime, several of his army officers entered the tent to pay him their respects. He responded to their deferential bows with a condescending nod of his head. Then he gave his judgement. Among the four prisoners there was one who had entered a house and slain a mother and her three children. He was condemned to have his hands and feet cut off and be thrown by the roadside to end his days. Another had stolen. The Nawab ordered him to be disembowelled and flung in a drain. As for the other two, whose crimes were probably even more serious, he ordered their heads to be cut off.

Mir Jumla used to take his daily meal at ten o'clock in the morning. Wishing to bid farewell to Tavernier and his companion, he invited them to share his meal. Then he gave them permission to leave for Golconda, and advised them to get in touch with his son and personal representative at court, Mohammed Amin, as soon as they arrived there.

As Governor of Karnataka, Mir Jumla ruled over a territory of 24,000 square kilometers, and enjoyed an annual income of 4,00,000 huns (sixteenth century Deccan currency). The legendary diamond mines of Golconda were within his jurisdiction. He farmed most of them under borrowed names in order to spare the susceptibilities of his sovereign. It is said that he possessed 20 man (around 11.6 kilos) of diamonds, which is about 232.5 kilos. However, even though the conditions of farming specified that the larger stones had to be handed over to the ruler, Mir Jumla kept the most beautiful ones for himself, sending the scrap to Abdullah Qutb Shah.

He also possessed many vessels that he had acquired when he was the Havildar of Machilipatnam , and was thus able to control a large part of Golconda's trade with South Asia and the Persian Gulf. European merchants, fearing his power, regularly sent him gifts to stay in his good books. The Portuguese viceroy, Don Felipe Mascarenhas, a great lover of diamonds, tried to win his favour by suggesting that Portugal would come to his aid should his fortunes ever change. As for the British East India Company, whose head office was located at Madras, it supplied him with cannons in exchange for new concessions in the Bay of Bengal. Emboldened by these connections, as well as by his personal power, Mir Jumla went on plundering Hindu temples and forcing the inhabitants of Karnataka to hand over their gold and precious stones to him, killing those who, according to custom, buried their treasure. It also appears that he expected a promotion. Perhaps he coveted the official position of Peshwa, as he was already discharging the responsibilities of that office since the death of his protector, Sheikh Mohammed Ibn Khatun. Disappointed at not being able to realise this ambition, he nursed, according to British sources, the plan of taking over the conquered lands. A representative of the East India Company observed: "If he were to succeed in his designs, he would be as powerful a king as his master." Other sources would have us believe that Mir Jumla wished to go to Mecca and end his days there.

Not unnaturally, Mir Jumla's growing prosperity aroused the jealousy and anger of the Sultan of Golconda. Inevitably the two men quarrelled in 1654. Summoned to Hyderabad, Mir Jumla complied reluctantly, rightly sensing a plot against him. Tavernier tells us that the Sultan intended to have him poisoned or blinded. However, warned in time by his son and probably by the Queen Mother, he managed to escape and returned to his fief.

From that moment Mir Jumla began looking for allies. He entered into secret and parallel negotiations with the Sultan of Bijapur and Prince Aurangzeb, Viceroy of the Deccan. But Mughal policy in the Deccan was to profoundly affect Mir Jumla's future. And with it, the fate of Babur's diamond.

Once the coronation ceremonies were over and a rebellion in Bundelkhand had been put down, Shah Jahan and his family were leading a relatively quiet life in Agra, when fresh trouble broke out in the Deccan. Although the Emperor had restored order in the region ten years earlier, the Deccan remained a hotbed of intrigue against the interests of the Mughal state. The latest conspiracy had been hatched by Khan Jahan Lodhi, a former Mughal governor of the Deccan, with the blessings of the King of Ahmadnagar. Shah Jahan decided to personally lead the imperial army against the rebellious chief, and put an end to the intrigues of the Ahmadnagar kingdom.

In December 1629, he left Agra for Burhanpur at the head of a powerful army, accompanied by his wife Mumtaz Mahal, who, despite an advanced state of pregnancy, had insisted on going along. The campaign against Khan Jahan Lodhi ended with the latter's death in January 1631, while the fate of his ally, the King of Ahmadnagar, was sealed two years later with the occupation of his new capital Daulatabad, the annexation of his kingdom to the Mughal empire and his imprisonment in the fortress of Gwalior.

Shah Jahan now met with great personal tragedy. On the torrid night of 7 June 1631, while he waited impatiently for the birth of his fourteenth child, he was called urgently to his wife's bedside. She had just given birth to a daughter whose lusty cries testified to her good health. But Mumtaz Mahal lay dying of internal hemorrhage. The Emperor sat by her side, his eyes filled with tears and held her hands while she asked him in a barely audible voice to look after her children and aged parents. Then, staring into the face of her companion, as if she wanted to take away its image for ever, she breathed her last, "three hours before sunrise". Her mortal remains were interred for some time at Zainabad, on the banks of the river Tapti, before being carried to Agra, to be buried in the gardens where the Taj Mahal was to be built.

In early 1636, Shah Jahan was obliged to return to the Deccan. The incompetence of his representatives on the one hand and his prolonged mourning on the other, had encouraged Golconda and Bijapur to encroach upon the territories of the former state of Ahmadnagar which was now a part of the Mughal empire.

Another regional factor which was to considerably embarrass the Mughals in the years to come was the growing power of the Marathas. Their chief, Shahji Bhonsle, had taken over a series of strategic fortresses from where his light cavalry harassed Mughal garrisons.

Arriving at Daulatabad, the new capital of the Mughal province of the Deccan, on 21 February 1636, Shah Jahan divided his army into three divisions of fifteen thousand men each, ready to swoop down on Bijapur and Golconda, should these two kingdoms refuse to accept his dictates. A fourth army of eight thousand men, led by Mumtaz Mahal's brother, was given the task of neutralising the Maratha horsemen.

The news of these preparations caused panic in Hyderabad. The Sultan of Golconda, Abdullah Qutb Shah, immediately surrendered and undertook to pay the Emperor the rupee equivalent of 2,00,000 huns, at the rate of four rupees per hun, as annual tribute. He also undertook to replace the name of the Shah of Persia in the Khutba as well as on his kingdom's coins, with that of the Mughal Emperor's.

On the other hand the Sultan of Bijapur, in a bid to defend his honour, put up stiff resistance to Shah Jahan's troops. The troops released from a second front by Golconda's surrender, had invaded his country from three different points, and threatened his capital, Bijapur. In desperation, the Sultan ordered that the dam situated on the Shahpur lake be destroyed in order to flood the approaches to the city. Taken aback by this move and also war weary, Shah Jahan accepted a compromise. Bijapur recognised his sovereignty in exchange for half the territories of the former state of Ahmadnagar.

The Emperor left the Deccan on 11 July 1636, after appointing his son Aurangzeb as viceroy with the mansab or rank of 10,000 horsemen. The young prince was eighteen years old. He had already distinguished himself by his courage on the battlefields of Bundelkhand and won the admiration of his father. By giving him this troublesome province to handle the Emperor meant to reward his courage.

But Shah Jahan had another, darker reason. He knew from personal experience that there was no love lost among Mughal princes. Fearing the acrimonious atmosphere which had poisoned his youth, he preferred to keep his sons away from the court by conferring upon each the viceroyalty of a province. Dara Shikoh was the exception. Being the eldest son, the favourite, and the chosen successor to the throne, he was granted the provinces of Allahabad, Multan and the Punjab, with the rank of 12,000 horsemen, soon to be increased to 20,000, and was allowed to rule them by proxy. This favouritism exasperated Shuja, Murad Baksh, and above all, Aurangzeb, who suffered deeply from this unequal dispensation of paternal affection. From then on, an implacable hatred was to keep the two brothers apart. Nothing predestined them to get along with each other: neither their diametrically opposite natures, nor their behaviour, nor particularly their conception of Islam.

The French philosopher and traveller François Bernier, who, like Manucci and Tavernier, stayed for a long time at the court of the Great Mughal, has this to say about them:

"Dara was not deficient in good qualities. He was courteous in conversation, quick at repartee, polite and extremely liberal; but he entertained too exalted an opinion of himself; believed he could accomplish everything by the powers of his own mind, and imagined that there existed no man from whose counsel he could derive benefit. He spoke disdainfully of those who ventured to advise him, and thus deterred his sincerest friends from disclosing the secret machinations of his brothers. He was also very irascible; apt to menace; abusive and insulting even to the greatest Omrahs; but his anger was seldom more than temporary.

"Aurangzeb was devoid of that urbanity and engaging presence, so much admired in Dara: but he possessed a sounder judgement, and was more skillful in selecting for confidants such persons as were best qualified to serve him with faithfulness and ability. He distributed his presents with a liberal but discriminating hand among those whose goodwill it was essential to preserve or cultivate. He was reserved, subtle, a complete master of the art of dissimulation. He affected contempt for worldly grandeur while clandestinely endeavouring to pave the way to future elevation. Even when nominated Viceroy of the Deccan, he caused it to be believed that his feelings would be better gratified if permitted to turn dervish and that the wish nearest his heart was to pass the rest of his days in prayer or in offices of piety."

Only Dara really saw through his younger brother's character. ". . . He would sometimes say to his intimate friends, that, of all his brothers, the only one who excited his suspicion, and filled him with alarm was that Namazi— or, as we should say, that bigot, that ever-prayerful one."

Whether he was a bigot or not, Aurangzeb was certainly what one would today call a fundamentalist. He desired, with all his soul, a return to orthodox Islam, which he felt had been neglected for far too long. On the other hand, Dara Shikoh, a free thinker, adhered to the religious eclecticism of his great-grandfather, Akbar. In his book *Majma-ul-Bahrain* (The Mingling of Two Oceans), he tried to show the similarities between Hindu philosophy and Muslim mysticism. His quest for spiritual enlightenment would even lead him to study the principles of the Catholic faith with the Flemish priest Henri Buzée, of the Jesuit mission in Delhi, who became one of his closest friends.

In April 1644, Aurangzeb suddenly left the Deccan for Agra. His sister Jahanara had suffered serious burn injuries when her muslin dress caught fire from a candle. It was a natural impulse as she had become, since the death of their mother, the first lady of the court, and wielded as much influence over the Emperor as Dara Shikoh.

However, the haste with which he left the Deccan gave rise to a rumour which, once verified, incurred the wrath of his father. Aurangzeb, it turned out, had decided to abandon his charge without his father's permission.

It must be said in his defence that Aurangzeb had spent eight years in the Deccan whereas the normal length for such a mission was never more than three. He had shown himself to be a capable, talented administrator who had brought peace and prosperity to the province. But this was no reason, he felt, for keeping him away for so long from the court, where his rival Dara's influence over their father was growing with each passing day.

This act of independence, if not rebellion, earned him the disfavour of Shah Jahan, who stripped him of his title and his revenues. Pardoned seven months later thanks to Jahanara's intercession on his behalf, Aurangzeb was once again sent away from court, though this time at his own request. He confided to Asaf Khan's successor, the Grand Vizier Saadullah Khan: "Send me as far away as possible from court, for here I have lost sleep and peace of mind."

From February 1645 to August 1652, Aurangzeb was constantly on the move. First, he became Viceroy of Gujarat. He then went to Balkh, where in spite of the unfavourable outcome of the war with the Uzbeks, tales of his fearlessness won him the admiration of his enemies. It is said that one day, while battle was raging between his troops and those of the King of Bukhara, the time for the evening prayer arrived. Aurangzeb dismounted from his elephant, knelt down on the ground and calmly began to pray in full view of both armies. His adversary, on hearing of it, cried out, "Fighting such a man is to court one's own ruin", whereupon he put an end to hostilities.

Aurangzeb was subsequently seen at the gates of Kandahar, fighting for the city against the Shah of Persia's army. The

Shah had recovered it in February 1649 after ten years of Mughal occupation. Aurangzeb's mission failed. Neither he, nor Dara after him, were able to dislodge the enemy, whose artillery was superior to theirs. However, whereas Aurangzeb met with his father's rebuffs before he was once again sent to the Deccan, this time in semi-disgrace, his elder brother received new honours and soon reached the zenith of his power.

Meanwhile, half-a-dozen incompetent and cowardly governors had succeeded each other in the Deccan, whereas the complex problems of the region required firm authority. This impression of weakness was furthered by the losses of the Mughal army in Balkh and Kandahar. As a result, tax collections fell, the King of Golconda shied away from his commitments and constantly deferred the payment of the annual tribute, and the Marathas began to raise their heads anew.

Aurangzeb was required to restore order in the province but he was not given the financial means to do so. This was hardly surprising. Most of the empire's resources had been sunk in Shah Jahan's grandiose architectural schemes: the construction of the Taj Mahal, the embellishment of the Agra palace and finally the foundation of Shahjahanabad, the new capital he had built to the north of the old cities of Delhi by the banks of the Yamuna.

Upon his arrival in Aurangabad (his newly-built capital of the Deccan province) on 28 October 1663, the new viceroy's first concern was to quickly overcome the budgetary deficit. To achieve his end, he dreamed of annexing Bijapur and Golconda, for he approved neither of their Shiism nor of their closeness to Persia. However, he was restrained by the treaties of 1636 from open aggression and fell back on guile.

Aurangzeb first took on the Sultan of Golconda. He was determined to strip him of his wealth, if he could not overthrow him. He learnt that since the treaty of 1636, the value of the hun had appreciated without Abdullah Qutb Shah taking this increase into account. Aurangzeb therefore demanded over and above the arrears, the difference due to the increase in the exchange rate for the period under review, that is, an additional two million rupees. He then blamed the Sultan for conquering Karnataka without the prior authorisation of his sovereign, but let it be known that he could make amends by presenting the Emperor with a generous amount of money. Finally, as the Raja of Chandragiri, a vassal of the Sultan of Golconda, had sought Shah Jahan's protection in exchange for an annual tribute of precious stones and two hundred elephants, Aurangzeb made it clear to the Sultan of Golconda that even this tempting offer could be reconsidered.

A compromise was indeed reached on all points of contention. However, to Aurangzeb's anger the negotiations were held in Delhi between Shah Jahan's ministers and the representatives of the Sultan of Golconda, without the Viceroy of the Deccan having a say in the matter. His bitterness was deepened by his father's growing indifference towards him. Not once during his second term as viceroy was he invited to court, nor did official chronicles mention any of the presents he sent to the Emperor on his birthday and the anniversary of his coronation.

But Aurangzeb held a master trump: Mir Jumla. The neglected Mughal had heard a lot about this ambitious minister, although they had never met. His agents in Golconda and Karnataka had spoken of Mir Jumla in such glowing terms that he immediately suggested to the Emperor the advantage that could be gained by using the Persian. He wrote to Shah Jahan: "Mir Jumla controls a populous country, composed of fortresses, ports, and gold and diamond mines. He is of average height, good-looking, wise, intelligent and shrewd. He is polite to others and has very capable officers under his command. In brief, even though his rank is one of a nobleman, he has the power, the wealth and the stature of a ruling prince."

Rumour has it that it was Aurangzeb who made the first move, sending several secret messages through the Mughal ambassador to the court of Golconda. He promised Mir Jumla and his family protection and special favours should they enter the service of the Emperor. Mir Jumla was in a dilemma, not knowing which side to choose. It was only when the Sultan of Bijapur got wise to his double game and allied himself with the Sultan of Golconda that Mir Jumla accepted Aurangzeb's offer and wrote to him: "I am the servant of Shah Jahan and solicit his protection."

It was now Aurangzeb's turn to be fussy. After conveying Mir Jumla's reply to Shah Jahan, he decided to wait till the former was provoked by his enemies before coming to his rescue.

It was at this point that an unforeseeable incident hastened the course of events.

Mohammed Amin, Mir Jumla's son and personal representative at the court of Golconda, was an arrogant and pretentious young man. Puffed up with pride by the achievements and power of his father he blatantly flouted every rule of the court. One day, he completely lost all sense of propriety, and entered the royal court intolerably drunk. Then, reeling before the stunned eyes of the Sultan and his courtiers, he fell onto a sofa and vomited thoroughly and noisomely. This affront to royal prestige was too flagrant.

The King ordered his arrest and the seizure of his and his father's property.

That was the moment Aurangzeb was waiting for. He immediately reported back to the Emperor and asked for his permission to act.

Meanwhile, on 3 December 1655, Shah Jahan had sent

a robe of honour and a firman to Mir Jumla, honouring him and his son with the mansab ranks of 5000 and 2000 respectively in the Mughal army. At the same time, in a letter to the King of Golconda, he warned him not to harm the life and property of his new protégés.

As soon as he learnt of the fate of Mohammed Amin, Shah Jahan ordered Abdullah Qutb Shah to release him immediately. A few days later he authorised Aurangzeb to invade Golconda, should his orders fail to be executed. However, before the letters could reach him, Aurangzeb, anticipating his father's reaction, declared that the Sultan's refusal to obey Shah Jahan's injunction justified the invasion of Golconda.

On 10 January 1656, the Mughal cavalry under the command of Prince Mohammed Sultan, the eldest son of Aurangzeb, crossed the borders and dashed towards Hyderabad.

In the meantime, the King of Golconda had received Shah Jahan's second letter. He immediately released Mohammed Amin, his family and his servants, and sent them to Mohammed Sultan's camp, hoping that his submission would put an end to the invasion of his country. However, he did not reckon with Aurangzeb's hypocrisy. The latter ordered his son to continue his advance under the pretext that the property of Mir Jumla and his kin had not yet been restored to them.

On 22 January 1656, at dawn, the Mughal cavalry reached the gates of Hyderabad. Taken by surprise, Abdullah Qutb Shah took refuge in the citadel of Golconda, carrying with him the few valuable objects that he had hurriedly managed to retrieve.

The story goes that a seven-kilometre-long passage linked Hyderabad to Golconda. Whether this is true or just a legend, the fact remains that even today, tourist guides, pandering to their clients' desire for romance and adventure, take visitors to the site of the old citadel. Then, pointing to a hole closed with bricks, they claim it to be the entrance to the famous tunnel, closed today for reasons of security. It is through this passage that the Sultan is supposed to have escaped from his enemies.

It was none too soon. Aurangzeb's secret instructions to his son would have given the Sultan no respite: "Qutb-ul-Mulk is a coward and will not put up any resistance. Besiege his palace with your artillery and post a detachment to stop him from escaping to Golconda. But before doing anything, send him a trustworthy person with the following message: 'I was expecting you to meet me and offer me hospitality. But as you have failed to do so, I have come to you.' Immediately after having had this message delivered, attack him with impetuosity, and if you can, relieve his neck of the weight of his head. The best way to carry out this plan is to show ingenuity, diligence and flexibility."

On 23 January 1656, Mohammed Sultan set up camp on the banks of the Hussein Sagar lake, three kilometres to the north of Hyderabad. In the meantime, a large detachment of his men were sent to the city centre to put an end to the looting of the previous evening. However, this did not stop the prince from helping himself to the treasures of the royal palace.

In the following days, a succession of emissaries were sent to the invader to offer him surrender and fabulous gifts, including the hand of the Sultan's daughter, in exchange for peace. It was to no avail. The young prince was not authorised to negotiate. As for Aurangzeb, who arrived in Hyderabad on 6 February, he did not have the slightest intention of making peace. He had come as a conqueror, not as a peacemaker. "Qutb-ul-Mulk", he wrote to his father, "is a scoundrel with no taste for imperial favours; he wallows in vices unworthy of a king and violates the doors of his subjects. He is a despot against whom the people invoke the heavens, an infidel who has turned his subjects from the straight road of Sunni faith; and lastly an ally of the Shah of Persia. An emperor faithful to Muslim orthodoxy would be failing in his duty should he not punish such a renegade. To miss the opportunity to crush such an enemy would be a serious political blunder. I hope that Your Majesty will order annexation."

On 7 February 1656, the sentinel standing guard over the roof of the bardari of Bala Hissar, the highest point of the citadel, saw a cloud of dust on the horizon. As the dust settled, thousands of horsemen came into sight, galloping towards the fortress. He immediately clapped his hands, the echo carrying the expected signal to the entrance of the fort. The Abyssinian guards rushed to lock the huge wooden gates with iron bars, while the eighty-seven bastions on the enclosure wall were placed in a state of defence.

The siege of Golconda had begun. It was to last till 30 March. At the time, Aurangzeb had only a light artillery, incapable of reducing a fortress reputed to be impregnable. He contented himself by encircling it, while awaiting the arrival of reinforcements of men and siege guns, as well as Mir Jumla's formidable army.

In the meantime, the ambassador of Golconda in Delhi had spared no effort to save his country. Aurangzeb's followers went as far as saying that he tried to buy over Prince Dara Shikoh and Princess Jahanara. Be that as it may, Shah Jahan was persuaded to put an end to hostilities and make peace in return for important concessions.

On 21 February Aurangzeb's uncle joined him with considerable troop reinforcements. The cannons were expected to come by the first of March. Success seemed certain because the King of Golconda had his back to the wall. He implored the grace of the viceroy, declaring himself ready to give the hand of his daughter to Mohammed

Sultan and make him his successor. He promised elephants and precious stones plus the payment of considerable damages and proposed to send his mother to work out the terms of a peace settlement.

Aurangzeb would have preferred to reject any compromise but he received fresh instructions from his father, along with a letter of grace addressed to Abdullah Qutb Shah. Now he had no option but to negotiate. Nevertheless, he was careful not to convey his father's message for fear that the imperial pardon would embolden the Sultan to water down his initial proposals.

On 20 March, Mir Jumla finally arrived at the gates of Golconda. Aurangzeb's agents were right. His army was not that of a nobleman's, but of a reigning prince. It consisted of six thousand horsemen, fifteen thousand infantrymen, a hundred-and-fifty elephants and an impressive artillery, besides hundreds of camels carrying luggage and treasure. Also, there were gifts valued at several lakhs of rupees for the Viceroy of the Deccan and the Mughal Emperor.

Alas, the chroniclers have not left us any account of Mir Jumla's first meeting with Aurangzeb. Nevertheless, considering the circumstances which preceded it, we can surmise that their encounter was characterised not only by warmth and shared views, but also by a double disappointment: Mir Jumla's failure to take revenge upon his former master and Aurangzeb's frustration at missing an outright victory.

Just a few days before Mir Jumla's arrival, an agreement had been concluded between Aurangzeb and the Queen Mother, Hayat Bakshi Begum, by which the latter confirmed her son's proposals.

Aurangzeb left Golconda on 15 April 1656 in the company of Mir Jumla. Upon arriving at Nander, half-way between Aurangabad and Hyderabad, they parted ways; the one to his capital in the Deccan and the other to Delhi, where he was to succeed the Grand Vizier Saadullah Khan who had just died.

In Delhi, Dara Shikoh had moved heaven and earth to prevent this appointment, fearing rightly the advantage it would give to Aurangzeb. This time, Shah Jahan disregarded his favourite son's objection for he needed Mir Jumla. He wanted to use him to reconquer Kandahar, as he was convinced that the Persian, with his cunning and talent, would best his compatriots.

Mir Jumla's journey to Delhi was marked by great pomp and glory. Manucci tells us: "Wherever he went governors would rush to receive him with full honours and offer him gifts; this was done under orders from the Emperor. As he approached Delhi, the most important generals had been dispatched to welcome and escort him. Orders had been given that all along his route, roads and shops be decorated as if the Emperor himself was coming."

The oil merchant's son from Ispahan had come a long way from his obscure beginnings. And at his moment of glory he carried a unique gift for his new sovereign. An incomparable diamond.

On 7 July 1656, as the sun set on the high sandstone walls and white marble kiosks of the imperial palace, Mir Jumla and his impressive escort entered the capital of the great Mughal.

The next morning, at exactly 9.40, Shah Jahan was to receive him in the Hall of Private Audience, the Diwan-i-Khas, for Shah Jahan's days were meticulously planned. The Emperor always woke at four and showed himself to his subjects from the Jharoka-i-Darshan, one of the windows of his private apartments which overlooked the sandbank separating the Red Fort from the Yamuna. This ceremony, named from a Sanskrit word meaning "the sight of an idol or a saint", had been institutionalised in Akbar's time. It was intended to reassure the populace about the king's health. There was also a sect of Brahmins, the Darsani, who believed that it was a good omen to see the Emperor's face before beginning their day.

Shah Jahan spent an entire hour in front of the window, mixing business with pleasure. First, he received the homage of his subjects. Then, he listened to their complaints and dispensed justice. Once the sandbank was cleared of his morning visitors, he watched elephant fights in which he delighted, and inspected his cavalry. Afterward, he went to the Diwan-i-Am or Hall of Public Audience, where, surrounded by Dara Shikoh, his ministers and his generals, he devoted two hours to the affairs of the empire. Then he moved to the Diwan-i-Khas, the Hall of Private Audience, on whose arches was inscribed:

If there be a Paradise on Earth,
It is this, it is this, it is this.

It was at Shah Jahan's orders that this verse by Amir Khusro, poet to the Delhi Sultan of yore, had been inscribed. It perfectly described the magic of white marble inlaid with flowers and interlacing of lapis lazuli, onyx, carnelian, agate, jade and turquoise, in the midst of which shone the fabulous Takht-e-Taus, the Peacock Throne.

It measured 1.80 metres by 1.20 metres and stood on a platform raised by four steps, resembling a canopied bed. The canopy was made of gold brocade, fringed with fine pearls, supported by twelve pillars of pure gold and embellished with rubies, emeralds and diamonds. Above the canopy stood a peacock with a magnificent tail made of sapphires, rubies, emeralds, pearls and a blend of other stones. The whole was placed on six solid gold legs also inlaid with precious stones.

Shah Jahan sat there cross-legged, leaning on brightly coloured cushions. He wore a floral-patterned white satin gown, embroidered with gold threads, its collar being adorned with a set of diamonds. On his head he wore a turban of gold cloth encircled with two rows of fine pearls, topped by an aigrette or sarpech set with heron feathers and an extraordinarily large diamond.

Dara Shikoh sat on a chair installed at the foot of the imperial throne. This signal honour had been granted to him on the occasion of his father's last birthday, along with other favours, among which were the title of Shah-i-Buland Iqbal, "highly fortunate king", and the rank of 40,000 horsemen. He had in fact become the co-ruler of the Mughal empire.

In these magnificent surroundings Mir Jumla had his first audience with the Emperor. The presents he brought for his new master were worthy of Mughal magnificence. Apart from the two hundred elephants which were led to the royal stables, he offered Shah Jahan a thousand pieces of gold and an unimaginable quantity of precious stones, including diamonds from his own mines in Karnataka and probably also from the Hindu temples he had stripped of their ornaments.

"On this occasion it was", recounts Bernier, "that Mir Jumla presented Shah Jahan with that celebrated diamond which has been generally deemed unparalleled in size and beauty." A description which fits closely with that of Babur's diamond.

We are also in possession of an extremely interesting letter from Shah Jahan to Abdullah Qutb Shah, in which the Emperor, after having extolled the virtues of Mir Jumla, refers to a large diamond of nine tanks offered by the latter, adding that he had never seen anything like it. The tank is an ancient Indian unit of weight which corresponds to about 0.3479 tola, another Indian unit of measurement. The tola at the time of Shah Jahan equalled 184.14 grains Troy, the English system of measurement used for precious stones. Accordingly, the diamond's weight would have been

576.56 grains Troy, i.e. 181.99 carats. The weight of Babur's diamond as well as that of the Koh-i-noor when it arrived in England were about 186 carats. We shall come back to the controversy that surrounds the origins of the Koh-i-noor. In the meantime, let us imagine for a moment that the diamond offered to Shah Jahan was none other than Babur's diamond. Mir Jumla may have discovered it somewhere in south India, where, as we remember, one Mahtar Jamal had sold it.

CHAPTER FIVE

The man who had returned Babur's diamond to the Mughals was rising rapidly in the world. Shah Jahan heaped honour and rewards on the Ispahani oil merchant's son. Mir Jumla was given the title of Diwan-i-Kul or Grand Vizier, the dignity of Muazzam Khan (the magnificent Khan), and promoted to the rank of 6,000 horsemen in the Mughal army. That was not all. He was granted the privileges that went with these honours: a splendid residence near the Red Fort, a beautiful pen-case laid with precious stones, two hundred horses and ten elephants from the imperial stables, as well as five hundred thousand rupees in cash. As a bonus, he was given the fiefdom of Karnataka for a period of seven years, without having to pay any tribute.

Upon hearing of the favours granted to his friend, Aurangzeb was delighted. "May God give you the power to satisfy the Emperor", he wrote to Mir Jumla, "which would be satisfying God."

The reader will remember that Shah Jahan was toying with the idea of sending his new prime minister to reconquer Kandahar. At least it was the reason he gave for having preferred Mir Jumla to other candidates. However, Mir Jumla did not relish the idea of a campaign against his compatriots. On the one hand, he feared that military failure would tarnish his reputation. On the other, he wished to spare Persia, his birthplace, so that he could return there should the need arise. Another consideration was that he held the monopoly over trade between Golconda and Persia through his fleet of merchant ships. So he did his utmost to divert the attention of the Great

Mughal from Kandahar to places where their respective interests were likely to converge.

He had noticed Shah Jahan's amazement at the sight of Babur's diamond and the other gems when they were offered him. Now Mir Jumla whetted his appetite for wealth by pointing out that "the precious stones of the Deccan were worth much greater consideration than the stones of Kandahar", and added: "Your Majesty should not rest until his power extends from the Himalayas to Kanyakumari."

The idea of an expedition to Kandahar was thus laid aside, while no decision was forthcoming on the Deccan campaign either. During this period, Shah Jahan vacillated between the encouragement of his vizier and the objections of his son Dara Shikoh. Eventually, towards the end of 1657, he let himself be convinced of the necessity of annexing Bijapur, where the succession of Sultan Mohammed Adil Shah, who had died in November 1657, was being disputed by several claimants, including the viceroy of the Deccan, Prince Aurangzeb. The latter claimed that the new sovereign, a young man of eighteen, was in fact a bastard of obscure origins who had been brought up in the harem of the former sultan.

Mir Jumla was placed at the head of the expeditionary corps, in spite of the opposition of Dara Shikoh, who once again feared that this appointment would be to Aurangzeb's advantage. But Shah Jahan held by his decision. The crown prince was not discouraged. He convinced Shah Jahan that the prime minister's family should be retained at court, as proof of his loyalty. This decision was a serious insult to Mohammed Said, even though he had suffered worse affronts in order to satisfy his ambitions.

Sensing his minister's bitterness, Shah Jahan took him aside and assured him that this had been done only to appease Dara's whims. He promised Mir Jumla that he would soon be joined by his wife and children.

The Bijapur campaign with Aurangzeb and Mir Jumla began in January 1657. Bidar and Kalyani, two strategic fortresses, fell in quick succession into the hands of the royal army. These successes emboldened Aurangzeb, but just as he was preparing to besiege the city of Bijapur, an imperial firman enjoined him to put an end to hostilities and conclude peace in exchange for the places already conquered and a few additional crumbs of territory. Although appalled, he complied and left for Aurangabad but his heart was full of rancour against his father, and even more against his eldest brother, the principal source of his frustrations.

In early September 1657, Shah Jahan fell seriously ill. His lower limbs were swollen, his tongue and palate dry, his body burning with fever.

Bernier recounts cryptically that it was a disease "disgraceful to a man of his age, who, instead of wasting, ought to have been careful to preserve the remaining vigour of his constitution." But the gossipy Neapolitan physician and traveller, Gemelli Careri, and the equally avid Venetian traveller, Manucci, have much more to say. According to Careri, Shah Jahan had fallen "hopelessly in love with a beautiful Moorish girl to whom he had given himself entirely, without bothering about the infirmities of his age", while Manucci recalls that the Emperor "still wanted to enjoy the pleasures of the flesh, like a young man. To this end he took various kinds of stimulants which for three days caused him urinary retention and took him to the brink of death."

For a whole week (from 6 to 13 September 1657), he missed the ritual of Jharoka-i-Darshan, whereas his subjects, faithful to the daily rendezvous, looked up every morning at an empty window. In consternation, they began to fear the worst, when suddenly, on September 14, at dawn, the Emperor, who now felt a little better, put in a short, weak appearance. However, it was too late to deny the rumour of his death which had spread like wildfire first in the city and then to the provinces. Some even whispered that the person seen at the window was really an old eunuch dressed in imperial robes to fool the people.

On 24 October 1657, Shah Jahan left Delhi for Agra because of his failing health. His doctors advised him to move to this more salubrious former Mughal capital. Feeling, however that his days were numbered, Shah Jahan gathered all his courtiers and pronounced Dara Shikoh the regent of the empire.

This decision, coupled with the rumour of his illness, even his imminent death, inflamed the passions of his other three sons and each one reacted instantly.

Prince Shuja, the viceroy of Bengal for twenty years, was a capable and generous man who had embraced the Shiite faith to win the sympathy of the Persian clan at court. In November 1657 he proclaimed himself Emperor and marched on Agra, convinced that his father's illness was due to a slow poison given by Dara.

A few days later, on 5 December, the youngest son, Murad Baksh, the viceroy of Gujarat, a bold but debauched young man, attacked and plundered the port of Surat after having murdered his minister Ali Naghi, who had tried to dissuade him. He also assumed the imperial title, had coins struck in his name, and waited impatiently for his ally Aurangzeb—with whom he maintained a secret correspondence. But this clever brother was in no hurry to lay his cards on the table. He was not ready. He even let it be known that it would be misplaced to take any action while Shah Jahan was still alive.

Dara Shikoh was not fooled by the "bigot's" scruples. He feared his apparent calm more than the open hostility of Shuja and Murad Baksh, all the more so since Mir Jumla and his army were still in the Deccan. Therefore, in a bid to ward off any collusion between the two accomplices as well as to demonstrate his authority, he stripped the grand vizier of his functions and ordered him to return forthwith to Agra with all his troops.

As soon as he was informed of this news, Aurangzeb, according to Manucci, sent his son Mohammed Sultan to Mir Jumla to remind him to honour the promise he had made in Golconda. "The time has come", recalled Mohammed Sultan, "to place Aurangzeb on the throne. You can do it and you have promised to do so. By joining your troops with his, you will give him military superiority over his brothers and help him win the crown that he desires from your hands alone."

It is not difficult to imagine Mir Jumla's predicament. He would have agreed unhesitatingly had he not feared reprisals against his family, still kept hostage in Agra. He managed to find a way out through a strategy which would have filled Machiavelli with admiration.

In January 1658, an astounding piece of news reached the court. Aurangzeb had arrested Mir Jumla and confined him to the Daulatabad fort, confiscated his property, his troops and his artillery. In a letter addressed to Shah Jahan, he justified his action by accusing Mir Jumla of siding with the ruler of Bijapur in a plot against Mughal interests. In reality, this measure was part of a scheme devised by Aurangzeb to secure his friend's continued support, without endangering the latter's family.

While, from the windows of his apartments at the Agra Fort, Shah Jahan's feverish and nostalgic eyes stared every day at the Taj Mahal, Mughal India was to witness one of the most tragic conflicts of her history: a war of succession. A battle fought in anticipation, one might say, for when it ended, Shah Jahan still had nine years to live.

In early February 1658, Aurangzeb at last revealed his strategy. It was not to promote his own cause, but to support the claims of Murad Baksh. In a letter addressed to his younger brother, where hypocrisy dripped from every sentence, cleverly hiding his political ambitions behind professions of religious fervour and altruism, he accused Dara Shikoh of idolatry and collusion with infidels of every sort. He also stressed the fact that, of the three brothers, Murad, with his noble qualities, was the most qualified to rule over the empire, Shuja being excluded because of his conversion to Shiism. As for himself, Aurangzeb, once he had seen his beloved brother on the throne, he would end his days in the hermitage of a dervish. In conclusion, he invited Murad to join forces with him near the village of Dharmat, a few kilometres south-west of Ujjain.

Meanwhile, at Agra, Shah Jahan, Dara Shikoh and Princess Jahanara had taken steps to thwart the rebellion of the three princes. Whereas Dara remained at court to handle the affairs of state and protect the Emperor, an army jointly commanded by his eldest son Suleiman Shikoh and Jai Singh, the Maharaja of Amber (Jaipur) marched against Shuja. The latter had left Bengal towards the end of November 1657 and taken over the holy city of Varanasi. At the same time, another army led by Jaswant Singh, the Maharaja of Jodhpur, was on its way to meet Aurangzeb and Murad.

Dara was convinced that the Rajputs cherished him for his liberal views and his overt sympathy for Hinduism, and would not hesitate to die on his behalf. That is why he had preferred them to the Muslim amirs, the more so because he feared that his younger sister Roshanara, an ardent supporter of Aurangzeb, would plot to win them over to his cause.

As soon as Aurangzeb heard that the imperial army was on its way, he tried to avoid confrontation by a ruse. He sent a Brahmin by the name of Kavi Rai to Jaswant Singh to persuade him to return to Jodhpur, trying to convince him that the two brothers were going to Agra only to pay a visit to their sick father. The Rajput chief refused: "I must execute the orders of the Emperor", he said, "I cannot retrace my steps without incurring his disfavour."

On 15 April 1658, at dawn, the two armies met near Dharmat. Jaswant Singh, faithful to the tactics of his race, launched his cavalry against Aurangzeb's artillery. To the shouts of "Ram Ram, Sita Ram", successive waves of horsemen, braving gunfire, swept over the rebellious forces and decimated their ranks with swords, capturing their arms and beheading the commander of the artillery. For a long time fortune smiled on the imperial army, leading every one to expect the final victory of Dara's supporters.

But, suddenly, came the surprise that was to be expected from a man of Aurangzeb's mettle. While thousands of Rajputs were basking in their victory, he had them mowed down to the last man by Mir Jumla's artillery, which until then had been kept discreetly in reserve.

Jaswant Singh survived and, gathering together the remnants of the imperial forces, he tried to change the course of the battle. However, Princess Roshanara had not remained idle. Thanks to her interminable intrigues, she had managed to persuade the Raja of Orchha, one of the rare Hindu mansabdars who had always preferred Aurangzeb, to rally round him at the appropriate time. This he did, followed soon after by Qasim Khan, the commander of the Mughal contingent.

Jaswant Singh nevertheless carried on the combat with what remained of his vassals and troops. At nightfall, thirty-seven thousand Rajputs lay dead on the battlefield. The Maharaja would have undoubtedly followed them, sparing himself the shame of surviving such a crushing defeat, but he was dissuaded from doing so by the entreaties of his minister.

The news of Jaswant Singh's defeat caused panic at court. But Dara had decided that nothing would be allowed to discourage him. He implored his father to let him head an army to Malwa in order to drive back the rebels. After much hesitation, Shah Jahan acquiesced, even though the decision went against his judgement.

Farewells between the father and his favourite son were truly touching. Before a gathering of ministers and generals assembled in the Diwan-i-Am, while the women of the harem watched the scene, hidden behind their curtained windows, the Emperor held Dara in his arms. So tight was his embrace that it seemed as if in a last surge of affection he wished to stop his son from leaving. Having at last released him from his clasp, he raised his hands to heaven to invoke god's help in his favour. The crown prince remained silent for a few seconds, overcome by emotion. Then, bowing ceremoniously before the Emperor, he was preparing to leave the hall when his pride got the better of him and he cried out: "Ya Takht ya Tabout"—the throne or the coffin!

A battle-honed strategist against the indulged crown prince: from the start it was an unequal fight. On 22 May, in the scorching heat of the Indian summer, Dara and his troops reached the banks of the river Chambal, near Dholpur. Without losing a minute, the prince had the fords fortified, to prevent the enemy from crossing the river. However, Aurangzeb counted among his officers one Subkaran Bundela, the Raja of Datia, who introduced him to the famous bandit Champat Rao Bundela. This man knew the region like the back of his hand and guided the rebel army to a ford he alone knew. Thus, before the unfortunate Dara could perceive the danger that threatened him, he was caught unawares by his brothers and forced to beat a retreat, leaving behind a large number of cannons.

On 29 May, both armies stood face to face on the plain of Samugarh, fourteen kilometres south-west of Agra.

The Rajputs in Dara's army had worn their legendary

saffron robes thus proclaiming that they were willing to die to the last man, rather than facing the humiliation of defeat. A chronicler recounts, "Thus, when they attacked the rebel soldiers, the latter felt as if a vast field of yellow flowers had invaded their ranks."

Dara Shikoh, dressed in a coat of shining armour, and seated on a richly caparisoned elephant, was leading the centre of the imperial army across a path cleared by the Rajput vanguard. Suddenly, Khalilullah Khan, the Governor of Delhi, who was commanding the right wing, advised the prince to mount a horse and to lead his cavalry against Aurangzeb. Without bothering to give a moment's thought to the advice of his officer who was, in fact, setting him a trap, Dara exchanged his elephant for a horse. This proved to be a fatal error. No longer able to see their commander on his howdah, Dara's men thought that he had been killed in the mêlée. Panic stricken, they fled the battlefield in large numbers, while the traitorous Khalilullah Khan, taking advantage of the confusion, switched his loyalties to the enemy. Once again, an almost certain imperial victory was transformed into a debacle.

When night fell, not a sound was heard on the battlefield of Samugarh, save the lamentations of the wounded and the dying. Farther away, on the road to Agra, the moon cast its pale beams on a small band of disheartened and wearied men. Dara and the debris of his huge army, mounted on their exhausted steeds, were slowly winding their way back to the capital.

His rebellious sons were just a few kilometres away from the imperial palace. Yet Shah Jahan did not seem worried about the threat that was looming large over his throne. All he could think of was how to console his beloved son, of telling him his defeat was due to a decree of fate rather than to any failure on his part. As for Dara, he didn't dare to look his father in the face. In fact, he would never see him again. After resting for a few hours in his residence on the banks of the Yamuna, he left Agra, accompanied by his wife Nadira Begum, his younger son Sipihr Shikoh and a handful of faithful followers. In a final outburst of indulgence and paternal love, Shah Jahan had allowed him to draw freely from the treasure contained in Delhi's Red Fort.

In the meantime, Sulaiman Shikoh, Dara's eldest son, and Jai Singh had managed to drive back Prince Shuja, and were on their way back to Agra. Had Dara waited for them before launching the battle of Samugarh, his own destiny and that of India would undoubtedly have followed another course.

On 5 June 1658, the rebellious brothers Murad Baksh and Aurangzeb occupied Agra. Mohammed Sultan Aurangzeb's eldest son, the newly appointed governor of the city, was sent to Shah Jahan to call for his abdication.

Even though the garrison stationed at the Agra Fort did not exceed one thousand, five hundred men, the Emperor decided to put up a defence, rejecting the impertinent demand of his grandson. He fell back on finesse, inviting Aurangzeb several times to call on him. It is speculated that he intended to have him assassinated by one of his famous Kalmuk Guard (which secured the imperial harem and was made up of a hundred Tartar women, armed with bows, daggers and scimitars). However, this plot, if it were ever hatched, was not carried out. A eunuch in Aurangzeb's pay unearthed it by intercepting a letter from Shah Jahan to Dara. He immediately informed his master who, after reinforcing the watch over his father, had the pipes supplying water to the palace reservoirs cut off.

On 8 June, Shah Jahan finally capitulated and handed over the keys of the fortress to Mohammed Sultan. The latter treated him with all the honour due to his rank.

Nevertheless, from that moment on, the Great Mughal was but a prisoner, confined to the harem of his palace.

Princess Roshanara, who had rendered precious assistance to Aurangzeb, left to join the victor. But his sister Jahanara Begum, Shah Jahan's favourite, stayed on with her father to share in his adversity just as she had in his glory.

After handing over Agra Fort and its illustrious prisoner to the trustworthy eunuch Itibar Khan, Aurangzeb left for Delhi, accompanied by Murad Baksh. Ten days later, on 23 June, they stopped at the small village of Kolighat, near the holy city of Mathura.

Although the battle of Samugarh had been won thanks to Aurangzeb's military and diplomatic skills, the latter artfully attributed the success of the operations to his younger brother. He praised his courage on the battlefield, recognised him as the legitimate Emperor of India and assured him that he owed the throne to his bravery alone.

The astrologers had even fixed a date for the coronation, 25 June 1658. The ceremony was to be preceded by a large banquet in Aurangzeb's tent of public audience.

On the appointed day, the trusting Murad Baksh mounted his steed and rode towards his elder brother's camp, escorted by some officers and by his faithful eunuch Shahbaz. Hardly had he left his camp that one of his lieutenants, sensing some misfortune, came galloping up to him and asked: "Where are you running to, Sire? And which star leads you to Aurangzeb?"

"I am running to the crown", replied Murad, "and it is from his hands that I shall receive it."

As soon as he reached the wall enclosing Aurangzeb's tents, he received a new warning. A mullah he had known for a long time came furtively up to him and whispered in his ear: "Sire, your entrance is a happy one. May it please the Almighty that your exit be as fortunate." Murad paid no heed to this warning, just as he had taken no notice of the first. While his escort was taken to another part of the camp, he jauntily entered his brother's pavilion followed only by Shahbaz.

Aurangzeb welcomed him effusively, led him to a place of honour and expressed his joy at being the host of his "sovereign". A magnificent table had been set for the occasion, where even wine, forbidden by Islam, flowed freely, although Aurangzeb did not touch it. He did none the less depart from his religious scruples to coax his brother to drink freely.

As beautiful dancing girls from Kashmir mingled with the guests to the sound of bewitching music and showered rose water on them, the elder brother lulled the younger one with tall promises. Every time his glass emptied, servants rushed to fill it with the potent wine of Shiraz. Under the combined effect of drink, perfume and the sensuous gyrations of the dancing girls, Murad began to doze off. At that moment Aurangzeb dismissed the guests, declaring that his brother needed rest before the tedious coronation ceremony. He then withdrew to his own tent.

Murad remained slumped in his armchair while his faithful eunuch, worried at the turn of events, sat crouched at his feet, sword in hand.

A few minutes later the curtain separating the banquet tent from the harem opened, and the viceroy of the Deccan appeared. He gestured to Shahbaz as if he wished to speak to him. The eunuch got up and began to move towards the prince when, suddenly, a powerful arm shot out and grabbed him by the sleeve, pulled him behind the curtain and strangled him with a lace under Aurangzeb's impassive gaze.

At the same time a slave from the harem slid up to Murad Baksh and began to massage his body so that under her skillful fingers he soon fell into a deep sleep. She then quietly removed his belt, sword and dagger, and darted back into the harem, leaving the unfortunate prince to the mercy of his enemies.

A few minutes later he was bound with silver chains, put on an elephant, locked up in a howda whose curtains were drawn, and taken to Delhi. Before leaving, it is said that he turned towards his brother and asked him bitterly: "Are these then the promises you had made to me on the holy Koran?"

Murad Baksh's arrest and his transfer to Delhi were carried out with such great skill that none of his followers realised what was happening. As the music filtered out of Aurangzeb's tent throughout the night, they thought that the feasting continued.

As day broke, the soldiers of both camps gathered in the vast enclosure where the coronation ceremony was to take place. Instructions had been given to come without arms in order to prevent the quarrels which sometimes broke out on such occasions.

While the audience was impatiently waiting for Murad, Aurangzeb's well-armed soldiers surrounded the enclosure, while people posted for the occasion shouted out: "Long live Emperor Aurangzeb!" Upon hearing these ovations, Murad's men switched camps, joined the victors, and repeated with the others: "Long live Emperor Aurangzeb!"

A little while later the latter appeared on the podium that had been put up for his brother. He sat briefly on the throne, then withdrew without drawing the slightest reaction from the crowd. Apart from the fact that the Indian character had no difficulty in accepting such changes, Aurangzeb's foresight had provided for all eventualities and he had won the loyalty of most of his brother's supporters. His success can thus be attributed to a meticulous plot, executed to perfection. (For seven months Murad Baksh remained imprisoned in the Salimgarh fortress, in the shadow of the Red Fort, before being transferred to

Gwalior. There, he was beheaded on 4 December 1661 by Aurangzeb's henchmen, after one of the sons of Murad's minister Ali Naghi, who had been assassinated in Gujarat, demanded revenge in accordance with *lex talionis.*)

After betraying his brother, Aurangzeb led both armies to Delhi. On 21 July 1658, he arrived at the Shalimar Gardens, seven kilometres north-west of the city, a pleasure spot built by Shah Jahan, where white marble kiosks stood among a profusion of canals, fountains, trees and flower beds. Here he was crowned Emperor of India with the grandiloquent title of Abul Muzzafar Muhiuddin Muhammad Aurangzeb Bahadur Alamgir Padishah Ghazi. The brevity and austerity of the ceremony, however, did not quite match this title. His "great enthronement", even more magnificent than his father's, was to take place one year later (on 5 June 1659) amidst the splendour and pomp of the Delhi citadel.

The unfortunate Dara was still hoping to regain the throne. After fleeing Agra he reached Delhi where, equipped with the firman signed by Shah Jahan, he appropriated the treasure of the Red Fort and was able to raise an army of five thousand men. He attempted for some time to hold on to the territories west of the Beas in the Punjab against the troops which were hot on his heels. Having failed, he withdrew with his wife, his younger son and his remaining soldiers to Lahore, then to Multan, Bhakkar and Tatta. Finally, after crossing the Sind desert, he arrived at the end of November 1658 at Bhuj, the capital of the territory of Kutch. He was given a warm welcome by the chief of the Jadeja Rajput clan, who gave to Sipihr Shikoh the hand of one of his daughters.

After a short and peaceful stay at Bhuj, Dara crossed the Rann, the great salt desert that separates Kutch from Kathiawar, and entered the state of Navanagar whose chief, also a Rajput of the Jadeja clan, received him just as cordially. From Navanagar he moved to Ahmedabad, the capital of Gujarat, where a wonderful surprise awaited him.

The governor of Gujarat, Shah Nawaz Khan Safavi, a Persian who belonged to the royal family of the Safavids, was not only one of the most famous officers of Mughal India, but also the father-in-law of both the new emperor and of his brother Murad Baksh. His daughter Dilras Banu had married Prince Aurangzeb in 1637 and had given him two daughters and two sons before dying in childbirth in 1657. Her husband had a tomb raised for her in Aurangabad—a replica of the Taj Mahal which, though nowhere near the original, still has a certain charm.

Shah Nawaz Khan hated Aurangzeb. He had never forgotten how his son-in-law had snubbed him just before the war of succession. He was then in the Deccan and out of loyalty towards Shah Jahan, he had refused to fight against Jaswant Singh's troops. Aurangzeb, furious, had him imprisoned in the Burhanpur Fort while awaiting the result of the battle. When Dara was defeated at Samugarh, Shah Nawaz Khan was appointed viceroy of Gujarat, due to the intercession of his granddaughter Zeb-un-nissa, who had refused to touch all food till her maternal grandfather was released. This did not prevent Aurangzeb from bearing a grudge against him. "I took this decision", he was to say, "because I had no choice, but when the time comes, I shall think the better of it. As he is a Sayyid (a descendant of the Prophet) it is hard to put an end to his days. Otherwise, as the old adage goes, a cut head does not tell any tales."

On reaching Ahmadabad on 9 January 1659, Dara discovered with surprise and joy that Shah Nawaz Khan was ready to put the troops and resources of Gujarat at his disposal. By allying himself with the fugitive prince to free Shah Jahan and then put him back at the head of his usurped empire, the old general believed he could avenge both himself and his second son-in-law, the unfortunate Murad Baksh.

While Dara was preparing a fresh campaign against Aurangzeb, an emissary from Jaswant Singh asked him to go to Ajmer. He assured him that his master and the Jodhpur army would give him full support.

Why would Jaswant Singh, who had, like Jai Singh, sworn allegiance to Aurangzeb, suddenly renounce his commitment? To understand this, we shall have to go back a few months. That will also allow us to follow the fortunes of Prince Shuja.

While Aurangzeb was chasing Dara across the Punjab, Shuja went up along the Ganga and recovered Allahabad and Varanasi in quick succession. The Emperor was thus forced to entrust the pursuit of Dara to Jai Singh while he himself took up arms against Shuja in the company of Jaswant Singh and Mir Jumla, liberated in the meantime from the fort of Daulatabad. However, on 4 January 1659, just on the eve of the final encounter with Shuja, it was learnt that the Maharaja of Jodhpur and his Rajputs had deserted, plundered the imperial camp and spread panic in the Mughal ranks.

Aurangzeb was on the verge of saying his evening prayer when Mir Jumla brought him the bad news. He listened calmly, completed his devotions and then said: "This incident is a sign of divine mercy. What would we have done if the hypocrite had acted in this way in the middle of the battlefield?"

The day after, Shuja suffered a crushing defeat at Khajwah, from where he once again fled to Bengal, pursued by Mir Jumla. He was later to take refuge with the King of Arakan (which is now a Burmese province), who treated him with great consideration, before murdering him for refusing to give him his daughter in marriage in 1660. Another version has it that Shuja managed to escape and took refuge in the wild forests separating Arakan from Pegu, where his trail was lost. An aura of mystery thus surrounds his fate. A Mughal historian wrote in 1771: "Till now, no one knows what happened to Shuja. No one knows where he is, what he is doing or whether he has died."

As for Jaswant Singh, he was but an opportunist who, notwithstanding his courage and loyalty on the battlefield of Dharmat, put his own interests before all others. Aurangzeb, who knew about this trait, had forgiven his act of betrayal and appointed him governor of Gujarat in place of the rebel Shah Nawaz Khan.

Unaware of this new realignment of forces, Dara Shikoh left Ahmadabad for Ajmer at the head of his armies, accompanied by Shah Nawaz Khan. A few days later they stopped at Merta where the prince invited Jaswant Singh to join him with his Rajputs, as promised. The Maharaja, playing for time, replied that he was awaiting some of his vassals and that as soon as they came, he would join the prince near Ajmer.

Dara was reassured and continued his onward march. However, when he arrived at Ajmer, he was astounded to learn that there was no trace of the warriors from Jodhpur. Worse still, he was informed that a huge army, commanded by no less than Aurangzeb in person, was coming to meet him.

Dara fell back on the Deorai pass, seven kilometres south of Ajmer. He hoped that his troops, deployed in a dominant position, with their flanks protected by high wooded hills, would manage to thwart his brother's attack.

Skirmishes, cavalry charges, artillery duels, hand-to-hand fights continued through 12 and 13 March 1659, without any decisive outcome. In the meantime, Aurangzeb had discovered, thanks to the complicity of a Rajput chief, a path which got around the positions occupied by his brother. He was thus able to move his cannons to a hillock which was behind the lines of Dara's left wing, commanded by Shah Nawaz Khan.

On 14 March, at nightfall, a shower of missiles tore apart the Emperor's father-law and a great number of his men and the rest of the army broke up in a state of indescribable chaos. Dara, completely shattered by the loss of his ally and a large chunk of his army, fled to Gujarat, pursued by a detachment of the imperial army, led by Jai Singh.

The news of the Deorai debacle had already reached Ahmedabad. Dara had just entered the city when he discovered with stupefaction that the officers he had left to guard the city had switched their allegiance to Aurangzeb.

Once again condemned to wander, he decided to take refuge in Persia, hoping that he would be welcomed as warmly as his ancestor Humayun had been. On the way he stayed with one Malik Jiwan, a Pathan whose fortress was fifteen kilometers from the entrance to the Bolan pass.

This Malik Jiwan had been condemned to death by Shah Jahan for high treason. He owed his life to Dara who had managed to save him from the hangman. The unfortunate prince thus expected Malik Jiwan to return the favour. But the ungrateful man, while welcoming his guests with open arms, sent a messenger to Jai Singh to tell him that he was ready to hand over Dara. This is exactly what he did a few days later.

Dara might have noticed the plot had he not been troubled by the death of his wife Nadira Begum, the mother of his two sons, Suleiman Shikoh and Sipihr Shikoh. Nadira died soon after their arrival at Malik Jiwan's fortress. Even though their marriage was one of convenience (Nadira was the daughter of Prince Parviz, Shah Jahan's brother), a deep and enduring tie united them. Her remains were taken under escort to Lahore to be buried near the tomb of Mian Mir, the Sufi saint of whom she, like her husband, was a follower.

Delhi had lived through many difficult, tragic, often bloody days. None, however was to be as moving as 29 August 1659. At dawn, Dara and Sipihr Shikoh, under heavy guard, reached the gates of the city. Even Malik Jiwan was there, enjoying the outcome of his misdeed.

In the meantime Aurangzeb and his ministers were deliberating about the appropriateness of parading the prisoners through the city before taking them to the Gwalior fortress. Opinion was divided. Some were against it. First, out of respect for the honour of the royal family. Secondly, because such a step might spark off riots in their favour and encourage attempts to save them. Others felt that they ought to be led through the streets of Delhi so that the people were convinced of their captivity and were impressed by Aurangzeb's might. The ayes had it.

François Bernier, who had been living for some time in Delhi as physician to a great Mughal dignitary, was witness to Dara's martyrdom:

"...The wretched prisoner was therefore secured on an elephant; his young son, Sipihr Shikoh, placed at his side, and behind them, instead of the executioner, was seated Bahadur Khan. This was not one of the majestic elephants of Pegu or Ceylon, which Dara had been in the habit of mounting, pompously caparisoned, the harness gilt, and trappings decorated with figured work; and carrying a beautifully painted howdah, inlaid with gold, and a magnificent canopy to shelter the prince from the sun: Dara was now seen seated on a miserable and worn-out animal, covered with filth; he no longer wore the necklace of large pearls which distinguished the princes of Hindustan, nor the rich turban and embroidered coat; he and his son were now dressed in dirty cloth of the coarsest texture, and his sorry turban was wrapt round with a Cashmere shawl or scarf, resembling that worn by the meanest of people.

"Such was the appearance of Dara when led through the bazaars and every quarter of the city. I could not divest myself of the idea that some dreadful execution was about to take place, and felt surprised that government should have the hardihood to commit all these indignities upon a prince confessedly popular among the lower orders, especially as I saw scarcely any armed force. The people had for some time inveighed bitterly against the unnatural conduct of Aurangzeb: the imprisonment of his father, of his son Sultan Mahmud, and of his brother Murad Baksh, filled every bosom with horror and disgust. . . I took my station in one of the most conspicuous parts of the city, in the midst of the largest bazaar; was mounted on a good horse, and accompanied by two servants and two intimate friends. From every quarter I heard piercing and distressing shrieks, for the Indian people have a very tender heart; men, women, and children wailing as if some mighty calamity had happened to themselves. Jiwan Khan rode near the wretched Dara and the abusive and indignant cries vociferated as the traitor moved along were absolutely deafening. I observed some fakirs and several poor people throw stones at the infamous Pathan; but not a single movement was made, no one offered to draw his sword, with a view of delivering the beloved and compassionate prince. When this disgraceful procession had passed through every part of Delhi, the poor prisoner was shut up in one of his own gardens, called Haider-Abad."

His fate was sealed that very night during a council held in the Diwan-i-Khas.

The religious dignitaries demanded the head of the "idolater and the infidel". Their view was supported by Princess Roshanara, who rejoiced in anticipation of the pain Dara's death would cause to her rival Jahanara. As for Aurangzeb, the least one can say is that he did not wait to be asked twice in order to confirm the sentence.

Dara, who in his leisure time had studied all the known religions, was drawn to Christianity. It is said that before dying he asked to see Father Buzée for the last time, a request that was turned down.

At seven o'clock in the evening, four men, led by a slave named Nazar Beg, burst into his cell. "My dear son", exclaimed Dara, "these men have come to murder us." While one of the assassins caught Sipihr Shikoh, the other three fell on Dara, threw him to the ground and held him, while Nazar Beg cut off his head.

The trophy was immediately brought to Aurangzeb. He ordered it to be placed in a bowl filled with water. The blood was then washed from the face, and when it could no longer be doubted that it was indeed Dara's head, the Emperor shed tears and said, "Ah Bad-bakht (*wretched one*)! Spare me this shocking sight. Take away this head and bury it in Humayun's tomb."

CHAPTER SIX

Once Aurangzeb became Emperor, Mir Jumla was duly rewarded for his "sacrifice". Freed from Daulatabad fort the day after Dara Shikoh's defeat, he joined his friend and sovereign in Bengal. He fought by his side against Prince Shuja and, on 6 May 1660, succeeded him as viceroy of India's richest province, Bengal. That was not all. Along with the title of Muazzam Khan, he acquired those of Amir-ul-Umara (the amir of amirs), Sipahsalar (generalissimo) and Yar Wafadar (faithful friend). He was promoted at the same time to the rank of 7,000 horsemen.

It was in Bengal that Mir Jumla was to reveal the full extent of his military genius, before meeting with a tragic end. But before dying, he was to offer Aurangzeb an even more extraordinary stone than Babur's diamond. This stone, probably lost or cut in several pieces, still evokes lively debates on the origin of the Koh-i-noor.

Soon after moving into the viceregal palace in Dacca, Mir Jumla, then sixty-nine, begged Aurangzeb to allow his family to join him, "Now that the war is over and I am, by virtue of my age and physical condition, in the twilight of my life, you surely cannot refuse me the consolation of spending what remains of my life with my wife and children." The Emperor hesitated. More suspicious than ever, he feared that once Mir Jumla was joined by his family, in particular his son Mohammed Amin, the ambitious general would try and become king of Bengal, just as he had once claimed supremacy over Karnataka. Aurangzeb, acting with customary cunning and caution, allowed his wife, daughter and grandchildren to go, but kept Mohammed Amin in Delhi, appointing him to the much sought-after post of Mir Bakshi (minister of defence), which required him to stay at court.

Aurangzeb's next concern was to keep Mir Jumla busy beyond the frontiers, fearing that idleness could turn his attention to the interior of the empire. He, therefore, put him in charge of the campaign against the Rajas of Assam and Cooch-Behar, whose principalities lay in the north-eastern extremity of the Indian subcontinent.

Situated in a marshy, humid, often flooded region, these principalities were protected by impenetrable forests, wooded hills, and the long valley of the Brahmaputra and its tributaries, and enclosed by the Himalayas in the north, the Arakan range and the Shillong plateau in the south. These natural barriers had spared them for a long time from Muslim invasions.

Taking advantage of the anarchy which reigned in Bengal during the war of succession (1656-58), the Rajas of Cooch-Behar and Assam sent separate troops to occupy the district of Kamrup. The Mughal garrison was sent away from the area, the Ahoms drove back their rivals before plundering the entire district and occupying its capital, Guwahati.

On 11 November 1661, Mir Jumla and his army of 12,000 horsemen and 30,000 infantrymen left Dacca on three-hundred-and-twenty-three ships of varying tonnage. Going up the Brahmaputra, they disembarked six weeks later at Cooch-Behar, whose capital they took without having fired a shot, as the Raja and his men had abandoned it as soon as they heard of the Mughals' arrival.

The invasion of Assam began on 14 January 1662. While the Ahoms fell back on their capital, Garhgaon, the imperial forces which were in hot pursuit took over a series of strategic fortresses along the Brahmaputra; on 17 March 1662, they occupied Garhgaon which had been hastily evacuated by its inhabitants. The booty was considerable:

82 elephants, 3,00,000 rupees, 675 pieces of artillery, 1,345 zamburak (a cannon on a pivot), 6,750 muskets and 1,000 small boats.

The king and his lieutenants had fled to the neighbouring mountains; as a result, Mir Jumla could dictate the conditions of a peace treaty. Meanwhile, the rainy season had set in and the entire region was flooded. The fleet, which was the only means of communication with Dacca, was anchored 30 kilometres downstream on the Brahmaputra.

On 20 May 1662 the Ahoms left their shelter in full force, attacked and occupied the Mughal outpost, and cut off Mir Jumla's line of communication with his ships. Isolated from his sole source of supplies, his reserves diminished rapidly. In August 1662 they were completely exhausted, while a terrible epidemic of plague broke out in the Mughal camp, reducing the expeditionary army to a fourth of its initial strength.

In the meantime the commander of the imperial fleet had remained in contact with Bengal; once the weather improved, he was able to send a large quantity of provisions to Mir Jumla, allowing the latter to resume his offensive. But his soldiers no longer had the heart for battle. Seriously ill and having failed to annex Assam, Mir Jumla contented himself with a highly advantageous peace treaty. It included an extremely handsome compensation, and a daughter of the Raja for the harem of Aurangzeb. Mir Jumla set out for Dacca on 20 January 1663; he died on 31 March, just before reaching the capital.

According to Manucci, it was at this time that Mir Jumla had offered Aurangzeb an extraordinary diamond. "When he returned from Assam, Mir Jumla fell ill. The Emperor, in a letter in which praise and scorn were heaped together, ordered him to prepare afresh for the conquest of Assam. Through the intermediary of a eunuch who brought him the letter, Mir Jumla replied: 'I am no longer in a state to give Your Highness proof of my loyalty and attachment. Mohammed Amin Khan, my son, does not seem unworthy till now of your protection. I would be very happy indeed if you would deign to count him among your slaves.'

"Along with the request the eunuch carried back a present that Mir Jumla had decided to give the Emperor just before he died. It was a diamond, the largest and the most perfect to be found in the Indies. Mir Jumla had acquired it when he was in the service of the king of Golconda and was the viceroy of this diamond-rich province. The eunuch added that the general was of the view that the Emperor neglected the conquest of Assam and only thought of that of Bijapur and Golconda."

The spectacular career of the Ispahani oil merchant's son, who, in the span of thirty years had occupied the highest posts of Golconda and the Mughal empire, had fired the imagination of Indians and his death plunged them into despondency. "It is only now", murmured the most spiteful, "that Aurangzeb is the king of Bengal."

The Emperor was not unduly affected by the death of his old ally. In reality, he could barely conceal his relief, declaring publicly to Mohammed Amin, the deceased's son: "You are weeping for the death of your father and I for the most powerful and the most dangerous of my friends." He nonetheless showered all kinds of privileges on the son. Instead of stripping him of his father's worldly possessions, as was the Mughal custom when a dignitary died, he allowed him to keep the whole. His title of Mir Bakshi was confirmed and his annual income increased by one thousand rupees. Finally, as an ultimate honour, he was ordered to consider Aurangzeb his second father.

On 12 September 1665 Aurangzeb granted an audience to Jean-Baptiste Tavernier who had arrived in Delhi a few days earlier. The latter presented the Emperor with splendid gifts among which was a large bronze shield, gilded and chiselled, whose carvings depicted the exploits of the Roman chevalier Marcus Curtius. All the dignitaries present praised the beauty of this masterpiece and suggested the Emperor should have it fixed on the caparison of the huge elephant which carried the imperial standard.

Towards the end of his sojourn, on 2 November 1665 the French traveller and jeweller was authorised to admire Aurangzeb's jewels including the extraordinary diamond that Mir Jumla had offered him before he died:

"The first piece which Akil Khan placed in my hands was the great diamond, which is a round rose, very high at one side. At the basal margin it has a small notch and flaw inside. Its water is beautiful, and it weighs 319.5 ratis, which are equal to 280 of our carats—the rati being $^{7}/_{8}$th of our carat. When Mir Jumla, who betrayed the King of Golconda, his master, presented this stone to Shah Jahan, to whose side he attached himself, it was then rough, and weighed 900 ratis, which are equivalent to 787.5 carats; and it had several flaws. If this stone had been in Europe it would have been treated in a different manner, for some good pieces would have been taken from it, and it would have weighed more than it does, instead of which it has been all ground down. It was the Sieur Hortensio Borgio, a Venetian, who cut it, for which he was badly rewarded; for when it was cut he was reproached with having spoilt the stone, which ought to have retained a greater weight; and instead of paying him for his work, the Emperor fined him 10,000 rupees, and would have taken more if he had possessed it. If the Sieur Hortensio had understood his trade, he would have been able to take a large piece from this stone without doing injury to the Emperor's jewel, and without having had so much trouble in grinding it; but he was not a very accomplished cutter."

In another part of his account Tavernier repeats that after having weighed the "diamond", he had noted that its weight was 319.5 ratis, that is 279.5 of "our carats" (he is talking about Florentine carats, which weigh four percent less than the French or English carat).

However, we don't know why he speaks of the diamond as having been presented to Shah Jahan, since we know for certain that the stone given to the latter by Mir Jumla was different from the one Tavernier saw in Delhi. In all likelihood the jeweller ignored the existence of the diamond given to Aurangzeb, whereas his friend Bernier had told him about the stone presented to Shah Jahan. He must therefore have deduced that Aurangzeb had taken it away, which was not the case. At least, not yet.

Confined to his apartments in the Agra Fort, Shah Jahan spent long hours in the magnificent Pearl Mosque in the company of a holy man, who acted as his chaplain and confessor and passed on his gifts to the poor of the city. The former Emperor had lost none of his love for the material things of this world, especially for jewels and precious stones.

After the capitulation of the Agra Fort, Aurangzeb had all the rooms containing clothes, furniture and household items sealed, and charged one of his trusted men to keep watch over them. As for the jewels and other precious stones, they were kept safely in a room near Shah Jahan's apartments, where the latter could from time to time admire them in the presence of a guard. But they were henceforth at the mercy of Aurangzeb who could dispose of them as he pleased.

However, Babur's diamond was not among them. It must have remained in Shah Jahan's room, together with the other jewels his son coveted.

In fact, Aurangzeb's greed was insatiable. According to Manucci and Khafi Khan, he asked one day for his father's rosary, made of a hundred round pearls, "all of the same colour and size", as well as the diamond ring that Shah

Jahan always wore, arguing that these objects "befitted a king, not a recluse". Shah Jahan sorrowfully parted with his ring but refused to give up the rosary. "I use them for my prayers", he replied bitterly, "and will only hand them over after grinding them in a mortar."

Shah Jahan spent his days with his daughter Jahanara. She was the disciple of Mian Mir, the Sufi saint from Lahore, and led a monastic existence, looking after her aged, abandoned father, as well as the welfare of the orphans of her brothers Dara and Murad, whom she had taken in ward.

The most magnificent of the Great Mughals lived till 22 January 1666. At the time of his death Shah Jahan was seventy-four years old. He was buried in strict privacy in the Taj Mahal, next to his beloved wife. The story goes that in his grand dreams he planned to build a monumental bridge across the Yamuna to link the Taj with a replica in black marble, where he himself wanted to be laid to rest.

"But", says Robert d'Humieres who visited India in 1904 "all one can see in place of so beautiful a dream is a flat river bank where large turtles bask in the sun; a plover gazing at the stones; nothing other unites the two banks of the river than a flight of green parrots diving sometimes to touch the water, emerald arrows stolen from the golden quiver of twilight, the message of Desire to Nothingness above the water which flows."

It was only three weeks after his father's death that Aurangzeb went to Agra to perform his last rites and beg for a posthumous pardon, even though some historians claim that Shah Jahan had forgiven him a few hours before passing away. It is probably during this journey that Aurangzeb laid his hands on the jewels he had been unable to take before. To presume that Babur's diamond was amongst them is a step only imagination can take.

Aurangzeb's rule provoked popular discontent from its

very start. He claimed to be the sole custodian of his faith and his measures of a rigid Islam were not well received.

Though music had been effectively banned in 1670, an incident, no doubt apocryphal, related by Manucci, reveals Aurangzeb's unpopularity. On a Friday morning Aurangzeb, now Emperor Alamgir, conqueror of the age, was going from the Red Fort to the Jama Masjid, the large mosque of Old Delhi, when from atop his elephant he saw a strange procession. A richly decorated coffin was followed by a thousand men dressed in mourning and sobbing loudly. He was told that they were the city's musicians who, unhappy with the imperial firman forbidding them to practice their art, were holding its funeral. Aurangzeb observed with a malicious smile that they ought to pray for the soul of music and see that it was properly buried. And yet, Aurangzeb had once been adept in playing the veena, the ancient lute of the south!

Another coffin could well have contained the solar calendar and the festival of Navroz, abolished and replaced by the lunar calendar. Khafi Khan, a historian as well as a good Muslim, observed: "Mathematicians, astrologers and historians know that the four seasons, the autumn and spring harvests, the ripening of wheat and fruits all depend on the solar calendar and cannot be governed by the lunar calendar. But all the same, his religious Majesty did not wish that Navroz and the years and months of the magus (priests of the former Persian empire) should lend their names to the anniversary of his accession to the throne."

In the tenth year of his rule, he also abolished the ceremony of Jharoka-i-Darshan, as he felt the adoration of idols went against Islam.

Aurangzeb was not content with purging morals and abolishing traditions, measures which affected the entire population. He also unleashed a policy of religious discrimination which spelt the end of the secular society so dear to Akbar and somehow spared, by default almost, by Jahangir and Shah Jahan.

The most hated measures of his policy were the destruction of Hindu temples, the re-instatement of the jeziya (a tax on non-Muslims), the abolition of custom duties for Muslims (now doubled for Hindus), and the ban on all Hindus, save Rajputs, on carrying arms, mounting elephants and Persian or Arab horses and travelling in palanquins. At the same time, with a single stroke of the pen, Hindu names were crossed from the list of state employees.

There were bound to be reactions. In 1669 a riot broke out among the peasants of the region of Agra and Mathura under the leadership of Gokla Jat, followed three years later by the Satnamis' uprising. The Satnamis were a group of Hindus who strove to reconcile the principles of Hinduism and Islam, very much like the Sikhs, who were also victims of the new policy.

These movements of revolt were put down with great bloodshed. However, they were to resurface a few years later with renewed intensity against both Aurangzeb and his successors. The torture and death of Teg Bahadur, the ninth Guru of the Sikhs, transformed this peaceful community into the implacable disciples of the Khalsa, the theocratic and military organisation founded by the tenth and last Guru, Gobind Singh, to combat the intolerance of the Great Mughal.

Meanwhile, the Rajputs, the legendary warriors who for over a century had been in the vanguard of the Mughal army, watched with horror and consternation this malefic course of events. They remained nonetheless faithful to the Mughal dynasty, though their loyalty towards Aurangzeb, sorely tested, hung by only their tradition of honouring oaths of fealty.

But in 1678 the Emperor snapped this tenuous link. On 10 December the famous Maharaja Jaswant Singh of Jodhpur, whose constant about-turns we have seen earlier, died near Peshawar without leaving a male successor. However, his queen was carrying a child. She was persuaded by her entourage not to perform sati—a custom whereby a woman sacrificed herself on the funeral pyre of her husband—and a little while later she gave birth to a son who was named Ajit Singh. Whereupon she wrote a letter to the Emperor, announcing her imminent arrival in Delhi to "receive from the hands of her suzerain a firman acknowledging Ajit Singh as the new Maharaja of Jodhpur".

She did not suspect for a moment that her husband's death had in fact provided Aurangzeb with the much awaited pretext of annexing the Rajput principalities in quick succession and striking a mortal blow at the Hindu heartland.

Before the news of the birth of Jaswant Singh's posthumous son became known, a Mughal army invaded Marwar, occupied Jodhpur and put the city to fire and the sword. They placed a figurehead on the throne, a great-nephew of Jaswant Singh. This unpretentious young man would have undoubtedly enjoyed a peaceful reign under the firm control of the Mughal governor had it not been for the courage and tenacity of one Durga Das Rathore in defending the rights of the legitimate heir.

Durga Das, a legendary figure in Rajasthan, was the son of Jaswant Singh's prime minister. Rallying around Ajit Singh's cause, he and a few faithful Rajputs helped Ajit Singh and his mother escape from house arrest in Delhi and took them to Marwar. On 23 July 1679 the small troop, swelled on the way by Jat and Rajput volunteers, reached the gates of Jodhpur. The Mughal governor of the city and his figurehead Maharaja having fled, Jaswant

Singh's wife was able to recover the city in the name of her son.

Aurangzeb's anger was terrible. He sent a powerful vanguard to Marwar and on 25 September 1679, he himself left Delhi for Ajmer, accompanied by his favourite son Mohammed Akbar, to beseige the Rathores. His reprisals were as terrible as his fury. He subjected the entire population of Jodhpur to the worst kind of privation before hoisting his Timurid standard, "a couched lion standing out against the rising sun", atop the great fortress of Mehrangarh that was Jodhpur's citadel.

After putting up a stiff resistance, Durga Das was forced to bow down to Aurangzeb's superior strength. He nonetheless succeeded in taking the young raja and his mother to Udaipur, where the latter, a princess from Mewar, asked for the help of her relative, Maharana Raj Singh.

Since 1614, when Raj Singh's father had concluded a peace treaty with Jahangir, Mewar had stayed away from any kind of interference in the affairs of the empire. The Maharana, therefore, hesitated until the month of November 1679 before agreeing to his guest's request and declaring war.

Mohammed Akbar was placed at the head of the expeditionary force to fight against Mewar. But his continuous failures irritated his father so much that Aurangzeb stripped him of his charge and transferred him to the less prestigious post of commander-in-chief in Marwar. There too, the prince did not prove to be up to the task and had to suffer the repeated rebuffs of the Emperor. This was the moment the Rajput leaders chose to worm their way between father and son, and to offer the latter their help in conquering the Peacock Throne.

Mohammed Akbar was in possession of an entire army, swelled by thirty thousand Rajputs, against the ten thousand men his father had stationed at Ajmer. The proposition was as tempting as it was realistic, and would probably have succeeded had the Emperor not taken recourse to a particularly cunning subterfuge. He sent his son a letter, making sure it would be intercepted by the Rajputs, who were made to believe that Mohammed Akbar was acting hand-in-glove with his father to lull them into complacency. The prince, abandoned by his allies, first fled to the Rathores; then, with the help of Durga Das, he took refuge in the Deccan, where the Marathas and their chief Shambhuji welcomed him cordially. He stayed there till 1687, when disillusioned by the turn of events and mercilessly pursued by his father, he finally fled to Persia and died there in 1704. As for Ajit Singh, he recovered the sovereignty of Marwar in 1698, thanks to an agreement concluded between Aurangzeb and the loyal Durga Das, and Aurangzeb recovered his granddaughter, Mohammed Akbar's child, who had been raised in purdah, as a Muslim, by Durga Das.

Aurangzeb returned to the Deccan in 1681 at the age of sixty-three. He would remain there for the rest of his days without ever returning to Delhi or northern India. It seems as if his destiny was forever intertwined with this province. It was in the Deccan he met with his first successes and frustration, and it was there that he breathed his last.

Fate now took the shape of a people who would leave an indelible imprint on the history of India: the Marathas, a caste of Hindu cultivators who became militant. They lived in the Konkan coast and in the Western Ghats. This region stretches along the Arabian Sea coast from Daman in the north to Goa in the south. It rises towards the high Deccan plateau in the east across jagged reliefs covered with wild forests and impregnable fortresses.

The Marathas were subjects of the Sultan of Bijapur.

Many of them served in his army, particularly in the light cavalry, and even reached high positions, such as Shahji Bhonsle, whose horsemen harassed Shah Jahan's troops in 1636. He later became governor of Pune and then of Mangalore. But Shahji's greatest glory is having fathered Shivaji, Aurangzeb's bête noire, whose equestrian statue now stands in the most beautiful square of Aurangabad, as if to defy the memory of his rival!

Shivaji, born in May 1627, was eight years younger than Aurangzeb. Their paths crossed for the first time in May 1657 when the latter, then viceroy of the Deccan, fought against Bijapur. At that time they settled their differences by a truce, before Aurangzeb left the Deccan to conquer the throne of India.

During the twenty-three years Aurangzeb spent in northern India consolidating his power, Shivaji had become a hero in the Deccan. In 1664, at the death of his father Shahji, he took on the title of Raja and had coins struck in his name. Then, taking advantage of the dissension caused by Aurangzeb's discriminatory policies, he united the Maratha people by exciting their religious fervour against the excesses of the Great Mughal.

Supported by an army of fifty thousand men, and with a clever combination of diplomacy and ruse, he dominated the Deccan till his death on 2 April 1680. His diplomacy consisted mainly of a series of short-lived alliances which he would conclude, depending on the need of the hour, with the Mughal empire, Bijapur or Golconda to play off one against the other, while he himself established his supremacy over the region. As for his courage and sagacity, the most telling example is his interview with Afzal Khan, commander of the troops sent by the Sultan of Bijapur to bring him to heel.

Shivaji, a master of guerrilla warfare, was too shrewd to face an army in an open field. As soon as he learnt that

Afzal Khan was on his heels, he hastened to send him his respects, together with rich presents and, to show his good faith, asked the general for a private interview. The latter, convinced of the sincerity of his rival, accepted immediately. It was agreed that they would meet the next day near the Maratha fortress of Pratapgarh without escort and armed with only a sword or a dagger.

The appointed day must have been particularly hot, as Afzal Khan wore only a muslin tunic with a sword belt. Shivaji too wore a light garment, but his dress hid a coat of arms. Besides the dagger attached to his belt, Shivaji hid in his left hand a formidable weapon. It was known as the *waghnakh,* "tiger claws" consisting of four curved claws of steel, attached to the first and fourth fingers, and hidden by rings.

When embracing Afzal Khan, Shivaji ripped open his belly with the claws and finished him off with his dagger. The Marathas, warned by a signal from their chief, appeared from behind the trees and massacred the Bijapur troops who were waiting calmly for their chief's return.

When Aurangzeb returned to the Deccan, Shivaji was dead But the Emperor pursued his son and successor, Shambhuji, just as relentlessly, especially because he had welcomed Prince Mohammed Akbar and participated in his rebellion. On 11 February 1689, the young Maratha chief who had neither the intelligence nor the sagacity of his father, was taken by surprise and captured by a Mughal patrol in the town of Sangameshwar, while indulging in a bout of debauchery in the company of a score of his lieutenants. He was taken to the imperial camp at Bahadurgarh, dressed as a clown and paraded to the sound of drums and trumpets. Then Aurangzeb promised to pardon him if he would give up his strongholds and tell where he had hidden his treasure. Not only did Shambhuji refuse, but he heaped insults upon the Emperor. He was then tortured for three full months before being cut into pieces and fed to dogs. Now Aurangzeb had no foe worth the name in the Deccan.

It was in 1698 that the physician from Naples, Gemelli Careri, went to one of the shifting imperial camps. He recounts:

"I was told that the army consisted of sixty thousand cavalrymen and a hundred thousand infantrymen; that for the luggage there were fifty thousand camels and three thousand elephants; but that the number of vivandières, merchants, sellers and workmen was even greater; that the camp was a moving city of five hundred thousand people where provisions were in easy supply and where one could get all that one desired. There were two hundred and fifty bazaars or markets, each omrah or general having one to meet the needs of his people. In this way, the entire camp was thirty miles in diameter."

Careri was received twice by Aurangzeb, the first time in his private apartments and the second in the tent for public audience:

"The king arrived on foot, using a stick which was forked at the top; he was preceded by several omrahs and an infinite number of courtesans. He was wearing a white tunic which was hooked under his right arm as all Mohammedans do to distinguish themselves from the gentiles who hook it under the left arm. His turban was of the same material; around it was a golden cloth on which a huge emerald shone in the midst of four small ones. His belt was of silk and hid on the right side a katari or Indian dagger. His shoes were Moorish, he wore no stockings. Two officers were chasing away the flies with white horse tails and another carried a green parasol to protect him from the sun. He was of small build with a long nose and seemed delicate as his eighty years had bent him. His olive coloured skin heightened his white round beard."

Aurangzeb was now an old man He had become the prisoner of his own creation: an empire, magnificent no doubt but too vast and unwieldy to govern. Deprived by his intolerance and suspicion of the traditional support of the Rajputs and the Afghans who had ensured the glory of his predecessors, it is hardly surprising that in spite of some brilliant successes he was unable for long to get the better of the Marathas.

In 1705 Aurangzeb, then eighty-seven, fell seriously ill. For twelve days he was confined to his bed in his camp on the banks of the Krishna, hanging between life and death. On 2 November, after he recovered, he was taken in a palanquin to Ahmadnagar where he arrived on 31 January 1706. It was in that city that he died a year later.

Some twenty kilometres to the north-west of Aurangabad lies Khuldabad: a small village surrounded by a medieval wall whose large avenue is bordered by houses, shops and lime-washed mosques. It would probably have remained unknown to the tourists who flock to India had it not been on the way to the famous Ellora caves.

At Khuldabad Emperor Aurangzeb's mortal remains lie in a modest tomb covered with earth, not imperial marble, in the shadow of the mausoleum of a holy man who was his spiritual master.

One would imagine that the last of the Great Mughals, the man who, after his grandfather, was undoubtedly the most powerful monarch of the Mughal dynasty, would be buried in a sepulchre matching his greatness. But he himself, a few days before his death, had opted for austerity. In his last will he had desired that only four rupees, the earnings from the sale of caps he had stitched with his own hands, be spent on his funeral. As for the three-hundred-and-five rupees he had earned from copying the Koran, they were to be distributed to the fakirs on the day of his death.

In this manner died the prince who was completely devoid of scruples; who had killed three brothers before usurping the Peacock Throne from his father, the absolute monarch whose audacity and tenacity stretched the frontiers of his empire to unheard of limits; the religious fanatic whose bigotry had escalated the conflict that persists to this day between Hindus and Muslims. This man, in the twilight of his life, tried to seek forgiveness for his sins through humility and charity.

KOH–I–NOOR

CHAPTER ONE

Aurangzeb's death was the beginning of the end of the Mughal empire. None of his successors, a series of weak, indolent kings, could match his stature. An Indian author, Muni Lal, has very aptly described them as the "Mini Mughals". They were mere puppets who occupied the centre stage for a brief spell only to fall into oblivion, blinded, assassinated or incarcerated. Power belonged to omnipotent coteries of ministers who took advantage of the prevailing anarchy to feather their own political and material nests at the expense of the people and the empire.

During this entire period Babur's diamond remained locked in the imperial treasury at the Red Fort, though a nineteenth century author claims that it was set in the eye of one of the peacocks which decorated the famous Mughal throne. We have thus no account of the period to tell us what became of it, and must move on to the morning of 22 September 1719, when the inhabitants of Delhi woke to the beating of drums, announcing the accession of a new Emperor, Mohammed Shah, the twelfth Mughal ruler, and in the twelve years since Aurangzeb's death, the sixth "emperor" to be crowned.

The new ruler was barely seventeen years old. He was handsome, affable, intelligent and, above all, clear-sighted. His first concern, after coming to the throne, was to avoid the fate of his predecessors. So, handing over the reins of power to his advisors before being compelled to do so, he sank into a state of utter debauchery, and has been described as a man "who was never without a mistress in his arms nor a cup in his hand" earning the sobriquet "Rangila"—literally "colourful" and meaning "a debauch".

He ruled in this manner for twenty-eight years.

It is hardly surprising then that the Rajputs, Marathas, Jats and Sikhs, who had been wronged for so long by the harshness of Islam, should seize the opportunity to rebel against the central government.

While the Mughal empire was sinking inexorably into a state of decadence, its rival Persia was like the proverbial phoenix rising from the ashes. Invaded, occupied and plundered in 1722 by the Afghan tribe of the Ghilzais, it would recover its past glory due to the providential arrival on the scene of Nadir Shah Afshar.

Few destinies compare with Nadir's. A humble shepherd's son, in the space of thirteen years he would raise Persia to the zenith of her power, conquer India, take away her fabulous treasures, and rename the Mughal diamond he captured the Koh-i-noor (Mountain of Light). From this time the gem ceased to be an elusive legend and became a tangible part of history.

Nadir's parents belonged to a branch of the nomadic tribe of Afshars, actually Turks from Azerbaidjan who had settled since 1502 in Khorasan. Every autumn the tribe would migrate towards their winter pastures, situated to the north of the Allah-o-Akbar mountain range at the border between modern Iran and Turkmenistan. It was during one such journey, on 22 November 1688, that the future sovereign of Persia was born.

As a teenager he entered the service of the governor of Abiverd, a small locality in Khorasan. In a short space of time his skill and bravery won him the esteem of his master who raised him not only to the rank of commander of his personal guard but also gave him his daughter's hand in marriage. His eldest son, Reza Qoli, was born on 15 April 1719. In the following year his wife died and Nadir married another daughter of his protector, by whom he had two sons.

Meanwhile, the year 1722 was proving to be fatal for the long-ruling Safavid dynasty. On the throne was Shah Sultan Hussein Safavi, a pious, gentle but hopelessly weak monarch.

Taking advantage of Safavid weakness, the Afghan hordes invaded Persia on several occasions, trying the strength of her once formidable army. At last, in 1722, they pushed their conquests till Ispahan where their chief, Mahmud deposed Shah Sultan Hussein and, much to the humiliation of Persia, was crowned king by the fallen sovereign.

The Afghan occupation and the ensuing anarchy enabled the Russians and Turks to satisfy their own territorial ambitions. A few years earlier a Russian trade mission had visited Ispahan. It informed the Czar of the decline of the Safavid dynasty, adding that the country would surely be ruined if Shah Sultan Hussein was not replaced by a more competent man. As for the Turks, the Sunnis of north-west Persia asked for Turkey's protection against the bigotry of the Shiite clergy, which was all powerful in the Safavid court.

While the western part of the country was occupied by the Ottoman empire, Peter the Great of Russia, freed at last by the Treaty of Nystadt from his long war with Sweden, took possession of the ports of Derbent and Baku, as well as of the border provinces of Daghestan, Mazandaran, Guilan and Astarabad, fulfilling his long cherished dream of converting the Caspian Sea into a Russian lake.

Meanwhile, Shah Sultan Hussein's third son, Tahmasp Mirza, then eighteen years old, had managed to escape from Ispahan before the Afghan arrival, and taken refuge at Qazvin, the second capital of the Safavids. As soon as he learnt of his father's fall, he proclaimed himself the legitimate heir to the throne and started raising an army to recover his kingdom.

Wandering from one city to another in the company of

a hundred odd followers, mercilessly pursued by the Afghans who had nicknamed him Saghzadeh (son of a dog) to make fun of his title of Shahzadeh (prince), Tahmasp at last reached the province of Mazandaran. There he received the valuable assistance of the chief of the Kadjar tribe and his two thousand partisans. He immediately appointed the latter as his principal advisor and the commander-in-chief of his small army. Their first objective was to reconquer Khorasan and its capital Mashad, whose governor had declared himself an independent sovereign.

Meanwhile, Nadir had acquired quite a reputation in the province of his birth. His tall stature, robust constitution, tanned complexion, black beard and alert eyes hooded by thick eyebrows, his stentorian voice and his iron will, and above all his prodigious strength, left a lasting impression on all those who met him. At the death of his father-in-law in 1720, he gathered several hundreds of the members of his clan as well as those of a friendly tribe under his banner. It is said that this group indulged in acts of banditry.

When Prince Tahmasp reached Khorasan, he heard about Nadir's exploits and invited him to join forces to save the country from the Afghans. The ambitious young man had no hesitation in accepting, though he had taken full measure of the irresolute character of the claimant to the throne. He also knew that it would not be easy to establish himself as Tahmasp's chief advisor. To succeed, he would have to first supplant the powerful Kadjar chief and then eliminate the schemers hanging on to the prince's cloak.

Nadir did not take long to achieve his ends. In October 1726 Tahmasp executed his first friend in need—the man Nadir considered an obstacle on his path. Some historians are of the view that the Kadjar chief was a victim of a rumour spread by Nadir. Whatever be the case, Nadir inherited his titles. He, however, managed to hide his all-consuming ambition by putting on an air of total abnegation showing the utmost devotion to his master. He went to the extent of asking the prince to do him the favour of calling him Tahmasp Quli which in Turkish means "Tahmasp's slave".

It is under this name, or, to be more precise, under the title of Tahmasp Quli Khan, that he became a living legend in Europe. Some, pushing fantasy to absurd heights, claimed that he was Irish or even Belgian, the former insisting that his real name was Thomas O'Kelly, while the latter supported the idea that he was born in Tirlemont in the Belgian province of Brabant. One anecdote, quoted in an anonymous book published in Amsterdam in 1740, tells us that a person worthy of trust who was passing by Tirlemont had heard over there that "Quli Khan" was born in that city. It was said that in his youth he was a bit of a libertine and one day when he asked his brother, the pastor in a neighbouring parish, for money, the latter refused. Furious, the future Nadir Shah waited for the holy man in the church with a stick and cruelly beat him. Then he ran away to Holland, from where he moved on to Smyrna and finally to Persia.

The French were to discover him thanks to *Nadir,* a tragedy dedicated to him by Pierre Ulric Dubuisson, which was first staged in the *Theatre des Nations* in Paris on 31 August 1780.

Between 1727 and 1729 Nadir subjugated the Abdali Afghans who, from their stronghold of Herat, posed a constant threat to Khorasan. He also drove out from Persian soil their compatriots and rivals, the Ghilzai Afghans. He achieved this in spite of Prince Tahmasp's intrigues, for he had in the meantime become jealous of his "slave", and never missed an opportunity to put a spoke in his wheel.

Nadir did not hold it against him. On the contrary, as

soon as the Afghans had been driven out from Ispahan, he placed Tahmasp on the throne of his ancestors as Tahmasp II. He obviously felt at the time that legitimacy took precedence over a coup d'état. Tahmasp, however, was but a figurehead. Persia's new strongman presided over the nation's destiny to the point of claiming the right to marry one of the king's sisters without his prior authorisation.

It was in Ispahan that Nadir first came into contact with Europeans, amongst whom were agents of the British and Dutch East India Companies, priests, missionaries, as well as the French consul, Chevalier de Gardane, the grandfather of Napoleon Bonaparte's future envoy to the court of Persia. The chevalier was extremely impressed with the personality of the Persian general and describes him in glowing terms:

"A man of about forty, trained since childhood in the use of arms; bravest among the brave; a man of understanding, frank and sincere, rewarding those who are valiant and punishing with death those who fall back before the enemy when there is a means to resist. He first gave proof of his talent, valour and loyalty each time his services were called upon, and when he was in the good graces of the king he taught him to distinguish flatterers from traitors and forced him to punish the former and distance himself from the latter."

After Nadir had defeated the Turks in the first half of 1730, Gardane, who had left Ispahan for France and had crossed the regions in which battle was raging, found that "from Bassora till Baghdad, and from Baghdad to the gates of Aleppo, everyone trembled when hearing the name of Tahmasp Quli Khan."

These military successes together with the iron discipline their commander-in-chief had imposed upon them restored the morale and strength the Persian troops had lost during the twilight of the Safavid empire.

However, like all Oriental potentates, the Shah wanted to rule and govern at the same time. His dithering provided Nadir with the much awaited opportunity to inch his way towards the throne. He had just vanquished the Abdali Afghans and occupied Herat when he received a piece of news which made him furious. During his absence the sovereign, encouraged by his courtesans to resume hostilities against the Turks, had been defeated. A peace treaty had been imposed by the enemy whose terms, Nadir presumed, must have been extremely humiliating for the Persians.

He rushed back to Ispahan and called a meeting of the dignitaries of the empire where he demanded that the king be dethroned for incompetence. On 23 August 1732 the Shah was replaced by his eight-month-old son Abbas. A few days later the deposed king, his harem and servants were sent off to Mashad under armed guard, while a strange ceremony was taking place in the great hall of the palace. The imperial "brat" was brought from the harem in his cradle, Nadir lifted him up and placed him on the throne. Then he managed to put on his head the egret, the mark of sovereignty, and place at his side the sword and shield, that are the symbols of royal power. Nadir himself gave up the title of Tahmasp Quli Khan and took on the more prestigious one of Viceroy and Benefactor of the People.

Why did Nadir go through this charade when we know that he himself had been aspiring for so long to become king? The entire capital was buzzing with rumours of his ambitions. "Ispahan, the people, the court, the king himself", recalls Gardane, "all fear his ambition of climbing higher and that he would no longer be able to take a step forward without seizing the throne."

In reality, Nadir was far more prudent than was thought. He wanted to be absolutely sure of the loyalty of his troops before mounting the Safavid throne. Another victorious campaign and the bloodless recovery of the provinces occupied by Russia were to secure it for him.

On the evening of 22 January 1736, he arrived in the Moghan plain, in the north-west of the country, between the rivers Kour and Aras. All the dignitaries of the empire had gathered there upon his invitation to confer the crown of Persia on the person they felt was the most capable of wearing it. Naturally Nadir expected to be the happy recipient. He nevertheless feigned indifference, pretending that he was tired of fighting and that he desired nothing more than to withdraw to his native Khorasan. But when the Sheikh-ol-Islam, the seniormost cleric, suggested that his friends choose from among the members of the Safavid family, Nadir had him brought to the large tent of the council and had him strangled on the spot, right in front of all present. Thereupon everyone got the message and he was unanimously proclaimed sovereign on 8 March 1739, with the title of Nadir Shah Afshar. Meanwhile, his young predecessor was taken to his father in the Mashad prison, where four years later both would be murdered.

After the Navroz festivities were over, the new monarch debated with his generals over the plan to recover Kandahar and questioned the Afghans in his service about the state of affairs in that area. On 21 November 1739, after spending five weeks in Ispahan, he marched at the head of an army of eighty thousand men, cavalry for the most part, and a light artillery commanded by European mercenaries. Among them were a Dutchman, Vanderen—who was to later become the grand master of artillery of Persia under the name of Soleiman—as well as a German, Roth, and a Frenchman, Bonnal.

Two years earlier Nadir had sent emissaries to Delhi requesting that Mohammed Shah forbid Afghan refugees from entering his territory when the Persian campaign began against Kandahar. The Mughal Emperor had promised to abide by his demand.

However, when a detachment of Persian troops drove out the Ghilzai Afghans from Kandahar, the survivors took refuge in India without the Indian authorities making the slightest move to stop them. Thus, on 11 May 1737 Nadir Shah sent a new ambassador to Mohammed Shah to remind him of his earlier promise. The Persian envoy was ordered to return from India within a period of forty days.

Forty days extended to February 1738. Nine months had gone by without the Emperor giving any reply to the Persian ambassador. It cannot be said that the latter was bored in Delhi. Everything there reminded him of his native Persia: the language, the culture, the architecture, the origin of several state dignitaries, and even the Chandni Chowk boulevard, which he often traversed on foot or in a palanquin to go to the Jama Masjid or to the Red Fort. At that time it was lined on both sides with hundred-year-old trees; in the middle ran a waterway; the place bore an uncanny resemblance to Tehahar Bagh, the main thoroughfare of Ispahan. Our diplomat is even supposed to have had a mild fling. Rumour had it that it was the love of a courtesan which kept him in the capital of India.

In fact, Mohammed Shah and his ministers were in no hurry to answer Nadir. On the one hand they did not want to recognize his title as Shah of Persia. On the other, they were waiting for the outcome of the siege of Kandahar, hoping that the man they considered the usurper of the Safavid throne would be vanquished and driven back. Thus, despite the protests of the Persian envoy, who rightly feared his master's wrath, they refused to allow him to leave Delhi.

Nadir Shah was then at his camp situated three kilometres to the south-east of Kandahar. It was an immense settlement enclosed by walls and equipped with a citadel, bazaars, mosques, public baths and inns. He had ordered each one of his men to build a house there. He himself occupied a modest room in the citadel. This city was called Nadirabad or Nadir's colony.

The siege of Kandahar had gone on for over a year and yet success seemed to elude the Persian army. It was only in March 1738 that luck switched sides. Thanks to informers within the citadel, Nadir Shah managed to discover the weaknesses of the Afghan defense and broke down one wall after the other. The governor and his troops were forced to take refuge in a fortress to the north-west of the town.

The Shah was exultant. In a letter to the governor of Ispahan, he boasted about his success: "The mountains seemed to be stalks and the sea a valley before our royal face . . . I pointed my mortars to them and threw bombs in the city without stopping, one after the other, at the speed with which thunder follows lightning."

A few days later, the unfortunate governor of Kandahar, threatened in his new retreat by Persian cannons, sent his sister in the company of several dignitaries to ask for mercy. Nadir was not insensitive to the distress of the young woman, all the more so since he wished to recruit the Afghans into his army. He spared the lives of the chiefs, contenting himself by banishing them to Mazandaran, in the north of Persia. The city was razed and its inhabitants shifted to Nadirabad, near the present site of Kandahar. Many young men were recruited in the Persian army, and among them was a precocious teenager named Ahmad. He was to win glory for himself as the founder of Afghanistan, and become another monarch to fall under the spell of the Koh-i-noor.

For Nadir Shah this victory was the fulfillment of a long held ambition and the beginning of another dream—India. Now that Kandahar had been recaptured, not only was

Persia's territorial integrity restored, but the gates to India and her fabulous treasures were opened to the "last great conqueror of Asia".

He knew that India would be easy prey. His ambassadors had informed him of the internal dissensions tearing the Mughal empire apart and of the incompetence of its rulers. They had also told him about the legendary wealth stored in the vaults of the Red Fort. Moreover, the large fresco which adorned one of the walls of the audience hall of Ispahan's Forty Column Palace, depicting the second monarch of the Safavid dynasty with Emperor Humayun in 1544, must have reminded Nadir of the latter's exile to Persia. He might even have known the story of the incomparable diamond the Great Mughal had offered Shah Tahmasp in exchange for his aid, and which the Shah sent as a gift to the Shiite Sultan of Ahmadnagar.

Although Mohammed Shah had been informed of the conquest of Kandahar and the Shah of Persia's designs on his country, he did not allow the news to bother him unduly. He contended himself by recalling to his side Nizam-ul-Mulk Asaf Jah, on whom he conferred the charge of "regent". A prestigious title indeed but devoid, as we shall see, of any authority. This grey-haired septuagenarian from Samarkand, one of the last survivors of Aurangzeb's time, was not only an experienced general but also a fine diplomat and he founded the Nizam dynasty of Hyderabad that ruled over a part of the Deccan till 1948. In 1722, after briefly serving as grand vizier, and disgusted by the intrigues at court, he had withdrawn to his province of the Deccan. His return might have saved the empire had he been given a free hand in commanding the army. But he had to share this task with three others: his cousin Kamar-ud-din Khan, his successor as grand vizier and a drunken, indolent old man; Khan Dauran, the Emperor's favourite and his advisor on military affairs, "one of the rare members of the nobility who did not react to an insult but laughed as if it were not worthy of attention"; and lastly, the fiery, impetuous Saadat Khan, the governor of the province of Oudh.

On 10 January 1739, Nadir Shah took Lahore. He had earlier conquered Ghazni, Kabul and Jalalabad, and crossed the formidable Khyber Pass to occupy Peshawar. The governors of these regions, who had been victims of moral and material neglect from Delhi, only put up a token resistance. Meanwhile, Nadir appointed his son Reza Qoli as regent and sent him back to Persia with some of his troops. He did not want his campaign in India to be hampered by lack of time.

The news of the fall of Kabul reached Delhi in early July 1738. But an unperturbed Mohammed Shah waited until 2 December before deciding to send an army against the invader. The army, commanded by Nizam-ul-Mulk, Kamar-ud-Din Khan and Khan Dauran, gathered first at Shalimar Gardens. Chroniclers of the time give out divergent estimates of the number of troops. Considering that the most important contingent, that of the Nizam, counted only three thousand men, one can deduce that the Mughal forces never exceeded seventy-five thousand horsemen and infantrymen and an artillery detachment. There was also, as was usual in every Mughal military camp, a large number of non-combatants: stewards, the royal harem, the families of dignitaries, all totalling up to one million souls.

Nadir Shah stayed for sixteen days in Lahore. On learning that Mohammed Shah was preparing to meet him with a considerable army, he sent him a letter which contained both veiled threats and placatory remarks. As a Turk who belonged to the same race as the Mughals, he wrote, his intentions towards the Emperor of India were entirely peaceful. He had violated Mughal borders solely to punish the Afghans, an enemy common to both India and Persia.

He went on to blame Mohammad Shah for treating his ambassadors without any regard for the rules of friendship and diplomacy. Finally, he warned the Mughal court against the consequences of a war, adding nonetheless that he would be magnanimous towards those Indian officers who, after their defeat, would surrender to him.

It is difficult to imagine that Nadir cared to justify his invasion of India. In all probability he wanted to gauge the reaction of his foes. However, before his letter reached Mohammed Shah, the Mughal army had already left Delhi. Presuming it was too late to save Lahore, Mohammed Shah and his advisors decided to entrench themselves near Karnal, a fortified city located 120 kilometres north-west of Delhi, and wait there for the governor of Oudh and his men.

The imperial camp was set up to the north of the town, on a vast plain bordered to the east by the Ali Mardan canal, thus ensuring an adequate supply of water and providing the cavalry enough room for manoeuvring. An enclosure made of cob, bristling at regular intervals with watch towers equipped with cannons, surrounded the camp.

The Shah of Persia and his army left Lahore on 26 January 1739. At dawn, on 11 February, they reached Sarai Azimabad, an abandoned caravanserai situated some twenty kilometres north of Karnal. An inhospitable jungle stretching over several kilometres, cut by a solitary path, was all that separated them from the Mughal lines. This ruled out a frontal attack. Using the information provided by his spies and scouts about the position of the Mughal army and the geographical layout of the area, Nadir decided to provoke his opponents out of their trenches and meet them on a terrain of his choice. The next day he skirted the jungle and set up his camp on a plain that lay between the Ali Mardan canal and the Yamuna, some seven kilometres to the east of the Mughal camp, and near the road that links Delhi to Karnal, effectively cutting the enemy lines without the latter even noticing it.

At nightfall Persian scouts sent out on a reconnaissance mission heard a pack of horses galloping past. This was Saadat Khan and the contingent from Oudh. As it was too late to intercept them, Nadir Shah ordered his men to take over their artillery and luggage, which were lagging at some distance behind the main army.

On 13 February, just before noon, while Mohammed Shah was presiding over a council of war, a eunuch swept in to the tent and announced the bad news to Saadat Khan. Dismayed, the governor of Oudh picked up his sword which he had placed on the carpet at the Emperor's feet, and begged, leave to depart. His colleagues did their best to caution him arguing that his soldiers were tired and the hour was late. But he would have none of it. Sending messengers to notify his army to be ready for an early battle, he dashed towards the Persian camp with the troops he had on hand: a thousand cavalrymen and a hundred infantrymen.

Due to this thoughtless impetuosity of the governor of Oudh, the Shah of Persia was going to reap the seeds of his strategy. Far from its base, the Indian army was easy prey for the Persian generals who excelled in tactical warfare.

Nadir arranged his troops to make sure that the enemy could not escape until its defeat was total. Then, dressed in a coat of mail, exchanging his legendary tahmazi (headgear in the shape of a cross with the four sides covered by a white woollen cloth for helmet), he mounted his grey steed and galloped towards the enemy followed by a thousand horsemen chosen from among the best of his tribe.

Showered by arrows, he feigned a hasty retreat, hoping that Saadat Khan would follow him. The latter, overjoyed at the prospect of an easy victory, sent a messenger to the camp asking for more troops and artillery reinforcements.

Then, without waiting for them to arrive, he fell headlong into the trap that had been laid for him a few kilometres ahead: a shield of cavalrymen hiding three thousand artillerymen, armed with long pivotal cannons, capable of firing shots of one to two pounds. Hardly had the governor of Oudh reached the spot where the enemy troops had gathered than the shield opened, exposing his men to the artillery at close range.

Meanwhile, he had been joined by Khan Dauran and part of the right wing of the Indian army, made up of horsemen, infantrymen and combat elephants. There was no sign of the Mughal artillery which was to remain absent till the end of the battle.

As for the Nizam, who was by far the best of the Mughal generals, he had stayed close to the Emperor like his cousin Kamar-ud-din Khan and did nothing to help his colleagues. This has led more than one historian to conclude that he wished to see them die so that he could usurp their power at court.

While the deadly fire of the Persian artillery continued to slay the poor Indian soldiers armed with just bows and swords, mobile torches invaded the battlefield. These torches were a masterstroke by Nadir. He knew that in India the elephant was considered to be the ultimate in weaponry. He also knew that most animals, with the exception of camels, were allergic to the sight of fire and strong smells. He, therefore, had a number of platforms made and fixed each across a pair of camels. On these platforms were laid naphta and a mixture of combustibles with orders to set them on fire during the battle. With the wind blowing the nauseating smoke towards them, the elephants began trumpeting with fear. Inspite of the efforts of their drivers, they scrambled helter-skelter, crushing soldiers and causing panic on all sides. It was not long before the plain was strewn with corpses.

Saadat Khan had for some time been suffering from a leg injury, hence he could not ride on horseback. Instead, he had mounted on an enormous elephant. Injured once again during the battle, he could have managed to save himself but his mount, scared by the flames, fled towards the enemy lines. He continued to fire arrows from his elephant when a Persian cavalryman galloped towards him, calling him by his first name, "Mohammed Amin, are you mad? Whom are you fighting? On whom are you relying?" Then, driving his spear into the ground, and throwing the reins of his horse round it, he climbed on to Saadat Khan's howda by the rope hanging down from it, and led the latter to Nadir Shah.

Khan Dauran, who had also mounted an elephant, was hit in the face and fell inert on his howda. He succumbed the next day, murmuring before dying: "I have done my duty. Now do yours. In no circumstance should you take the Emperor to Nadir, nor conduct Nadir to Delhi. Send that evil away from here by all the means that you can devise."

At sunset, Mohammed Shah withdrew to his tent without lifting a finger to save his throne or his people. Flanked by the left wing of his army and most of his artillery, he had remained a spectator throughout the battle.

The massacre by Nadir Shah's troops was terrible. The Shah of Persia's historiographer estimated the number of Indian dead at a hundred officers and thirty thousand soldiers. An Indian historian assesses the losses of Khan Dauran and Saadat Khan at five and three thousand respectively, figures which seem to be closer to reality. On the Persian side then, were two thousand five hundred dead and five thousand wounded.

The Battle of Karnal had lasted no more than three hours. It had begun after the noon prayer and ended before the evening one. The bulk of the Mughal army, including the artillery, was intact. But the soldiers were tired of fighting. Their morale, worn down by the capture of Saadat Khan and the death of Khan Dauran, could not withstand the apathy of the Emperor and Nizam-ul-Mulk or the tactical and strategic superiority of the enemy.

Returning to his tent, a tired but triumphant Nadir Shah sent for Saadat Khan to consult him on the best way to take advantage of his victory. The latter advised him, not without a bit of malice, to call Nizam-ul-Mulk, "the key of the Indian state", and discuss the conditions of peace with him.

The next day, 14 February, at nightfall, the old man came to the Persian camp where the Shah received him warmly. After long negotiations in which the prime minister of Persia participated, they came to an agreement. The Persian army would withdraw from Indian territory in exchange for war reparations of fifty lakh (five million) rupees of which twenty were to be paid immediately, ten when the troops reached Lahore, ten in Attock and the rest in Kabul.

On Thursday, 15 February, just before noon, Mohammed Shah, seated in a palanquin of gold and silver, accompanied by a handful of his nobles and escorted by two thousand horsemen, moved towards the Persian camp. Nadir Shah had invited him to lunch, through Nizam-ul-Mulk, to celebrate their reconciliation. The Shah's son, Nasrollah Mirza, welcomed the Emperor half way and led him to his father. Nadir Shah was standing outside his tent, flanked by his ministers and generals. Hoping to appease the adversary, Mohammed Shah presented him six splendid Tartar horses and two elephants, one laden with jewels and the other with rupees. Nadir thanked him; then, taking him by the arm, he led him to his tent and bade him sit by him on a magnificent Persian carpet.

The meeting lasted till "three hours before sunset". The story goes that while lunch was being served, Nadir proudly announced: "I practice open warfare and not treacherous assassination." Whereupon he exchanged his plate for the Emperor's in order to reassure him that the food was not poisoned.

After Khan Dauran's death, Nizam-ul-Mulk's son had been given charge of the army to the great displeasure of Saadat Khan. To take his revenge, he told Nadir that knowing of the fabulous wealth stashed away in Delhi, he should never have been satisfied with a mere fifty lakh rupees as damages.

The Shah of Persia was, of course, in complete agreement. He nonetheless made it clear that he could not go back on his agreement with Mohammed Shah without a valid excuse.

In the meantime the Persian troops continued to occupy the Mughal camp while waiting for the settlement of the first instalment of the reparation. As payment was being delayed beyond the deadline, Nadir made it a pretext for reinforcing the siege. The condition of the inhabitants became unbearable. Wheat was scarce, even at the very high price of six or seven rupees a seer. The stocks of ghee were exhausted. There seemed to be no end in sight. The Persian soldiers, the kizilbashs, patrolled the road to Delhi and slaughtered or took as slaves anybody who dared to venture beyond the camp.

On 22 February Nizam-ul-Mulk was summoned again by Nadir Shah. He came to the Persian cantonment without suspecting the surprises which awaited him. As soon as he crossed the threshold of the royal ante-chamber, he was arrested by the guards on duty, bound hand and foot and put in solitary confinement.

Then, as a second surprise, Nadir sent him a message ordering him to procure twenty crore (two hundred million) rupees over and above the amount stipulated in the agreement and twenty thousand men to serve under his banner. He also insisted on a fresh meeting with Mohammed Shah. The Nizam was dumbfounded. He did his utmost to convince the Shah that the Mughal empire had never possessed that kind of money and that another interview with the Emperor went against protocol. His protestations were in vain. Finally, fearing that famine would wipe out his fellow countrymen, he bowed to the demands of the conqueror.

On 24 February Mohammed Shah came to meet the Persian Emperor for the second time, accompanied this time by a few ministers, eunuchs and servants. On this occasion there was no one to welcome him. After some minutes—which for an Emperor must have seemed like an eternity—the Nizam and Saadat Khan, their jailers by their sides, joined him and conducted him to Nadir Shah's tent.

The Persian's manner towards his guest had changed radically. It was no longer the behaviour of a king with his equal, but clearly that of a victor versus a vanquished foe. Taken aback by the haughty demeanour of his counterpart, Mohammed Shah waited for a few minutes, then, presuming that all that was required was to reconfirm the agreement concluded two days before with the Nizam, he declared that he accepted the suggested preliminaries.

"If this be the case", replied Nadir, "the treaty will soon be drawn up. All that remains is to agree upon the reparation of the damages I have been forced to incur to wage this war as well as upon an annual tribute that you shall pay me." This time he fixed the amount at forty crores, that is twenty crores above the amount he had asked from the Nizam.

How can one doubt that all this bargaining was nothing but a pretext to occupy Delhi and take over the imperial treasure? Mohammed Shah could hardly believe his ears. He protested bitterly that he would prefer giving up the whole of India rather than undertake to pay such exorbitant sums. "You will be giving me nothing but what belongs to me", retorted Nadir, flushed with anger. "Do you not know that the outcome of the battle has rendered me master of not only your estates but also of your freedom and your life?" Having said that, he gestured to his soldiers to remove the Emperor from his presence and confined Mohammed Shah and his harem to the tents adjoining his own.

A few days later he dispatched his loyal lieutenant, Tahmasp Khan Jalayer, to Delhi in the company of Saadat Khan, the former as his personal representative and the latter as Mohammed Shah's plenipotentiary. Escorted by four thousand kizilbashs, they were given the task of taking possession of the city and the Red Fort.

Both sovereigns left Karnal on 1 March 1739 in the following order: Nadir's harem escorted by twenty thousand cavalrymen; Mohammed Shah, his sons and his wives, perched on elephants, under the guard of twelve thousand Persian soldiers; the Indian rajas, viziers and khans whose contingents were intact, each being separated from the others by detachments of Persian troops, and finally, the Shah himself, riding in front of his personal guard and a large cavalry. A witness tells us: "No less than three hundred and fifty thousand men slowly proceeded in this manner, and a space of four leagues in length by more than one in width was occupied by this crowd."

One wonders, if on his triumphant journey towards Delhi Nadir Shah thought of the legendary diamond in the Red Fort treasury and schemed en route to seize it.

CHAPTER TWO

The people of Delhi were stunned to learn that just two days after the Battle of Karnal all was lost to the enemy. Convinced of the power of their leaders and the invincibility of the Mughal troops, they never expected the Mughals to buckle down so easily before the will of a "shepherd's son".

As a worried, impatient Delhi waited and wondered what fate now had in store, the procession of the Persian and Indian sovereigns reached the outskirts of Shalimar Gardens. It was Wednesday, 7 March 1739, a little before daybreak. Even though the capital was close by, Nadir decided to postpone his entry till the next day, to give Mohammed Shah time to get to Delhi first and organise a rousing welcome for the conqueror. Meanwhile, he settled down in the magnificent pavilions of the Shalimar Gardens.

The avenue which used to connect that site to the gates of Delhi must have been a beautiful sight. "As far as the eye could see". recounts a traveller at the end of the eighteenth century, "the horizon was covered with traces of gardens, pavilions, mosques and mausoleums in ruin." This is the road—probably then at the height of its splendour—that Nadir Shah followed on Friday, 9 March, at dawn, to reach the capital.

It is said that when he mounted the traditional, richly caparisoned elephant, he began to search vainly for the reins. When told that they were held by the mahout, he immediately climbed down, refusing to ride an animal over which he had no control. This anecdote, even though some dispute it, shows us the mettle of the man.

Mohammed Shah had seen to it that his guest was

provided with every comfort. He himself settled in a relatively modest apartment on the south-west corner of the palace walls, giving Nadir his luxurious apartments next to the Diwan-i-Khas.

The sun was already high when the Shah of Persia and his impressive escort entered Chandni Chowk. From the ramparts of the imperial palace whose cyclopean mass of red sandstone stood out against the horizon, a hundred gun salute boomed out to mark the arrival of the conqueror. The four thousand kizilbashs, who came with Saadat Khan, formed a double line along the famous avenue as petrified crowds saw their new master go by.

Mohammed Shah received his guest in front of Lahori Gate, the main entrance to the citadel, with great pomp and ceremony. The ground had been covered with carpets, brocades and other precious fabrics on which he would tread when he dismounted. "This habit of spreading a carpet on the path which kings and great princes tread", relates Chardin, "is one of the oldest customs of the Orient and the most universal."

In the meantime Persian soldiers had scattered all over the city, some taking quarters around the citadel, others on the banks of the Yamuna, some in houses confiscated for this purpose, among which was Khan Dauran's residence. The majority stationed themselves at the gates of the capital in order to keep an eye on the people.

Once the welcoming ceremony was over, the Emperor led Nadir Shah to his apartments. After crossing a series of marble rooms with latticed windows, they stopped in the Diwan-i-Khas where they were served a hearty breakfast. The Shah of Persia was wonderstruck by the profusion of precious stones which decorated the Peacock Throne: diamonds, rubies, emeralds, pearls. Did they not augur more prizes hidden in the vaults of the imperial treasury? And why not Babur's diamond? Nadir, as we have mentioned earlier, must have known about its existence. Hence it is extremely likely that he hoped to find it during his stay in Delhi.

He was dazzled by the prospect of such magnificent booty. However, everything pointed to the fact that Nadir Shah had no intention of lingering in this "paradise". Once he had collected the war indemnity and achieved the political goals of his conquest, he intended to go back to Persia. Furthermore, he had no illusions about the feelings of the people of Delhi towards him. Hadn't he been warned that they were in a restless and rebellious mood? That is why he had ordered his men to take the strictest precautions to ensure that nothing would disturb law and order. Any misbehaviour, he had warned, would lead to very harsh punishment, the mildest being the amputation of the nose and ears.

To maintain his influence over the conqueror, Saadat Khan followed him like his shadow. Nadir ordered him to collect the war indemnity as quickly as possible. The tone of his voice was so abrupt that one would have thought he held Saadat Khan responsible for the delay. Then, without giving him an opportunity to reply, he dismissed him with a nod of the head. The governor of Oudh was deeply disturbed. The consideration which he had enjoyed since Karnal had inexplicably turned into contempt. He saw the intrigues of his rival Nizam-ul-Mulk behind it. It is also possible that he was full of remorse at having kindled the appetite of the conqueror and tempting him to take over Delhi. Overwhelmed with despair, he poisoned himself the minute he returned to his quarters.

Id-ul-Zuha, the great festival commemorating the day Abraham sacrificed his son, Isaac, to God, fell on 10 March. It promised to be a happy day in Delhi in spite of the invader's presence. Just after the Muslim festivities, the Hindus were going to celebrate the festival of Holi. The previous day, a Friday, had been a holiday and the khutba had been recited in the name of Mohammed Shah, reassuring the inhabitants of the capital that the Mughal dynasty would live on forever.

Imagine their surprise when the next morning every mosque echoed with the sermon being recited to the glory of the conqueror, the Emperor of Persia, while new rupees, exceeding by twenty grains those of the Great Mughal, were put in circulation, bearing the legend: "Nadir Shah, the King of Kings".

Flabbergasted, the population of Delhi thought that the rule of the Mughals had come to an end. It was an unbearable prospect as the Great Mughals had ruled over India much longer than any other dynasty, Muslim or Hindu, leading to a feeling of permanence among their subjects. Further, the presence of the nasakhchi, the members of the Persian mounted police, who strutted proudly through the streets, did not help matters.

As the first rumours of discontent mingled with the sounds of the festivities, Nadir went to visit his host on what has officially been described as a courtesy call. But reading between the lines of the account given to us by the Shah of Persia's historiographer, it becomes clear that the main aim of the interview was to strip Mohammed Shah of his wealth under the guise of the greatest generosity: "Nadir Shah graciously remarked that the throne of Hindustan would be left to Mohammed Shah, in the terms of the agreement made on the first day, and that the Emperor would enjoy the support and friendship of the Persian monarch, because both were of the same Turkoman stock. Mohammed Shah bowed low in gratitude and gave profuse thanks to the victor for his generosity. He had received no small favour: it was the gift of his crown added to the gift of life. As a mark of his gratitude he laid before Nadir Shah the accumulated treasure stores and rare possessions of the rulers of Delhi as presents to Nadir and offerings for his health. But the gracious sovereign of Persia refused to take any of these things, though the piled-up wealth of all the other kings of the world did not amount to a tenth part of a tenth part of this immense hoard. At last he yielded to the importunity of Mohammed Shah and appointed trusty officers to take delivery of the money and other property."

The officers in question, Nizam-ul-Mulk, Kamar-ud-din Khan and a few other Mughal dignitaries, headed by Nadir's chief lieutenant Tahmasp Khan Jalayer, debated into the early hours of the morning over the best way to raise the tribute. Apart from this, they dispatched a group of nasakhchi to Pahar Ganj, the seed merchants' quarters, to open the silos and fix the price of wheat at one rupee for ten seers (about nine kilos). Judging this price to be too low, the merchants played for time till nightfall. Then, with the support of some hoodlums, joined by a rabble, they slit the throats of the Persian agents.

At the same time, in a house which was not far from the imperial palace, four generals of the Mughal army under the surveillance of twenty kizilbash got drunk in spite of orders forbidding them wine. Along with their servants, they jumped on their jailers, knocked them out with clubs and ran into the streets, shouting that Nadir had been assassinated by a dagger wound from Mohammed Shah.

Meanwhile, in the alleys of the bazaar, thugs who were just waiting for an opportunity to fish in troubled waters, spread the word that the Shah of Persia had been killed by an arrow aimed at him by one of the famous Kalmuk guards of the imperial harem while returning from his visit to Mohammed Shah, supposedly at the Emperor's behest.

These rumours spread across Delhi like wildfire. The

people, arming themselves with whatever they could find, rushed towards the Red Fort with a deafening din, crushing and massacring the Persian soldiers who had not taken refuge in the citadel. Then, from atop the palace walls, the thundering of cannons and the crackling of arquebus guns answered the clamour of the crowd, dispersing it for a short while.

The next day at about eight o'clock in the morning, while the revolt continued to rage, Nadir Shah crossed the palace court without bridling his mount, galloped across the domed passage which opened onto Lahori Gate, then, followed by an impressive escort, dashed towards Chandni Chowk to take stock of the situation. The sight could not have pleased him. The main thoroughfare was strewn with the corpses of his men. They had been beheaded, disemboweled or impaled. Keeping his cool, he dispatched patrols to put down the insurrection, authorizing them to take harsh measures if all else failed. Nonetheless, they were to spare innocent lives. But the indulgence of the Persians was taken to be a sign of weakness and the insurgents, bolder than ever before, received them with volleys of arrows and a barrage of fire from their muskets.

In the meantime, Nadir Shah had reached the foot of the Sunehri Masjid or golden mosque, with its gilded domes. Had it not been for the events that followed, this unimpressive monument would never have found a place in the guide books on Delhi.

Nadir climbed up the steps and reached the platform of the mosque, from where he could see the main pocket of tension, the heart of Chandni Chowk. What he witnessed did nothing to appease his anger. From the rooftops and windows of neighbouring houses a barrage of stones was being thrown down on the street, killing or wounding the troopers and horses of his escort, and then a bullet whistled past his ears and lodged in the head of one of his officers.

Foaming with rage, he pulled out his sabre and brandishing it above his head, gave the signal to sack the city.

For six hours, Persian troops, encouraged by the presence of their chief, struck, killed, raped, plundered and burned. The blood of their victims flooded the narrow streets of Dariba Bazaar (the gold merchants' mart), so that the gate which led into it was called Khuni Darwaza, or the gate of blood. People ran about in terror trying to escape the explosion of the kizilbashs' fury.

All across the town were scenes of desolation: smoking ruins, mutilated bodies and plundered houses. The Vezir Kamar-ud-din Khan's secretary who had witnessed the carnage from his terrace tells us: "Chandni Chowk, the fruit market, the Dariba Bazaar and the buildings around Jami Masjid were set fire to and reduced to ashes. The inhabitants, one and all, were slaughtered. Here and there some opposition was offered, but in most places people were butchered unresistingly. The Persians laid violent hands on everything and everybody. Cloth, jewels, dishes of gold and silver were acceptable spoils . . . Since the days of Hazrat Sahib-Kiran Amir Timur (Tamerlane), who captured Delhi and ordered the inhabitants to be massacred, up to the present time, a period of three-hundred-and-forty-eight years, the capital had been free from such visitations . . . For a long time the streets remained strewn with corpses, as the walks of a garden with dead flowers and leaves. The town was reduced to ashes and had the appearance of a plain consumed with fire."

At two o'clock in the afternoon Nizam-ul-Mulk and Kamar-ud-din Khan approached Nadir and begged him, in the name of their master, "to check his rancour and pardon their compatriots who had been led astray". The

Shah of Persia acceded to this request because, as another witness informs us: "It did not please him to spill blood wantonly and he had only ordered the carnage to prevent the threat of a general insurrection of the Indian population."

Nonetheless, this measure of "self defence" claimed the lives of tens of thousands of Delhiwalas as well as three to five thousand Persian soldiers.

While in the city the survivors were burying or burning their dead, in the imperial palace entertainment and festivities relieved the monotony of meetings held to raise the war indemnity. "Nadir Shah, it is told, was very taken up by women and did not disdain the charms of novelty, but this weakness had never harmed his affairs and he could move with admirable facility from pleasure to work." Once the insurrection had been put down and the process of collecting the indemnity had begun, there was nothing to stop him from taking his pick from the zenana of the Great Mughal as well as from his own harem.

It has been said—and unfortunately there are no documents to support it—that it was a concubine abandoned by Mohammed Shah who, in her desire for revenge, disclosed the hiding place of Babur's diamond to Nadir Shah. She told him that the emperor hid it in the folds of the turban which he always wore. The authors who have written accounts of the Koh-i-noor have preferred this version to another, which is totally devoid of romance and presumes that the vanquished emperor offered the diamond to the victor in exchange for his kingdom.

Whatever be the case, the Shah of Persia's booty grew in size. To the fabulous treasures that he had extorted from Mohammed Shah and his generals, among which was the Peacock Throne, nine other thrones and a vast amount of precious stones, were added each day the fines levied on the inhabitants of Delhi: jewellery, vases, vessels of gold and silver, silk carpets and precious fabrics, not to mention the millions of rupees in cash.

On 26 March Nadir Shah married his son Nasrollah Mirza to the daughter of Dawar Baksh, Aurangzeb's grandson. Tradition required that at the time of the marriage proposal the aspirant states his lineage, going back seven generations. Nadir Shah let it be known that his son was the son of the sabre, the grandson of the sabre, the great-grandson of the sabre and so on. However, he was clearly keen on wetting this sabre in Mughal blood to upgrade his descendants' lineage and also cement ties with India before he left.

For a week the city and the court lived to the rhythm of festivities. There were so many that the massacre of 11 March seemed nothing but a bad dream. On the sandbank which separated the Yamuna from the ramparts of the fort, illuminations and fireworks followed elephant, tiger and deer fights, while in the palace every night the most famous courtesan of Delhi captivated the heart of the Shah of Persia.

Her name was Nur Bai, a beautiful, cultivated woman with the gift of pleasant conversation. Cherished as a princess by Mohammed Shah, she was his favourite dancing girl. The latter had gone as far as to allow her the royal privilege of riding a magnificent elephant, escorted by two hundred armed men. Nadir was so taken by her charms, her dancing and her voice that he is supposed to have told her: "The face of India has been blackened. Come with me to Iran." It is easy to imagine how difficult it must have been for her to refuse the request.

April 1739 was drawing to a close. Nadir decided to return to Persia before the heat became unbearable. On 1 May, he held a great darbar where he honoured a hundred umaras—including Nizam-ul-Mulk and Kamar-ud-din Khan—with robes of honour, magnificently harnessed horses, and sabres and daggers of very fine workmanship. Finally he tied a sword inlaid with precious stones to Mohammed Shah's belt and ordered that the khutbah be once again recited in his name and coins carry his effigy. In fact, he was officially handing back his empire, reduced nevertheless by the provinces situated to the north-west of the Indus that he had annexed to Persia.

It was during this gathering that Nadir Shah is supposed to have taken the much-coveted diamond. Informed of its hiding place, he used an ingenious ploy to get it. He reminded his counterpart that according to an ancient tradition they were to exchange their turbans as a sign of friendship and fraternal ties. Mohammed Shah who had no choice but to comply carried through this gesture with such poise that Nadir was baffled. Was the diamond really hidden in the folds of the turban, as the concubine had suggested, or was it a hoax?

With a wave of the hand, he let it be known that the audience was over. Then he hurried to his apartments, quickly undid the turban and to his delight found the diamond hidden in its folds. Then, wonderstruck by the size, the beauty and the brilliance of the stone, he exclaimed: "Koh-i-noor" which in Persian means "mountain of light". And so this gem of fortune was named, thereafter.

On 5 May 1739, Nadir Shah left Delhi for Persia after a stay of two months. Apart from the fabulous wealth of eight generations of Indian kings, he took away with him a thousand elephants, seven thousand horses, ten thousand camels, a hundred eunuchs, a hundred-and-thirty scribes, three hundred masons, two hundred blacksmiths, a hundred stonecutters, two hundred carpenters, musicians and dancers.

Arriving in Khorasan, he had all his treasures with the exception of the Koh-i-noor taken to Kalat, his mountain den situated north of Mashad. At this place, known today as Kalat-i-Naderi, the king had built a residence for himself on a plain surrounded by rocky spurs, making it a naturally impregnable fortress. It could only be reached by two steep paths called the Gates of Kalat.

The last years of Nadir's reign were marked by calamities which leads one to believe that the bad luck associated with the Koh-i-noor did not spare him.

Upon returning to Persia, he began to feel the effects of an illness that he must have contracted in Delhi: frequent vomiting, constipation, a bad liver and a dry mouth. These discomforts would affect his essentially choleric and cruel temperament and soon transform him into a bloodthirsty monster whose first victim was to be his own son.

One day in 1741 as he was crossing a forest in Mazandaran, a man fired in his direction, missing him, but cutting the bridle of his horse. Suspected of having hatched the plot, the sovereign's nephew, Ali Qoli, the future Adel Shah, managed to extricate himself from the situation by shifting the blame on to Prince Reza Qoli Mirza who was also accused of having a hand in the attempt.

Nadir loved his son and intended him to be his successor. He ordered Reza to come and explain his actions, assuring him of his clemency. Rather than bowing down to his father's injunctions the prince, who was then governor of Khorasan, claimed his innocence in a letter whose impertinent tone irritated Nadir to such an extent that he had him brought in his presence, hands and feet tied, and had his eyes pulled out. He was then locked in the Kalat fortress where his cousin Ali Qoli, who later became king, had him executed after Nadir's death.

It is obvious that a man who did not spare his own son was not likely to waste much sympathy on the rest of his subjects. In the years that followed, neither foreigners nor Persians, princes nor governors, soldiers and officials were spared the effects of his deadly madness.

In 1746, Nadir Shah was sixty years old. The fatigue of his interminable campaigns and long marches across mountains and deserts had further aggravated his illness. Incapable of curing their ruler, Persian doctors had called upon Father Bazin, a French Jesuit missionary in Ispahan, who had a rudimentary knowledge of medicine, to look after him. Father Bazin diagnosed it as a case of dropsy and asked for two months to prepare the cure. The Shah gave him half that amount of time. Meanwhile, appointed as the monarch's chief physician, the priest accompanied him on an expedition to the south of Persia.

"All along the way", he recounts, "he committed acts of unheard-of cruelty. He knew that Shah Abbas the Great, one of his predecessors and a keen hunter, had in the past sent the heads of the animals he had killed to some cities to have pyramids raised with them; he too wanted to make a similar monument, not with animal heads, but with human heads. He himself fixed the height: it was thirty feet high in the city of Kerman."

On 19 June 1747, the Shah set up camp near the city of Qutchan, about fifty kilometres to the south of Kalat, from where he was planning to start a new campaign. He was in a very agitated frame of mind. He believed rightly that an attempt on his life was imminent. In fact, several of his officers and family members, in particular Prince Ali Qoli Mirza, his nephew and future successor, fearing his growing cruelty, had decided to get rid of him. The task had been entrusted to the commander of the guard and the grand chamberlain. But as the latter had no military position it was the former that Nadir suspected.

On the night of 19 June he summoned Ahmad Khan Abdali. By now the young Afghan, who had enrolled in the Persian army at Kandahar, had become a senior officer in the Afghan and Uzbek corps of the Shah. "I am unhappy with my guards", Nadir told Ahmad Khan. "Your devotion and courage are known to me. I order you to arrest tomorrow morning all the officers and clap them in irons. Do not spare the life of any one of those who dares to resist you. My personal safety is at stake, as I entrust to you the evening of my life."

However, the conspirators had spies in the king's entourage. No sooner had Nadir given these instructions than they learnt about them and decided to make a move at "moon set", with the sixty officers who were closest to them.

Their impatience, or perhaps their desire to distinguish themselves, led fifteen conspirators to go to the appointed place before the fixed hour. They entered the royal tent, breaking everything that came in their way. Awakened by the noise, Nadir exclaimed: "Who is there? Where is my sword? Give me my arms."

Upon hearing these words, and terrified at the voice of their master, the assassins fled, but turning back found themselves face to face with the two chief conspirators who persuaded them to go back to the tent with them. Nadir Shah was still not dressed. The commander of the guards ran in first and dealt him a sabre wound that knocked him over. Covered with blood, the Shah tried in vain to get up but he did not have the strength to do so. "Why are you killing me?" he cried out. "Spare my life, and all that I own shall be yours." He was still speaking when his chamberlain jumped on him, sabre in hand, cut off his head and sent it over to Ali Qoli Mirza. According to Father Bazin: "Thus perished after ruling for thirteen years the richest prince of the world, the terror of the Ottoman empire, the conqueror of India, the master of Persia and Asia, the famous Nadir Shah, respected by his neighbours, feared by his enemies but who failed to be loved by his subjects."

The conspirators had wanted to keep Nadir's death a secret till the next morning, in order to arm themselves against the Afghan and Uzbek contingents, whose reaction they feared. However, one of Nadir's wives, an Afghan lady, heard the noise coming from the Shah's tent and guessed what was happening inside. She sent an urgent message to Ahmad Khan Abdali. The latter immediately called for his troops, dispatched a squadron to protect the imperial harem and rushed with the rest of his cavalrymen to the site of the crime, if not to save his master, at least to avenge him.

In the meantime the Persian soldiers were plundering the camp. Their first target was the huge tent for public audience. When the Afghan contingent reached the spot, this palace made of scarlet wool, lined inside with violet satin, embroidered with pearls, diamonds, emeralds, amethysts and other precious stones and supported by solid gold pillars, had been reduced to tatters.

The thrill of plunder did not stop the soldiers from putting up a stiff resistance to the Afghans. Ahmad Khan realised that with the entire Persian army against him, any idea of vengeance or resistance would prove futile. While his men protected his retreat, he went into Nadir's tent. Convinced of his death, he pulled off the imperial seal from his finger, took the Koh-i-noor and other objects of value, saluted his master for the last time and joined his men. One hour later, breaking through the Persian army, he was on the road to Kandahar with his troops.

According to another account, the future king of Afghanistan got the famous diamond after he intercepted a convoy on the road to Kandahar carrying treasure from Nadir's camp. In reality, this convoy, which was carrying the annual tribute from the Indian provinces that had been annexed by the Shah of Persia, could not have contained the Koh-i-noor which Nadir always kept with him.

Through the centuries the Koh-i-noor brought out a fatal avarice in whoever possessed it. Even the great Nadir Shah was not immune to its enchantment, while betrayals, horrific deaths and tragedy seemed to inevitably follow in its wake.

One of the saddest victims was Shahrokh Mirza, the young grandson of Nadir Shah who was blinded and then tortured and killed by the first Shah of a new dynasty, only because Shahrokh could not hand over the Koh-i-noor to him. No one would believe the unfortunate man when he pleaded that the diamond had been carried away to Afghanistan long before his time.

CHAPTER THREE

The journey of the Koh-i-noor now takes us to Afghanistan and the rising fortunes of Ahmad Khan Abdali. After Nadir Shah's death, his Afghan auxiliaries began looking for a charismatic leader capable of uniting them into an independent, sovereign nation. It was therefore decided to convene a jargah, or tribal council, to settle the issue. A spot next to a barley field was chosen for the occasion, where a tent was put up for the council to deliberate.

Each tribe, each clan, each family naturally wished to advance the claims of its own candidate. Considering the number of applicants, the debates went on for more than a week without any decision being reached. All this while Ahmad Khan Abdali held himself aloof from the discussions, listening to the arguments and observing with some bitterness the division which existed among his compatriots. At last, on the ninth day, Haji Jamal, the chief of the Barakzai clan of the Abdali tribe emerged with the largest number of votes. But they were still not sufficient to clinch the leadership.

It was then that a dervish named Sabir Shah put forward the claim of Ahmad Abdali, saying: "Why all this verbose talk? God has created Ahmad Khan a much greater man than any of you. He is the most noble of all the Afghan families. Maintain, therefore, God's work, for His wrath will weigh heavily upon you if you destroy it."

Ahmad Khan belonged to the Sadozai clan of the Abdalis. His ancestor, Sado, had once led an embassy to the court of Shah Abbas the Great of Persia, whereas his rival's forefather had merely been a member of the delegation. Another of Ahmad Khan's ancestors, Khawja Khizar, Sado's son, was considered a saint by the Afghan tribes. Haji Jamal had to give in to the dervish's arguments.

Sabir Shah took Ahmad Khan by the hand, seated him on a small earthen platform that he had raised in the centre of the plain and said to him: "This is the throne of your kingdom." He then picked some barley-shoots from the adjoining field and tucked them into his turban, adding: "And may this serve as the aigrette of your crown." To conclude the ceremony, the dervish declared: "Now you are the Padishah-i-Durr-i-Dowran (King, the Pearl of this Age). The new sovereign was content, however, to style himself as Durr-i-Durran, the Pearl of Pearls, from which was derived the new name of his dynasty and his tribe: Durrani.

The jargah broke up all ties of vassalage with Persia and declared the independence of the Afghan people under its new king. Kandahar was chosen as the capital of the new state.

Thus, towards the end of 1747, Nadir Shah's favourite bodyguard, at the age of twenty-three, became the founder of modern Afghanistan. His first concern was to consolidate his power without treading on the toes of the tribal chiefs who remained deeply attached to their traditional privileges. He managed to do so by leaving them with a semblance of independence and by consulting them on matters relating to the exercise of central power. At the same time all the responsible positions in government were made hereditary and entrusted to members of his own clan.

Abdali invaded India eight times and his fifth expedition was undoubtedly the most significant. By then the Marathas had reached the height of their power and were camping at the gates of Delhi. Inspired by a feeling of nationalism which the rest of their compatriots seemed to lack, they wished to crush the power of the Mughals who would have undoubtedly fallen had the new master of Afghanistan not come to their rescue.

The battle between the Marathas and the Afghans took place on 14 January 1761 on the famous battlefield of Panipat, where the latter won a decisive victory. "It is to Ahmad Shah", writes Maurice Fouchet, "that the British Empire owes the possession of India, for if the Marathas had won at Panipat, the English would have in all likelihood failed against Hindu unity." On 15 January the victor entered the city of Panipat, where after receiving the homage of its inhabitants, he prostrated himself before the tomb of a Muslim saint. On this occasion he wore a magnificent tunic on which shone the Koh-i-noor.

Ahmad Shah, a man of majestic stature whose dignity and strength of character were far beyond the average, died of cancer of the face on 23 October 1772 after appointing Timur, the second of his four sons, as his successor. The inscription engraved on his tomb at Kandahar is proof of the admiration and respect that his subjects bore him: "Ahmad Shah Durrani was a great king! So great was the fear of his justice that the lion lived peacefully with the lamb. The ears of his enemies were constantly deafened by the roar of his conquests."

At the time of his father's death, Timur, then governor of Khorasan, was far from the capital. Taking advantage of that, his brother Suleiman Mirza usurped the throne with the blessing of Shah Wali Khan, the prime minister.

However, he did not rule for long. The legitimate heir, supported by the majority of the Durranis and other Afghan tribes, immediately marched on Kandahar. Shah Wali Khan did his best to save his protégé but having failed, he went to Timur to beg his pardon. Timur, knowing that any indulgence towards an enemy only served to encourage further sedition, refused to receive him, and had his head cut off without further ado.

This harsh measure had the desired effect. The prince made a triumphant entry into Kandahar and was crowned King of the Afghans. Disgusted, however, with the loyalty the Kandaharis had borne towards his brother, he transferred his capital to Kabul.

The new owner of the Koh-i-noor was intelligent, determined and active on the domestic front. But he did not share his father's passion for conquest. He thus neglected the border provinces annexed by Ahmad Shah, which took the opportunity to defy his authority. This does not mean that he was totally spared from internal strife. In fact, he was nearly assassinated in 1779 and replaced on the throne by one of his nephews.

Timur was sleeping peacefully in his room in the Peshawar fort when he was suddenly woken by the sound of gunshots and the clash of swords. Sensing danger, he ran and locked himself in a room on the top storey of the palace. From there he waved his turban out of a window to alert his troops gathered together at the foot of the fort. Meanwhile, the conspirators had killed his bodyguard and would have assassinated him had his supporters not arrived in time to save him. All the conspirators were put to the sword except a tribal chief named Arsalan Khan, the instigator of the plot, who managed to escape to the mountains.

The fate of this man deserves a digression, for it illustrates remarkably the almost religious sentiment the Afghans felt for vengeance.

Arsalan Khan had tried to assassinate his sovereign, a crime that was unpardonable, deserving the worst form of punishment. However, he had to be arrested first. A difficult task, since he had taken refuge in arid passes which even the most hardened horsemen had difficulty in crossing. Timur, filled with a desire for revenge, laid a trap for him. He sent him a Koran on one of whose pages he swore to forgive him for his misdeed. As no promise could be more sacred than this, Arsalan Khan returned to Peshawar and surrendered. Timur immediately had him beheaded. This decision tarnished his reputation, for in the eyes of a people who considered revenge as a religion and an act of honour, the king's bad faith was taken for a crime as ignoble as that of Arsalan Khan.

Timur Shah died in Kabul on 20 May 1793 after a reign of twenty years. He was not as keen as his father on pomp and ostentation, and never wore the Koh-i-noor. Thus the diamond remained locked in the coffers of the Bala Hissar (the citadels of Afghan cities) with the other jewels of the crown.

Timur left behind twenty-three sons and thirteen daughters, and died without naming a successor. It fell, therefore, to the tribal council to elect the new monarch.

Zaman Mirza, Timur Shah's fifth son and one of the most tragic heroes of our story, won over his brothers thanks to the support of the zenana as well as the chief of the Barakzai clan, Payanded Khan, Haji Jamal's son.

The first act of the new king was to put down the rebellion of his elder brothers Humayun and Mahmud, who from their respective fiefs of Kandahar and Herat, were openly fighting for the throne.

It must be remembered that in this campaign, Zaman Shah was seconded by his full brother Shuja Mirza, another figure whose fate was closely linked to that of the Koh-i-noor.

After Kandahar had surrendered, Zaman Shah planned to lay siege to Herat, but trouble broke out in the Punjab. He was thus forced to reach a hurried agreement with his half-brother Mahmud before marching on the rebellious province.

The Punjab, "the land of the five rivers", which is now divided between India and Pakistan, stretches in the form of a scalene triangle from the Himalayas in the north to the Thar desert in the south and from the Indus in the west to Karnal in the east. Its population was made up of Hindus, Muslims and Sikhs. The latter were to become the standard bearers of Punjabi nationalism.

In the early days of 1699, Gobind Singh, the tenth and last Guru of the Sikhs, invited his disciples to gather around him at Anantpur, a town situated on the banks of the Sutlej, one of the five rivers of the Punjab. One morning, after the religious service was over, the Guru turned towards the crowd, pulled out his sword and demanded five men for sacrifice. After a long, tortured silence, one man stood up and offered himself as a volunteer. He was immediately taken into a tent. After a while, Gobind Singh, the blade of his sword dripping with blood, came out of the tent and asked for another victim. Thus, five men offered themselves in quick succession as volunteers. The Guru, who had in reality killed goats, then appeared with his "victims" and declared that these *panj piyare* (five beloved) were to constitute the core of a new community called *Khalsa* (the pure).

He baptised the five men by making them drink the water in which he had dipped the blade of his sword and gave them the patronymic of Singh (lion), thus acknowledging them as his own children. This ceremony came to be known as the Pahul. After initiating his five disciples, Gobind Singh asked to be also baptised in the new community, thereby giving up his prominent position to merge with the Khalsa. A little before his death on 7 October 1708, he decreed that the lineage of the gurus would come to an end after him and that in future the Sikhs should seek inspiration and advice from the Adi Granth or the Granth Sahib, the compilation of their sacred texts.

The Sikhs were no more safe from persecution in the time of Ahmad Shah Durrani than they had been under Aurangzeb. In fact, at the end of his fourth expedition to

India (1756-57), the king of Afghanistan was harassed on the way back by Khalsa horsemen. They would spring up like lightning from their dens and disappear after massacring his men and plundering his property. Ahmad Shah ordered his son Timur Mirza to occupy Amritsar and destroy their temple, the Hari Mandir.

Forced to defend themselves against a common enemy, be it Mughal or Afghan, the Sikhs formed armed groups called misl, each one under the command of a misldar acknowledged for his courage and audacity. There were twelve such groups. The five most important ones were the Bhangis who controlled Lahore, Amritsar and most of West Punjab; the Kanhayas who occupied the foothills of the Himalayas; the Phulkias who settled down around Patiala and Sirhind; the Ahluwalias, masters of the land between the Ravi and the Beas; and lastly the Sukerchakias who lived in the town of Gujranwala (sixty-five kilometres north-west of Lahore). It was here that Ranjit Singh, the future Maharaja of the Punjab and the most colourful of all the owners of the Koh-i-noor, was born on 2 November 1780. His father Mahan Singh, the chief of the Sukerchakia misl, came from a family of farmers and shepherds, while his mother, Raj Kaur, was the daughter of Raja Gajpat Singh of Jind. As tradition required that a mother give birth to her first child in her father's house, some authors claim that Ranjit Singh was born in the small fort of Budrukhan near Jind.

Soon after his birth, Ranjit Singh contracted smallpox. He recovered his health but lost his left eye, thus acquiring the nickname kana (one-eyed), while his face carried the indelible scars of the disease.

He was hardly twelve years old when he succeeded his father. Five years later he married Mehtab Kaur whose mother, Sada Kaur, a remarkable woman, had led the Kanhaya misl since the death of her husband who was killed in the course of a battle against Mahan Singh's troops. It was a marriage of convenience as Mehtab Kaur rarely consented to share the matrimonial bed of the man she considered to be the son of her father's assassin. In fact, she was to live most of the time with her mother whereas Ranjit Singh took a second wife, the daughter of another Sikh chief.

With the coming of Zaman Shah, Afghan imperial designs against India resurfaced. But whereas Ahmad Shah had occupied Delhi several times, his grandson was never able to go beyond Lahore.

In 1793, just after his coronation, Zaman Shah invaded the Punjab. However, he had barely reached Hassan Abdal, to the south-east of Peshawar, when he had to retrace his steps, his brother Humayun having taken advantage of his absence to recapture Kandahar. The royal revenge was terrible. Humayun, betrayed by his former subjects, was fleeing to Sind when the king's horsemen caught up with him and brought him back to their master. Zaman Shah ordered that his eyes be put out, hardly guessing that the future held the same fate in store for him.

In January 1797 the Afghan sovereign occupied Lahore after devastating the lands of the Bhangis and the Sukerchakias who took refuge in Amritsar in order to organise the other misls. It did seem as if no obstacle could stop Ahmad Shah's grandson from following in the footsteps of his grandfather. But as he was preparing to march on Delhi, he was informed that Mahmud Mirza had rebelled again and was threatening his capital with a considerable army. Zaman Shah immediately gave up the idea of invading northern India and returned to his kingdom, where he bought over one of his half-brother's main advisors, shaking the former's trust in his men and forced him to seek asylum at the court of the Shah of Persia.

Meanwhile Ranjit Singh, who had been entrusted by his

peers to command the Khalsa forces, inflicted a bloody defeat on the Afghan troops which had remained behind in the Punjab to protect their chief's retreat.

On 27 November 1798, Zaman Shah returned to Lahore to avenge the humiliation of his men. As he approached, the Sikhs fell back on Amritsar where, after lengthy discussions, they once again entrusted their fortunes to Ranjit Singh who had just turned eighteen. The latter had no difficulty in overcoming the Afghan troops, pursuing them till the very gates of Lahore where he had the crops burnt and the supplies to the city suspended. Sensing the futility of fighting the Sikhs, Zaman Shah decided to spare them by guaranteeing them full rights to live in their domains. Hardly had the negotiations with the Sardars begun than alarming news came from Kabul: Fath Ali Shah Kadjar, the Shah of Persia was threatening Khorasan. To overcome the fresh threat from Persia, Zaman Shah abandoned the Punjab and moved towards Herat, followed by Ranjit Singh's horsemen who harassed his troops till the banks of the Indus.

Lahore was re-occupied by the chiefs of the Bhangi misl who had owned the city before the Afghan invasion. However, they were so unpopular that the city's senior citizens secretly invited Ranjit Singh to take their place. He willingly accepted and, with the support of his mother-in-law's army, entered the citadel of Lahore on 7 July 1799 to the rousing welcome of the inhabitants. On 12 April 1801, at the age of twenty, he was proclaimed Maharaja of the Punjab.

The English traveller, William Forster, a perceptive observer of the inter-misl rivalry, wrote in 1783: "Should any future cause call forth the combined efforts of the Sikhs to maintain the existence of empire and religion, we may see some ambitious chief led on by his genius and success and absorbing the power of his associates, display from the ruins of their commonwealth the standard of monarchy."

The irresistible rise of Ranjit Singh, whose courage and exploits on the battlefield had won him the sobriquet of "Lion of the Punjab", amply bore out this prediction.

Meanwhile the Koh-i-noor still lay in the treasury of Zaman Shah. In a feudal country like Afghanistan, social harmony could only be maintained with the consent of the tribal chiefs. Ahmad Shah and Timur Shah realised this and did not take any important decision without consulting them. The same could not be said for Zaman Shah who not only scorned their counsel but also constantly irritated them with his condescension and arrogance. The chiefs decided to overthrow him.

The plot was hatched by Payandeh Khan Barakzai, the man who had in the past supported Zaman Shah's claim to the throne. In order to avoid arousing the suspicions of the royal secret police, the conspirators met at the home of a dervish who was famous for his holiness and whose home was considered to be a place of worship.

However, at the last minute, one of the conspirators, panic-stricken by a rumour that the plot had been discovered, went to the prime minister and let the cat out of the bag. The next day his unsuspecting accomplices were called to the palace, arrested and executed. One of the noteworthy victims was Payandeh Khan, the chief of the Barkazais.

His eldest son, Fateh Khan, a brave, intelligent and determined young man, was burning to avenge the death of his father. He immediately went to Prince Mahmud Mirza and, after promising his tribe's unconditional support, convinced him to resume the leadership of the opposition against the king.

Zaman Shah, busy with a fresh spate of uprisings in the Punjab and Kashmir, paid no heed to the event, for he no longer took his brother's machinations seriously. After leaving the bulk of his army at Peshawar under the command of his brother, Shuja Mirza, he went back to Kabul. A few days later, he learnt that Mahmud Mirza had entered Kandahar with the support of the main tribes of the country and was threatening to capture the capital.

Deprived of his best troops and fearing for his life, Zaman Shah gathered what remained of his followers and left for Peshawar, taking the Koh-i-noor and the rest of his treasure with him. On the way he made a last appeal to his people.

His speech, full of tempting promises, won him the support of a powerful tribal chief who had a following of at least fifteen thousand men. With this miraculously-won support, he faced the army of Mahmud Mirza, commanded by Fateh Khan Barakzai. This shrewd man, going one step further than Zaman Shah, managed to win over his followers who, once the hostilities began, changed sides.

Zaman Shah understood the extent of his misfortune. Accompanied by a small group of followers he continued his journey to Peshawar to join his brother Shuja Mirza. As night began to fall they halted at a fort that belonged to one Ashook, who welcomed them with open arms. They did not suspect for a minute that this show of sincerity masked the most sinister of plots.

In fact, Ashook, who had been informed of Mahmud Mirza's conquest of Kabul, was doing his best to enter the good books of the new master of Afghanistan. What better way to do this than handing over his brother and enemy?

At the stroke of midnight he had his guests surrounded by two hundred soldiers. Zaman Shah, smelling a trap, tried to escape but was quickly caught and imprisoned, while a courier was sent to Kabul to announce the news of his capture.

The next day, at dawn, the prisoner was taken under heavy escort to the capital. However, with the help of his warder he managed to hide the Koh-i-noor in a cavity in the wall of his cell and his other jewels in a hole he dug in the floor with the point of his dagger.

The convoy was welcomed at the gates of the city by the henchmen of the new king; one of them, a surgeon, immediately pulled out Zaman Shah's eyes with his lancet, because for his enemies there was "no difference between a dead king and a blind king".

Then, while his companions in misfortune were being beheaded, he was taken to his brother Mahmud, who before locking him up in the Bala Hissar citadel, tried in vain to extract the whereabouts of his jewels. The wretched man stoically maintained, even under torture, that he had cast them in the river before reaching Kabul.

Rather than devoting himself to the task of governing, as his predecessors had done, Mahmud Shah sank into indolence and entrusted his power to two powerful chieftains.

His reign was a period of conflict between the various tribal chiefs jostling for power and influence. One group supported a second claimant to the throne—Shuja Mirza, Zaman Shah's younger brother, and he finally triumphed in the internecine war.

In July 1803 young Shuja Mirza, mounted on a splendid steed, made his entry into the capital to the acclamation of the crowds and rode straight to Bala Hissar where the gates were opened to him without any resistance.

Before deciding the fate of his rival Mahmud, he hurried to free poor Zaman Shah who revealed the hiding place of the Koh-i-noor and the other jewels. Shuja immediately sought them out and ordered that the perfidious Ashook be executed with the rest of his family. They were blown from cannon, like common bullets.

CHAPTER FOUR

In the early nineteenth century, thanks to the expansionist policies of the Marquess of Wellesley, the English East India Company's domination, once limited to south India, extended to the north till the borders of the Punjab. The Governor General was able to justifiably claim on his return to England in 1805 that the Company and Government were "in a most glorious situation, as the sovereigns of a great part of India, the protectors of the principal powers and the mediators, by treaty, of the disputes of all."

These new acquisitions actively involved the Company in regional affairs, all the more so since the Franco-Persian rapprochement, sealed with the treaty of Finkenstein in 1807, had caused a great deal of concern in Calcutta.

Gilbert Elliot, the Count of Minto, who presided over the fortunes of British India from 1807 confided to a friend : "French diplomacy is very active in Persia. After having established relations with that kingdom to undermine our influence, it is now diligently seeking ways and means to spread its intrigues to the courts of the Indian princes."

The Treaty of Tilsit in 1807 aroused his fears even further. The new Governor General feared that with the cessation of hostilities between France and Russia, the plan for a common invasion of India might be revived. The First Consul and Tsar Paul I of Russia had in fact drawn up such a plan in 1802 before the latter was assassinated by the pro-British faction of his court.

Minto now decided to ward off the Franco-Russian threat. John Malcolm, once Wellesley's envoy to Persia, was sent back to Tehran to persuade Fath Ali Shah to break his ties with Napoleon. And in India, Charles Metcalfe and

Mountstuart Elphinstone, two young upcoming servants of the Company, tried to gain the friendship of Ranjit Singh and Shah Shuja.

Of the three ambassadors, only Charles Metcalfe fully succeeded in his mission. After lengthy, even tempestuous discussions with Ranjit Singh, where it often seemed that war would get the better of diplomacy, he managed to obtain a treaty of friendship in 1809. Apart from its specified object, it limited the territorial ambitions of the Lion of the Punjab to the north and west of the Sutlej, with the Sikh states situated south and east of the river coming under British protection.

According to the author and journalist Khushwant Singh, "The treaty of Amritsar was a grievous blow to Ranjit Singh's dream of a unified Punjab. Although for the rest of his life he professed friendship for the English nation, this friendship was strongly tinged with fear of their might. It is strange that despite the experience of dealing with Metcalfe, Ranjit Singh seldom distrusted the word of an Englishman."

Malcolm returned to Bombay empty-handed. It fell on his countryman Harford Jones Brydges—an ambassador dispatched to Teheran by the government in London, in spite of Minto's opposition—to take Persia away from the ambit of French influence. He then managed to bring it under the influence of Great Britain by the Preliminary Treaty of Friendship and Alliance in 1809.

Mountstuart Elphinstone and his delegation, most impressive with its escort of four hundred horsemen and six hundred camels, arrived in Peshawar on 25 February 1809, after four months' journey. They were immediately granted an audience by Shah Shuja who hoped to win their support to consolidate his power.

They found the king, who had a passion for pomp, seated on a golden throne with a crown on his head and wearing luxurious garments. His entire person was twinkling with jewels. The most remarkable of them, the Koh-i-noor, shone in a magnificent bracelet surrounded with emeralds.

In spite of the splendour that surrounded him, Shuja was living on borrowed time. Just before the arrival of the British mission, he had sent his best troops to Kashmir in order to curb the claims to independence of Ata Mohammed Khan, the son of his former prime minister Sher Mohammed Khan. Hardly had he begun negotiating with the English that he learnt that his men had suffered a crushing defeat. Depressing news indeed, the more so since it came on the heels of the occupation of Kandahar by the former king Mahmud, and his right hand man, Fateh Khan Barakzai!

Shah Shuja immediately began to raise new recruits from among the tribes, which, when added to what remained of the expeditionary corps to Kashmir, would allow him to confront his rival.

After signing the Anglo-Afghan treaty (1809), he left for Kabul, unaware that the capital had just fallen into the hands of his enemies who, learning of his imminent arrival, were marching against him.

The confrontation took place a few days later near Gandamak, some fifty kilometres south-east of Kabul. While Mahmud attacked his brother from the front, Fateh Khan charged against his flank. The result was almost immediate. The royal army was routed whereas its chief, leaving arms and baggage on the battlefield, fled across the mountains, taking with him only the Koh-i-noor and the rest of his jewels.

Thus Mahmud became king of Afghanistan for the second time, thanks to the support of Fateh Khan Barakzai. As for Shuja, who must have undoubtedly regretted the fact that he had not blinded his brother, he continued to fight for his throne, and even managed to control Kandahar for some time. He was, however, driven away by the tribal chiefs who realised with regret that, even in adversity, their former king had lost neither his pride nor his authoritarian manners.

Shuja was not one to give up. On 20 March 1810 he took over Peshawar, where he remained for six months, before being ousted by Fateh Khan's brother. He then fell into the hands of Ata Mohammed Khan, the governor of Kashmir, who humiliated and imprisoned him to avenge his father and tried to extract the Koh-i-noor from him. This proved futile. Shuja had entrusted the diamond to his principal wife, Wafa Begum, before making his last bid to recover the throne.

Wafa Begum lived in exile in Rawalpindi at the expense of Maharaja Ranjit Singh, in the company of three other legitimate wives and numerous concubines of her husband as well as the blind Zaman Shah and his harem. One day the Maharaja learnt that in spite of the obligation of reserve imposed upon him, Zaman Shah had sent emissaries to the English to negotiate the re-establishment of his younger brother Shuja on the throne of Afghanistan. As he did not appreciate secret negotiations taking place behind his back, he transferred his guests to Lahore, to keep a better watch over them.

At the time Ranjit Singh was planning an expedition to Kashmir with Fateh Khan Barakzai. Wafa Begum was frightened out of her wits. She rightly feared that Mahmud Shah's prime minister would capture her husband and he would meet the same fate as the unfortunate Zaman Shah. Knowing Ranjit Singh's interest in precious stones and the fact that he was aware of the existence of the Koh-i-noor, she promised to give him the diamond, if he saved her husband from the clutches of Ata Mohammed Khan.

The commander-in-chief of the Sikh forces, General Mokham Chand, knew that if the Afghans reached Kashmir first, it would mean the end of Shah Shuja. Taking a shortcut, he managed to get ahead of them and arrived first at the foot of the fort where the royal prisoner was held. The fort capitulated without much resistance. Meanwhile, the Afghans had also arrived. While they were busy plundering the neighbourhood, the Sikhs searched the dungeon, found Shuja and took him to Lahore.

Shah Shuja was welcomed in the capital of the Punjab with all the honour due to his rank and installed in a residence separate from his harem, to which he was forbidden access.

Two days later, Ranjit Singh's emissary called upon him to ask for the Koh-i-noor. Shuja stated that he did not have it with him, but in appreciation of the hospitality and assistance from the Maharaja, he would take his wish into consideration. The messenger came back the next day and received the same reply. Shah Shuja was then deprived of food and his residence was surrounded by Sikh soldiers.

After a month had gone by, Ranjit Singh tried to find out if his guest was ready to give up the diamond in exchange for a treaty of friendship and ready cash. The answer being in the affirmative, Ranjit Singh sent him fifty thousand rupees and once again asked for the Koh-i-noor, which Shah Shuja promised to hand over as soon as the treaty was signed.

Two days later, the Maharaja went to see him in person and after offering him his friendship, swore on the Granth Sahib and his sword that he would give him many provinces and provide him with the means to recover his kingdom. Shuja promised in return that should he once again mount the throne of Afghanistan, he would for ever consider Ranjit Singh as his ally. They then exchanged turbans to celebrate their eternal friendship. After which the Lion of the Punjab acquired the Koh-i-noor, while his guest recovered his freedom.

This account is taken from an article written by none

other than Shah Shuja himself in 1826-27 and published by the *Calcutta Monthly Journal* of January 1839. It is considerably milder than the version taken from other sources.

According to the latter, Shah Shuja's arrival in Lahore was followed by a long period of silence regarding the Koh-i-noor. It seemed as if the former king and his wife had completely forgotten their pledge to hand over the diamond to the Maharaja.

Ranjit Singh, who was getting more and more impatient, sent emissaries to demand the diamond. Wafa Begum, who had suggested the bargain in the first place, then told the emissary that she had pawned it with a Kandahar merchant to finance her husband's last campaign.

Ranjit Singh did not believe a word of her story, and decided to use force. He had guards placed around their residence and ordered that no one be allowed to enter or leave without being thoroughly searched. When this measure failed to yield any results, Shuja and his family were deprived of supplies for two days, but to no avail. Not willing to ruin his reputation, the Maharaja lifted the ban, while he looked for more subtle means to attain his end.

On 1 April 1813, he showed to his courtiers two letters, one supposedly written by Shah Shuja to Fateh Khan Barakzai and the other to Afghan chiefs to tell them of his sufferings, asking them to come to his rescue. Whether such a correspondence had really been intercepted or it was pure fabrication is something we shall never know. It nonetheless provided Ranjit Singh with an opportunity to tighten the screws under the pretext that he was obliged to guard himself against his guest's intrigues.

The guard on the former king was strengthened. He was threatened with a transfer to Govindgarh, the fortress that the Maharaja had built near Amritsar.

Shah Shuja tried to buy time and asked for two months

to get back the diamond from the pawnbroker. Ranjit Singh agreed even though he was highly sceptical of his guest's sincerity. The intimidation was suspended, but resumed soon after, as the Maharaja could wait no longer. Exasperated and fearing for his life, Shah Shuja finally agreed to hand over the Koh-i-noor, provided Ranjit Singh came in person to collect it.

The Maharaja accepted the proposal and on, 1 June 1813, he went to the former king's residence with some of his ministers. Once the courtesies had been dispensed with, the two men sat at two ends of an immense room, facing each other. Then followed an embarrassed, endless, oppressive silence, during which Ranjit Singh's single eye scrutinised the room's innermost recesses in search of the desired object. Nearly an hour passed by without a word being uttered by one or the other. Finally the Maharaja, who had by then lost all patience, whispered to one of the members of his entourage to remind the master of the house about the purpose of his visit.

Shah Shuja merely nodded to a eunuch, who left the room and brought back a small packet wrapped in scarlet velvet which he placed on the carpet, half way between the two princes. Ranjit Singh had it opened and the Koh-i-noor appeared, shining in its gold setting. When the Maharaja was certain that it was really the famous diamond, he put it in his pocket and left the room without a word.

The very next day all restrictions on Shuja's movements were lifted and he was sent with his family to Shalimar Gardens—a park laid out by Shah Jahan in Lahore. It was modelled on the Delhi garden which served as the setting for Aurangzeb's coronation. Shuja was allowed to move around the city freely and could often be seen riding in his ceremonial palanquin.

Some time later, however, he was subjected to new affronts. Ranjit Singh coveted what remained of his jewels but could not take possession of them without overtly breaking the rules of hospitality. He thus resorted to extremely devious methods.

He invited his guest to join him in ousting Fateh Khan Barakzai from Peshawar. The former king accepted the proposal with enthusiasm, hoping that it would be a prelude to his reconquering the throne of Afghanistan. But halfway through the trip the Maharaja left him in the care of one of his generals and returned to Lahore. The Sikh officer was in reality charged with stripping Shah Shuja of his property during the march, instead of helping him to recover Peshawar.

After several attempts through hired bandits, the Sikh officer decided to lay his cards on the table. He asked for and got from Shah Shuja a complete list of all his jewels and objects of value. Then, as soon as they returned to Lahore, he went to Shalimar Gardens and after settling the former Afghan royal family in a residence in the heart of the city, he confiscated all their possessions on behalf of his master.

Shah Shuja's ordeal did not end there. Dispossessed of every thing without getting the promised provinces and assistance, he went through further trials. After five months his situation became so intolerable that he decided to flee Lahore; but before taking such a step he had to organise the escape of his harem.

The venture proved fraught with danger as Ranjit Singh's spies, who had been placed in Shuja's entourage, had been following his slightest move. Therefore many of his attempts failed, till finally Shah Shuja caught the culprits and bought them over with bribes. He then dressed his relatives in Punjabi peasant clothes and had them carried on bullock carts to Ludhiana, where British authorities granted them asylum.

Ranjit Singh was dismayed to hear of their escape. He

immediately tightened the security around Shah Shuja to the point that the latter could not even satisfy his natural urges without being escorted by an armed guard. Five months passed before he was able to extricate himself from his predicament.

On an April night in 1815, he managed to deceive his guards and had a hole made through the seven walls that separated him from the outside world. He then disguised himself as a dervish and slithered through the narrow passage way, followed by three faithful servants. When they reached the street, the gates of the city had already been closed, so they were forced to escape by sliding along the sewers.

A few weeks later they reached Kishtwar, a mountainous country situated at the foot of the Himalayas, from where Shah Shuja tried to raise an army to conquer Kashmir. The expedition would have succeeded but it coincided with the arrival of winter. His ambitions frustrated by bad weather and the thick snow which blocked his supply line, he was forced to give up and take the path of exile, arriving at Ludhiana in September 1816. The British government gave him an annual pension of forty-eight thousand rupees whereas the blind Zaman Shah who was later allowed to share his exile was to get twenty-four thousand rupees.

It was in Ludhiana, some fifteen years later, that the French botanist and traveller, Victor Jacquemont, was to meet the two former owners of the Koh-i-noor. Jacquemont was first received by the elder brother, Zaman Shah:

"He is nearly sixty, but does not seem so old. His complexion is a clear sallow brown and his features quite handsome. His painted beard because of the extreme evenness with which it is etched across his face and because of its thickness resembles a false beard and perhaps hides his age. He was very simply dressed; I was only able to observe the extreme beauty of the shawl that he had rolled as turban around his head.

"In spite of his age and great devotion, he has not renounced women. He has a small harem, quite useless no doubt, but he spends several hours there every day; and I forgot to say that during the conversation he complained about his utter exhaustion, and knowing that I was a physician, he asked me for some medicine which would revive him. I sent him to Doctor Murray, who has been visiting him for quite some time over the years."

This was followed by an audience with Shah Shuja, who in spite of all his troubles, had lost none of his majesty:

"It is impossible to appear more kingly than this dethroned prince, to have more dignity without haughtiness or stiffness, more nobility and elegance without affectation. His dress was carefully chosen without being magnificent. Around his head was a light green Cashmere turban, whose cloth and design could not be more delicate. His body was wrapped in a large gown with huge sleeves of the same cloth as his turban, but with a white background covered with elegant palm leaves that looked as big as half of a hand; the robe was crossed at the chest with a huge bejewelled clip in the shape of a palm leaf. He wore a very simple dagger in his belt; a cane stick with a rock crystal handle; trousers of red silk and stockings of rainbow colour Cashmere; green slippers, similar to those worn by the members of his household."

He might have lost his haughtiness and stiffness but his ambition remained unchanged. He would never give up his claim to the throne of his ancestors.

Since 1812, when he had left his country, many events had taken place in Afghanistan. Most significant among them were the administrative reforms that had been brought about by the vigorous efforts of Fateh Khan Barakzai. But the prime minister's success and growing influence began to offend Mahmud Shah's cruel son, Prince Kamran, the governor of Herat. Fateh Khan did not enjoy his good fortune for long. He was blinded by Kamran before his throat was cut in 1818 in the presence of both father and son. His death caused a general insurrection of the Barakzais which plunged Afghanistan into a state of anarchy. While Mahmud Shah took refuge in Herat, where he died in 1829, the country was divided among Fateh Khan's numerous brothers who, still faithful to the Sadozai dynasty, preferred to govern under a prince of that house rather than to assume kingship.

They decided to recall Shah Shuja who, in spite of his past conduct and indecisive character, remained the sole Sadozai capable of re-establishing national unity. As soon as he received this proposal, he accepted, on condition that he received the unswerving loyalty of the Barakzais. Getting this assurance he resumed his haughty airs of the past, letting it be known in unambiguous terms that he intended to govern as well as to rule. This intention was not at all to the taste of the new masters of the country, who immediately turned towards another prince of the ruling family, the fourteenth in the order of succession.

The latter willingly accepted their offer. "Make me king", he confided to Mohammed Azim Khan, the eldest of the Barakzais, "and allow coins to be struck with my effigy. I shall be happy and you may govern as you please." His rule, however, did not last long. Implicated in a plot hatched by two of his brothers, he was dethroned and driven out of Kabul while the instigators of the conspiracy were put to the sword.

Mohammed Azim Khan then took over the reins of power without making any claims to the crown. But he was unable to impose his will. Meanwhile the general situation of the kingdom had degenerated considerably. Herat, Badakhshan and Afghan Turkistan had seceded, while Ranjit Singh threatened to take Peshawar after annexing Kashmir, Multan, Dera Ghazi Khan and Attock.

Now only a stunning victory over the Sikhs could have boosted the fortunes of the Barakzais. Mohammed Azim Khan mobilised the tribes and with his brother Dost Mohammed Khan, the future sovereign of Afghanistan, marched against the Khalsa. The two armies met in March 1823 at a spot situated one hundred kilometres south of Peshawar. The Afghans were superior in number, but their main asset, the cavalry, could not handle the assaults of Ranjit Singh's disciplined troops and the firepower of his artillery. During this encounter, the Maharaja's entourage included two men of whom we shall speak later: Jean Baptiste Ventura and Jean François Allard, former officers in Napoleon's army who, with other Europeans, contributed to the greatness of the Sikh kingdom of the Punjab, and added to the vividness of Ranjit Singh's court.

Mohammed Azim Khan did not survive his defeat. His death was followed by a bitter fight among his brothers, leading to Dost Mohammed Khan's ascendancy over Kabul and Ghazni, without settling the question of national unity. The persistent Shah Shuja took advantage of this to once again claim his rights.

In January 1834 he left Ludhiana with a handful of followers, crossed the Indus, raised a small troop on the way and took over Shikarpur, a city which dominates the road linking Sind to Afghanistan through the Bolan Pass.

While Shah Shuja was strengthening his army with a view to besieging Kandahar, the governor of the city, one of the Barakzai brothers, begged his younger brother, Dost Mohammed Khan, to come to his rescue. Dost Mohammed put off his decision, wanting to know beforehand if the former king's venture had the blessing of the British authorities. A few days later his emissary returned from Ludhiana with a reply that could not have been more misleading: "The Indian government is not participating in the expedition, but expresses its best wishes to Shah Shuja."

Dost Mohammed Khan, a master in the art of ambiguity, rightly surmised that Britain did not care a fig for the outcome of the conflict. He immediately went to meet the enemy and, after a long indecisive battle, managed to oust him from Kandahar. At the same time he managed to impose his authority over his brothers to become the uncontested master of what remained of the great empire of Ahmad Shah Durrani: Kabul, Ghazni, Jalalabad and Kandahar. When someone suggested that he assume the title of Shah, he answered: "I am too poor to even support my dignity of sardar (chief of a tribe). What would I do with the title of king?" Finally, he accepted the title of Amir-ul-Momenin (commander of the faithful).

Amir Dost Mohammed Khan ruled over Afghanistan from 1835 to 1838 and then from 1842 to 1863. This break, provoked by British diplomacy, provided the persistent Shah Shuja with the opportunity to make a final and tragic appearance on the political scene of his county.

Dost Mohammed Khan had never been resigned to the annexation of Peshawar by the Sikhs. His prime concern was to drive them away. His military endeavours failed and so he decided to resort to diplomacy.

Meanwhile, Britain's hesitation in respecting its commitments towards Persia had thrown this country "hands and feet tied" into the arms of an interested Russia. The Russians encouraged the grandson and successor of Fath Ali Shah, an ambitious, impressionable young man, to stake his legitimate claim to Herat.

The British reacted immediately. "If the Russians threaten the English in India with their manoeuvres in Persia", observed Lord Palmerston, the British foreign minister, "why should the English not threaten the Russians with their manoeuvres in Afghanistan?" adding: "Why shouldn't an Anglophile ruler in Afghanistan counterbalance a Russophile ruler in Persia?"

George Eden, the Count of Auckland, who was appointed Governor General of India in 1835, was given the task of implementing the new policy. Dost Mohammed Khan could well have been its instrument because he was avidly seeking a British alliance to oust the Sikhs from Peshawar and repel the attacks of the Persian troops against Herat, under siege since September 1837. But when he probed Auckland on the possibility of getting British assistance, the latter replied: "My friend, you ought to know that it is not the British government's habit to interfere in the affairs of independent states." In reality, he was refusing to sacrifice the solid friendship with Ranjit Singh for a more nebulous one with the Afghan ruler, whose overtures were in any case weakened by the opposition from his brothers.

The Governor General nevertheless sent a delegation to Kabul to negotiate with the Afghan government. But as was to be expected, the negotiations stumbled on the question of Peshawar, with the British representative persisting in his refusal to accept any compromise that could offend the Maharaja of the Punjab. Meanwhile, a Russian emissary arrived in the Afghan capital and as soon as the English left, he gave his unstinting support to Dost Mohammed Khan on the question of Peshawar.

This was to no avail because the Russians did not have the means to implement their policies, especially since on 8 September 1838 the Persians had raised the siege of Herat and withdrawn to their territory.

Even though this move had made British intervention in Afghanistan superfluous, Lord Auckland nevertheless decided to overthrow Dost Mohammed Khan and replace him on the throne of Kabul by Shah Shuja who, on account of his debt to Britain, seemed to be the "Anglophile king" that Palmerston had in mind.

The plan received the support of Ranjit Singh who accepted it on the condition that Shah Shuja would once and for all renounce all claims to Peshawar, Kashmir and the other places that the Sikhs had taken from the Afghans, and that he would send him every year as a present fifty-five race horses, twenty-five mules, swords and daggers as well as an abundant quantity of musk melons, pomegranates, apples, raisins and pistachio nuts. In order to soften his demands Ranjit Singh agreed to supply, in return, apart from the parsimonious annual gift of shawls, muslin and rice, military assistance "each time the English government, in consultation with the Maharaja, deemed it necessary".

Shah Shuja signed the agreement after protesting in vain against Ranjit Singh's demands. But he had no choice.

We shall not enter into the details of the 1842 Anglo-Afghan war that the commander-in-chief of the British expeditionary corps, General Sir John Keane has so rightly described as a "signal catastrophe". It deserves nonetheless to be treated briefly, as it will allow us to witness the tragic end of one of the most fascinating owners of the Koh-i-noor.

On 6 August 1839, the former king arrived in Kabul on the heels of the British army. It was an affront that his proud, impetuous and xenophobic countrymen would not forgive. Even more so because he was usurping the throne from a sovereign as popular as Dost Mohammed Khan.

It was obvious from the very outset that Shah Shuja, who was sixty years old at the time, could not survive without the active protection of his allies, at least during the first few months of his rule. The English then decided to leave a garrison of four thousand, five hundred men in Kabul, while the Governor General's representative, Sir William Macnaghten, took malicious delight in calling the shots in Afghanistan.

Macnaghten concentrated the powers hitherto enjoyed by the tribal chiefs in his own hands and the latter accused Shah Shuja of complicity with the infidels. Even the surrender and deportation of Dost Mohammed Khan did not succeed in rattling their unswerving determination to throw out the occupiers.

The English and their protégé now suffered a series of insults. The insurrection of the people of Kabul, Macnaghten's murder, the extermination of British troops in the solitude of the Afghan passes, and finally the assassination of Shah Shuja himself.

Shah Shuja feared the English as much as he dreaded the mob. So when the insurrection of Kabul broke out, he refused to take sides before knowing the result.

"Shah Shuja", says Sir John William Kaye, "was no hero and did not play a heroic part. The British Government had picked him out of the dust of Ludhiana, simply as a matter of convenience to themselves; and they had no reason to complain that, in a great and imminent conjuncture, he thought less of their convenience than his own. He proved himself at the last to be very much what we had helped to make him. We could not expect him to be an active workman, when we had so long used him as a tool."

Once the English had left, internal squabbles resurfaced. The tribal chiefs, envious of the ascendancy of Akbar Khan, son of Dost Mohammed Khan and the instigator of the Kabul riots, drew closer to Shah Shuja and gave him the opportunity to redeem himself by taking command of the troops charged with expelling the English from Jalalabad.

The king hesitated for a long time before accepting. He feared he might fall into a trap set by his enemies when he came out of his refuge of Bala Hissar. Zaman Khan (no relation of the blind Zaman Shah), a moderate member of the Barakzai clan, now the prime minister, understood his attitude. To calm his fears, he ordered his wife to go and meet the monarch and swear to him on the Koran that the Barakzais would remain loyal to him.

On 4 April 1842, a reassured Shah Shuja put on a

ceremonial uniform and was led in a palanquin to the camp of the Afghan army, situated on the heights overlooking the road to Jalalabad.

The procession was coming near the royal pavilion when suddenly gunfire broke out: a bullet hit Shah Shuja on the head, killing him instantly. A few seconds later a young and handsome horseman dismounted and looked at the corpse of the old monarch with a satisfied smile. Then, after removing his gem-inlaid belt and dagger, he threw him in a ditch and galloped away.

In the atmosphere of hatred and jealousy which prevailed in the Afghan capital, even the goodwill of the prime minister, sealed by the oath of his wife, could not withstand the lack of filial respect. For the assassin was none other than Zaman Khan's own son who, bearing moreover the name of Shuja, was the assassinated king's godson.

Questioned one day by Fakir Azizuddin, Ranjit Singh's minister of Foreign affairs, on the real value of the Koh-i-noor, Shah Shuja is supposed to have replied: "Its value is good fortune, for whoever owns it triumphs over his enemies."

He must have said this in a moment of euphoria, for, as his tragic end demonstrates, he too was a victim of the curse attached to the diamond even though, by then, it had been taken from him.

CHAPTER FIVE

While Shah Shuja's body lay in a ditch in a Kabul suburb, awaiting an honourable burial, the Lion of the Punjab had passed into legend.

Ranjit Singh died in the afternoon of 27 June 1839, after ruling for forty years. During his reign he not only founded the first Sikh kingdom but also became, through his vivid personality, one of the most colourful owners of the Koh-i-noor.

Victor Jacquemont, who met him in March 1831, paints a glowing picture of him:

"Much had been said about him. He was famous for his courage and wisdom. I had often seen Bonaparte, and wished for a long time to meet this Bonaparte of the Orient. All my wishes were fulfilled when I was in his presence.

"He is a small, thin man, cutting a rather pretty figure in spite of his being blind in one eye as the result of an attack of smallpox which has left him few marks. His remaining right eye is large, his nose fine and very slightly turned up, a well-defined mouth with superb teeth, small moustaches that he is constantly twirling in his fingers, and a long, thin white beard which falls straight onto his chest, without movement. His face expresses constant mobility of thought, great finesse and deep insight.

"He had a small turban of white muslin inelegantly rolled around his head, a sort of long tunic with a short cape falling on his shoulders, like those on French horsemens' coats, narrow trousers, and was barefooted. His dress was of white Cashmere with small borders and golden embroidery on the cape, the facings and the seams, of a very practical but unusual cut, or so it seemed to me. As ornaments, he wore huge golden earrings with enormous pearls, a pearl necklace and ruby bracelets hidden under the sleeves of his dress. At his side was a sabre whose golden point was enhanced with diamonds and emeralds.

"The maharaja is an old fox and next to him, the most cunning of our diplomats is harmless. His conversation is a nightmare. He is the first curious Indian I have seen but he pays in curiosity for the apathy of his entire country. He asked me a thousand questions about India, the English, Europe, Bonaparte, this world in general and the other, hell and heaven, the soul, God, the devil and several other things."

Ranjit Singh was a mixture of virtue and vice. His contemporaries either hated or loved him but none could be indifferent to him. His critics accuse him of being selfish, hypocritical, deceitful, greedy, superstitious and debauched even though they acknowledge that he was neither cruel nor bloodthirsty. His admirers boast of his intelligence, his courage, his shrewd judgement of men, and above all his tolerance that the following anecdote will bear out.

One day a calligrapher went to the Maharaja's palace and asked to see his advisor and Foreign Minister Fakir Aziz-ud-din, a Shiite Muslim. He hoped to sell the minister a manuscript of the Koran that he had copied out. Fakir Aziz-ud-din appreciated his work, praised his talent, but said that he could not pay the required price.

Ranjit Singh must have heard the conversation, for before the man could leave the palace he had him called back. When he learnt that the calligrapher had presented his work to all the Muslim princes except the Nizam of Hyderabad, without being able to get the right price for it, he took the manuscript in his own hands, respectfully touched it to his forehead as he would have done with the Granth Sahib, and ordered that the calligrapher be paid his price.

Then turning towards Fakir Aziz-ud-din who was stunned by this gesture, he remarked: "God has wanted me to look at all religions with the same eye. That's why he has deprived me of one of them. This is a holy book. I have not just paid the price of the man's labour but above all a tribute to God."

This open-mindedness won him not only the loyalty of his own subjects—Sikhs, Muslims and Hindus—but also that of several foreigners who rushed to Lahore to serve under his banner.

Among them, the most remarkable were the Frenchman Jean François Allard, the Italians Jean-Baptiste Ventura and Paolo Avitabile, and the Hungarian Martin Honigberger.

Allard came to Punjab in March 1822 at the age of thirty-six. He was of average height, had an imposing presence, and a proud, soft face. His greying hair and long beard contrasted with his black moustaches and sideburns. He spoke with assurance in a modest tone, with a slight accent of his native South France.

In 1815 he was a cavalry captain and Marshal Brune's aide-de-camp. When the latter was assassinated in Avignon, he withdrew for some time to Saint-Tropez, then went to Persia, where the crown prince, Abbas Mirza, took him on as a military advisor.

However, he soon tired of the opulent indolence in which the prince maintained him and left his service in the company of Jean-Baptiste Ventura who, like him, was tired of doing nothing. Travelling together in eastern and southern Persia, it was not long before they heard of the military fame of the Maharaja of the Punjab and they decided to go to Lahore to offer their services.

Ranjit Singh, who had never employed Europeans, was somewhat wary, especially after the problems he had had with the English. But Allard's military prowess soon allayed his fears. Allard organised the Sikh cavalry and distinguished himself in many battles before dying in 1839 in Peshawar. His tomb stands in the old Anarkali area of Lahore.

Speaking of the Koh-i-noor during his stay in Paris, he is supposed to have said: "Our Regent is but a bourgeois diamond in comparison to that one."

Little is known about Ventura's origins except that he was the son of an Italian rabbi. His bravery in the battle of Wagram won him the sobriquet of "fighting cock of Wagram" and after the departure of Emperor Napoleon into exile at St. Helena, he followed Allard to Persia and then to the Punjab. An infantry officer and an excellent strategist, he took part in several campaigns and at one time even became commander-in-chief of the Sikh army.

His amorous exploits were as notorious as his military feats. He was the only foreign officer in the service of the Maharaja to maintain a harem composed of some of the most beautiful women of the kingdom. This did not prevent him from having an occasional fling with the members of the king's harem.

Legend has it that Ranjit Singh, madly in love with a Kashmir belle called Lotus, thought that she returned his feelings. On a festive evening, after she had danced before a wonderstruck audience, he proudly turned to Ventura and told him of the love that his young mistress bore him. The Italian was unable to hide his disbelief and an indignant Ranjit Singh challenged him to seduce her. Two days later the old lion's illusions went up in smoke. Ventura had bribed the guard, entered his harem and transplanted the beautiful Lotus into his own garden.

Paolo Avitabile, a colossus who was almost seven feet tall, with hard sensuous features and a greying tufty beard, had also served in the Persian army with Allard and Ventura. Full of admiration for his strength and courage, Ventura invited him in 1826 to join the ranks of Ranjit Singh's army. He was first appointed governor of Wazirabad and then of Peshawar where, from the very outset, his harshness won him the respect and fear of the Afghan tribes. This is hardly surprising. In the first three days after his arrival he had fifty brigands hanged every morning before breakfast as a warning.

Martin Honigberger, a native of Transylvania, had lived for thirty-seven years in the east, fifteen of which were in Lahore as the court physician. Ranjit Singh had also assigned him the jobs of managing his gunpowder factory and of preparing his favourite drink: a strong mixture of cereal alcohol, meat juice, opium, musk and pearl powder, which he used to drink in great quantities at sundown.

After dispossessing Shah Shuja of the Koh-i-noor, the Maharaja returned to his palace where, during an impressive reception he proudly showed it to his courtesans. Then he entrusted the diamond to the care of Misser Basti Ram, the treasurer, who had served his father and his grandfather before him and enjoyed Ranjit Singh's full trust.

A few days later Ranjit Singh went to Amritsar and called for the town's best jewellers to estimate the value of the Koh-i-noor. After examining it attentively, the jewellers concluded that its size and brilliance made it priceless. The Maharaja then ordered that it be set in the ornament of his turban. This was done in his presence for he could not tolerate losing sight of the diamond. Once the work was done, the Maharaja put on his headgear, mounted his elephant and went through the streets of the city to allow his subjects to admire it.

The Koh-i-noor accompanied him wherever he went. It was locked—a secret shared only by the treasurer and his deputies—in a wooden coffer placed on the back of the first of the long line of camels which, under heavy guard, carried the luggage of the Maharaja and his entourage. At every stage of the journey the coffer would be placed between two identical replicas near Misser Basti Ram's bed, and later near that of his son and successor, Misser Beli Ram.

Ranjit Singh wore it on his turban three or four times before it came to decorate the right side of the bridle of his favourite mount, Laili. In this way, his good eye could contemplate it at leisure when he went on the long horse rides which he loved. Finally, mounted between a pair of smaller diamonds, it would adorn the bracelet that he wore at official functions.

Baron Charles Hügel saw it in this form during his interview with the Maharaja in January 1836.

"I am sure you would like to see the famous diamond", Ranjit Singh told him. Then without waiting for his guest to reply, he called for the four trays on which were placed one of the most beautiful assortments of jewels ever to be seen. None, however, struck Hügel as much as the Koh-i-noor which he compared to a hen's egg in size and form and whose brilliance, he felt, was "beyond description".

Two years later, another foreign visitor had the privilege of seeing and touching this fabulous stone. That was William Godolphin Osborne, Lord Auckland's nephew, who as military secretary to the Governor General, took part in the talks between his uncle and Ranjit Singh.

"The Lion of Lahore", relates Osborne, "was sitting cross-legged in a golden chair, dressed in simple white, wearing no ornaments but a single string of enormous pearls round the waist, and the celebrated Koh-i-noor, or mountain of light, on his arm. The jewel rivalled, if not surpassed, in brilliancy the glance of fire which every now and then shot from his single eye as it wandered restlessly round the circle."

The Maharaja at first repelled him. But he changed his mind, and concluded after his second meeting that so enchanting was Ranjit Singh's intelligence and so captivating the incessant wandering of his single eye that it did not take long to get used to his physique.

Osborne saw him again on 13 July 1838, on the occasion

of a farewell audience. The ceremony took place in the baradari, a pavilion with twelve arched openings made entirely of white marble, built in 1818 in the garden which separates the royal mosque from the Lahore Fort.

"After having talked for half an hour about different subjects, I reminded him of his promise to show me the Koh-i-noor, which he ordered to be brought forthwith. It certainly is a most magnificent diamond. It is about an inch and a half in length and upwards of an inch in width, and stands out from the setting about half an inch: it is in the shape of an egg, and is set in a bracelet between two very handsome diamonds about half its size. It is valued at three million sterling, and without a flaw of any kind. Ranjit Singh was anxious to know how much it would be worth in England and whether we had ever seen so splendid a diamond."

But Ranjit Singh's reign was drawing to a close. Ever since an attack suffered on the night of 17 August 1835 had paralyzed a portion of his face, he was but a shadow of his former self. "I am growing old", he was to tell Baron Hügel, "I am at the end of my strength."

His infirmity made him adopt a somewhat strange strategy for riding. While an equerry knelt before him, he would put his legs around his shoulders. Then the man stood up and carried him to his horse. The Maharaja would then put his right foot in the stirrup, hold on to the horse's mane, and moving his left leg above the head of the equerry and the back of his mount, would find the other stirrup.

Two fresh attacks, at the beginning of 1837 and the end of 1838, finally sapped his strength and deprived him of his speech. Six months later most European and local physicians, who took turns at his bedside, lost all hope of saving him.

He then gave in to divine mercy and distributed alms to the poor, sending expiatory offerings to the Brahmins of the Punjab and India. Even the Koh-i-noor was nearly given away.

A few days before his death one of his main lieutenants came to him and whispered in his ear: "Sire, you have often expressed the desire to send the Koh-i-noor to the temple of Jagannath, as an offering to Krishna. Do you still wish your will to be carried out?" Ranjit Singh nodded his approval and Misser Beli Ram was called and informed of the decision. The treasurer hesitated for a minute, then refused to comply, arguing that the diamond was the property of the state and as such belonged to the Maharaja's successors. Besides, the Brahmins had already received twenty-one lakh rupees as well as an abundance of gold and precious stones. This refusal provoked the animosity of Dhian Singh, Ranjit Singh's Hindu prime minister, and he was put in jail soon after the Maharaja passed away.

Thus the Koh-i-noor remained in the Lahore treasury waiting for fresh events to once again change the course of its destiny.

Only a man of Ranjit Singh's calibre could dominate the Sikh chiefs and impose total submission on them. Under his indolent, debauched successors, discipline got lax, factionalism began to raise its head, the army posed as arbitrator, and assassinations and internal strife got the better of compromise. The Punjab fell into a state of chaos which was soon to bring its end as a sovereign state.

Ranjit Singh is supposed to have asked a cartographer after looking at the map of the Indian subcontinent: "What does the red mean?" "This is the extent of British possessions, Sire", replied the cartographer. The Maharaja took a quick look at the map and found that almost the whole of India had been painted in red with the exception of the Punjab. He then turned towards his courtiers and said cynically, "One day it will be all red." Ten years later his prophetic words came true.

Three of his seven sons and his grandson were destined to rule over the Punjab before it was integrated into the British empire. They were his sons Kharak Singh, Sher Singh and Dalip Singh, and his grandson Nau Nihal Singh.

The eldest son, Kharak Singh, was the fruit of the Maharaja's second marriage, the one he had contracted after the break up of his conjugal ties with his first wife, Mehtab Kaur.

Six years after Kharak Singh's birth, Mehtab Kaur gave birth to two boys whom she called Sher Singh and Tara Singh. This event gladdened the heart of her husband but gave rise to a wild rumour claiming that the newborn were in reality adopted children that Mehtab Kaur was trying to pass off as the legitimate sons of the Maharaja. It was a rumour to which Kharak Singh was to give credence in order to neutralise Sher Singh's influence on their father.

As for Dalip Singh, he was born of Jindan Kaur, whom Ranjit Singh had married towards the end of his life. Speculation veers wildly on Jindan Kaur's origins, from a theory that she was a palace porter's daughter to the claim by the Sikh scholar, Professor Ganda Singh, that Jindan Kaur was the daughter of a respectable Sikh zamindar, of the Aulakh Jat tribe of Sialkot district.

Ranjit Singh's successors ruled over the Punjab for as long as they enjoyed the backing of the Sikh army and the support of the main factions that had come into being at the court of Lahore just before the Maharaja's death.

The most powerful faction was that of the Dogra brothers: Dhian Singh (Ranjit Singh's prime minister), Ghulab Singh and Suchet Singh, Rajputs and Hindus from the Jammu province (south-west of Kashmir). After playing an important role under the previous regime, they now aspired for absolute power under the new one. It is even said that they intended to place Hira Singh on the throne. Hira Singh, the son of Dhian Singh, was a very handsome youth who had been Ranjit Singh's pet and was favourably viewed by the army.

The Dogras faced the fierce hostility of another important faction led by the generals Ajit Singh, Lehna Singh and Attar Singh, the chiefs of the Sikh clan of Sandhawalia.

It is, therefore, hardly surprising that in this atmosphere of jealousy and intrigue, the lives of Ranjit Singh's legitimate successors should be as ephemeral as their rule. Apart from Dalip Singh who would die peacefully in 1893 in a Parisian hotel, they all met with a tragic end.

Kharak Singh died on 5 November 1840 of acute dysentery accompanied by high fever whose real cause, the rumour went, was premeditated poisoning. A year earlier, a palace revolution fomented by the Dogra brothers with the benevolent neutrality of the English had dethroned him in favour of his son Nau Nihal Singh, an intelligent, determined young man who might have followed in the footsteps of his illustrious grandfather had he lived longer.

Unfortunately, while returning to the palace after his father's funeral, in the company of Dhian Singh and Ghulab Singh's son, the huge arched gateway of the Lahore fort suddenly crumbled over the procession. Fragments of stone and wood smashed the head of the young Maharaja, while the prime minister and his nephew escaped with slight injuries.

Even though Doctor Honigberger concluded that it was an accident, a large number of English and Sikh historians blame the Dogras for the calamity even though two of their most important members almost lost their lives.

Dhian Singh ordered that the death of the ruler be kept a secret until a successor was appointed. Then, with the consent of the principal members of the Council of Ministers, he invited Prince Sher Singh to come immediately to Lahore to take power.

Sher Singh was considered to be Ranjit Singh's ablest

son. He also enjoyed the support of the Sikh army and was looked upon favourably by the English, whose policies required a friendly presence at the head of the Punjab.

Dhian Singh's choice nonetheless met with the opposition of his rivals who favoured Maharani Chand Kaur, Nau Nihal Singh's mother. Dhian Singh then tried to come to a compromise which would have protected the unity of the country under its new sovereign, even going to the extent of suggesting a marriage between Sher Singh and the widow of his brother. His efforts proved to be futile. Encouraged by people's sympathy at her son's tragic death, she staked her claim to sovereignty, inviting the Sandhawalias and Ghulab Singh Dogra, Dhian Singh's brother, to support her claim.

On 2 December 1840 she was proclaimed Maharani of the Punjab, in spite of the opposition of the army and the European officers who continued to support her rival. Besides, the tension among the troops, whose wages were depleting the treasury, had come to a boiling point. The soldiers took to plundering, selling their services to the highest bidder and disobeying their officers. The situation could have hastened the disintegration of the country had discipline not been re-established immediately. With the consent of the English, Sher Singh swung into action, reaching the suburbs of Lahore in February 1841 at the head of contingents made up of deserters from the regular army and European officers, including Jean-Baptiste Ventura.

Maharani Chand Kaur, who was protected by the Sandhawalias and Ghulab Singh Dogra's men, appointed Ghulab Singh as commander-in-chief of the army and ordered him to defend the city against Sher Singh's forces. She also settled the outstanding wages of the troops and showered their officers with gold, precious stones and Cashmere shawls, while at the same time she forbade local bankers to give loans to her rival.

These measures were, however, construed as signs of weakness on her part. Sher Singh seized the opportunity to win the troops over to his side and promised them a raise the minute he mounted the throne.

On 15 January 1841 he entered the capital followed by twenty-six thousand infantrymen, eight thousand cavalrymen and forty-five canons, subjecting the fort for two days to heavy artillery fire. He was, however, unable to break Ghulab Singh's resistance and the latter responded by bombarding the bazaar located outside the ramparts.

On 17 January Dhian Singh, who was to be retained as prime minister, arrived on the spot and obtained a cease-fire, which was followed by a negotiated agreement. According to the terms of the arrangement, the Maharani was to give up her claim in exchange for an important fief, whereas Sher Singh, now the ruler, undertook to grant amnesty to his rival's supporters. The Sandhawalias managed to escape from Lahore. When the British agent at Ludhiana refused them asylum, they went to Calcutta where the Governor General agreed to their demand. As for the unfortunate Maharani, she was assassinated a little while later in her bath by the orders of her successor.

Meanwhile, what had become of the Koh-i-noor of which nobody had heard since it had been worn on one or two occasions by Kharak Singh? It was apparently kept safely in the treasure room of the palace before it fell into the hands of Ghulab Singh who eagerly presented it to the new Maharaja and once again found favour with him by taking credit for saving the famous stone.

Sher Singh's rule began badly. He was unable to fulfill the promises he made to his troops. The soldiers continued to plunder the bazaars and massacre the army's accountants whom they accused of misappropriation of funds and complicity with the English. They also called for the establishment of the panchayat, a council of wise men elected by the soldiers. They threatened to overthrow the king if he did not accede to their demand.

Instead of putting down the mutiny as his lieutenants expected him to do, Sher Singh gave in to the whims of the army rabble, and began to indulge in excesses of all kinds, especially alcohol. Rumours of his scandalous conduct spread far and wide, ruining his stock not only with his own people but also with the British authorities.

The Maharaja for his part blamed Lord Ellenborough, Lord Auckland's successor, for settling the Afghan problem without considering the Punjab's interests. Relations certainly did not improve with the British takeover of Sind in March 1843.

This quarrel, interspersed with mutual protestations of friendship, did not stop the Governor General from obtaining from Sher Singh an amnesty for the Sandhawalias, who were allowed to return to Punjab and take possession of their estates.

On 15 September 1843 Sher Singh was to seal his reconciliation with the Sandhawalias with an inspection of their troops. As he did not come on time, the three generals Ajit Singh, Lehna Singh and Attar Singh, went to the palace and jokingly blamed him for keeping them waiting. Ajit Singh was armed with a magnificent double-barrelled rifle he had bought during his stay in Calcutta. The Maharaja asked to have a look at it. The general handed it over with the barrel pointed towards him, and pulled the trigger, and the bullet pierced his chest "What perfidy!" cried out the unfortunate king before succumbing to his wounds.

Sher Singh's murder, followed by that of Dhian Singh, the prime minister, plunged the army into consternation. Acting in the name of the Khalsa, it chose Hira Singh, the son of the assassinated minister, as its leader. The day after, the conspirators were put to the sword, while Dalip Singh, Ranjit Singh's youngest son who was six years old, was put on the throne, with the government entrusted to Hira Singh.

Having virtually grown up in Ranjit Singh's lap, the new prime minister was well versed in the affairs of state. He went about his task with energy and wisdom. However, he was unable to withstand the incessant intrigues of the many factions at court and particularly the anger of Jindan Kaur. The Queen Mother, furious at the slanderous words uttered against her by one of the confidants of Hira Singh, exposed him to the condemnation of the people and the army. Soon after, the unfortunate prime minister and his confidant suffered a complete reversal of fortune. They were killed on 21 December 1844 as they fled from Lahore. Their heads were planted on the points of Sikh cavalry lances and taken round the streets of the capital.

The Sikh army was now an all-powerful institution that no government could handle. Maharani Jindan Kaur, who had been appointed regent, contented herself with dealing with day to day affairs with the help of her brother Jawahar Singh, and some say her lover, one Lal Singh, while waiting for an opportunity to assert herself.

Unfortunately, she was confronted a little while later with the revolt of Peshaura Singh, another of Ranjit Singh's sons, who after capturing the fort of Attock, disputed the right of his younger brother Dalip Singh to the throne and called upon the army and the people to support his claim.

Jindan Kaur nonetheless managed to thwart his plans through her alliance with powerful Sikh chiefs. One of them persuaded the prince to accompany him to Lahore and even though he promised him safety, killed him on the way.

The army, furious that the blood of a descendant of Ranjit Singh had been spilled, accused the Maharani's brother of hatching the plot and ordered him to appear before the council of wise men to clear himself.

In September 1845, at sundown, Jawahar Singh, pale with

fright, landed at the army headquarters, perched on an elephant and holding in his arms his nephew, the young Maharaja Dalip Singh. Maharani Jindan Kaur followed on another elephant, hidden behind the closed curtains of her golden howda.

The procession was welcomed with a gun salute in honour of the young king after which Jawahar Singh was called upon to dismount from his howda. When he refused to obey the injunction, he was separated from his nephew and killed with a lance. The Maharani, shaken by the murder of her brother, returned to the palace swearing revenge.

According to Colonel Alexander Gardner, an American officer who served with Ghulab Singh Dogra and died in Kashmir in 1875, Jindan Kaur provoked the First Anglo-Sikh War simply in order to avenge her brother. He claims that the Maharani's policies were inspired by an old Sikh motto: "Throw the snake in your enemy's bosom." For her, the snake was certainly her own army, with England the enemy.

In reality, this policy found favour with several personalities of the Lahore court who, scared by the excesses of the army rabble, were quite happy to sacrifice it to feather their own nests. This is borne out by the perfidy of some Sikh generals on the battlefield.

On 11 December 1845 the Sikh army crossed the Sutlej in the early hours of the morning. Two days later Sir Henry Hardinge, Ellenborough's successor, a career soldier who had lost a hand during the battle of Waterloo, declared war on the kingdom of the Punjab, accusing the Sikhs of having invaded British territories without any valid pretext.

In reality, the movement of English troops south of the Sutlej had prompted the Sikhs to take up offensive positions. Between the spring of 1844 and the beginning of hostilities, the strength of the British army grew from seventeen thousand, five hundred men to nearly forty thousand men and its firepower increased from sixty-six to ninety-four pieces of artillery. Apart from this, an advance base had been set up at Ferozepur, to the west of Ludhiana, from where the English cavalry and artillery could reach Lahore within a matter of hours.

The First Anglo-Sikh War ended with the English victory at Sabraon on 10 February 1846, a battle that the British commander-in-chief described as "the Indian Waterloo" before praising the valour of his adversaries.

There is no doubt that the valour and devotion of the Sikh soldiers at Sabraon and in earlier skirmishes were outstanding and that the outcome would have been very different had the army not been betrayed by its generals.

The Governor General, rewarded for his success with the title of Viscount, wanted the Punjab to remain independent even though severed of a portion of her territory, to serve as a buffer between British possessions and the countries of Central Asia. During his ceremonial meeting with Dalip Singh on 15 February 1846 he explained British policies to the latter and placed on his turban a diamond aigrette that was a gift from Queen Victoria.

Lord Hardinge received in exchange several presents from the young Maharaja, and then asked to see the Koh-i-noor which was shown to him. He examined the jewel for quite some time, showed it to his officers and then fastening it to Dalip Singh's right arm, congratulated him on possessing such a marvel.

By the treaties of Lahore (March 1846), the Sikh army was reduced to twenty-five infantry battalions, each consisting of eight hundred men, and twelve thousand cavalrymen. The kingdom of the Punjab had been stripped of a large part of its territory by England, and the Lahore court was made to pay war damages amounting to one-and-a-half million rupees. As it was in no position to pay such an amount, instead it surrendered Kashmir and Hazara, the mountainous region situated in the north of the country between the Beas and the Indus. Kashmir was sold to Ghulab Singh Dogra who, as a reward for his neutrality during the war, was recognised as the independent sovereign of Jammu and Kashmir.

As for Jindan Kaur, she was to bitterly regret her tacit collaboration with the English. Stripped by the latter of her title of regent, she was pensioned off with an annual allowance of a hundred-and-fifty-thousand rupees and then confined to a fortress near Lahore for having intrigued against the army of occupation.

The Treaties of Lahore were completed in December 1846 by the Treaty of Bhairowal. By these the administration of the Punjab was handed over to a regency council composed of local chiefs acting under the authority and control of the British resident, Sir Henry Lawrence. Moreover, while a contingent of English troops was to remain stationed at Lahore to protect the Maharaja, the Governor General was authorised to occupy any other region that he deemed necessary to maintain peace.

These provisions were to expire at the latest by 4 September 1854, the sixteenth birthday of the Maharaja, unless the Governor General decided to put an end to them before that date.

The British government would have been satisfied with this ambiguous situation if it had continued to enjoy the support of the Sikh leaders. However, the latter, hurt by the social, administrative and financial reforms of the occupying power and repenting its betrayal of the memory of Ranjit Singh, would soon rally together for a popular uprising which was the prelude to the Second Anglo-Sikh War and the English annexation of the Punjab.

CHAPTER SIX

As the year 1847 drew to an end, a regrettable incident—which in a less surcharged atmosphere could have been settled through diplomacy—shook the Punjab.

In December, Dewan Mulraj, the governor of Multan, resigned from office, as he could not pay the British resident taxes on the revenues of his province. He remained in office until the Regency Council appointed his successor, a Sikh general, who arrived in Multan in April 1848 accompanied by Lieutenant Anderson and Vance Agnew, the English agents responsible for overseeing the transfer of power.

Once the formality was over, units of the regular army of the Punjab took over from the local garrison whose members were sent back home. A few days later the demobilised soldiers mutinied. Dewan Mulraj, who was persuaded to lead the insurrection, managed to entice their replacements to join forces with them and expel the foreigners. At nightfall the rebels invaded the British cantonment and, in the general mêlée, killed Vance Agnew and his colleague.

On 29 April 1848 the British resident at Lahore, who was informed of the event, went to the court and demanded that immediate measures be taken to punish those who were responsible for the offence committed against the British government.

After lengthy discussions, the Sikh chiefs replied that they could depend neither on their troops nor on the regular army of the state to act against Mulraj.

In the meantime, Viscount Hardinge was succeeded by James Andrew Brown Ramsay, the tenth Count and first Marquis of Dalhousie, a thirty-five-year-old Scottish aristocrat whose expansionist policies were in sharp contrast to those of his predecessor. Even though of average height, so strong was his personality and so majestic his bearing that people would say "he had in all manner the allure of a king"

When he heard of the Multan rebellion, he and the commander-in-chief of the British forces, General Gough, decided to allow the situation to deteriorate in order to take advantage of it. His decision was probably also influenced by the summer heat that excluded all possibility of a large scale military operation. The heat, however, did not deter some stormy English officers from spontaneously marching on Multan to avenge the death of their compatriots.

Moreover, Frederick Currie and John Lawrence who managed the affairs of the Punjab, further inflamed the passions of the people by confining the Queen Mother to Chunar, a fortress on the banks of the Ganga, not far from Banaras. They accused her of complicity with the insurgents.

Even though Jindan Kaur was not particularly loved or respected by the notables—her love of debauchery had won her the nickname of the Messalina of Punjab—her banishment shook their confidence in the good faith of the British government. Thereupon, except for a few who continued to temporise to protect their interests, most of the Sikh chiefs joined the rebellion.

This was the moment Dalhousie was waiting for. In a speech delivered on 5 October 1848 before the officers of the Calcutta garrison, he declared in a firm, determined voice: "I wished for peace, I desired it fervently, I did all my best to achieve it. But, insensitive to the lessons of the past, the Sikh nation has wished for war, and, I will give you my word, Gentlemen, she will have it with a vengeance."

However, he did not go as far as to implicate the Lahore court so that British reinforcements could enter the Punjab, not as enemies but to re-establish law and order.

The Sikh army, now reduced to twenty thousand men

and five thousand cavalrymen, was later joined by a great number of soldiers demobilised after the First Anglo-Sikh War. The English aligned fifty thousand soldiers along the Sutlej, nine thousand in Lahore, and nine thousand in Ferozepur.

In early 1849, while British detachments were putting down the rebellion around Multan, the bulk of the English army faced the Khalsa forces in the first of the two major battles that were to decide the future of the Punjab.

Fearing the superior firepower of the British artillery, Sikh troops abandoned their positions on the Chenab to fall back on the northern bank of the Jhelum, where an expanse of thick brushwood intersected by deep ravines separated them from the enemy.

The first encounter took place in the afternoon of 13 January 1849 near the village of Chilianwala. As the Treaty of Lahore had deprived the Sikhs of much of their artillery, they decided to rely on lightning cavalry charges under the cover of the brushwood, inflicting on the English their most terrible defeat since their occupation of India. As thousands of soldiers from both camps lay dead on the battlefield, torrential rains began to fall, flooding the brushwood and ravines and hampering the movement of the Sikh cavalry. This moment of respite enabled the English troops to withdraw until the arrival of reinforcements. On 21 February 1849, at dawn, hostilities resumed near Gujrat, a town situated a few kilometres from Chilianwala, on the northern banks of the Chenab.

The Sikhs replied to the English assault with a heavy fire of artillery that in no time exhausted their ammunition and revealed the position of their cannons, which were reduced to silence by the British artillery. Now it was only a question of days before the Khalsa forces succumbed to the numerical and material superiority of the opponent.

On 13 March 1849, after a series of bitter encounters

where the bravery and sacrifice of the Sikhs won them the admiration and respect of the British, the Khalsa army laid down its arms.

On 29 March 1849, at twilight, Dalip Singh, barely twelve years old, entered the Sheesh Mahal (the hall of mirrors) of the Lahore fort, where he was welcomed by his local and English counsellors, as well as by Mr. Elliot, the Secretary-General of the British Government of India. The latter waited for the young Maharaja to sit on his golden throne. Then, by the light of the candles that the stalactite-shaped cut-glasses decorating the room reflected indefinitely, he read the proclamation of Lord Dalhousie that ended the independence of the Punjab.

What it said in substance was that the British had not aspired to conquer the Punjab. Forced, however, to protect themselves from the recurrence of expensive and unprovoked wars that compromised their safety and interests, it had decided to subordinate the entire population of the Punjab.

From that day onwards, concluded the proclamation, all the territories of Maharaja Dalip Singh were incorporated in the British Empire of India. As for the fallen sovereign, he would continue to be treated with respect and honour.

The proclamation was then read in its Persian and Hindustani translations following which a dignitary of the court of Lahore moved away from his peers and in a voice choked with emotion acceded to the will of the conqueror. "This is an order from Lord Sahib", he said, "and we must obey". Another advisor of the Maharaja then handed over to his master the note containing the conditions of the annexation, which he signed immediately, having been told of its content a few hours earlier:

1. His Highness Maharaja Dalip Singh shall resign for himself, his soldiers and his successors, all rights, titles and claims to the sovereignty of the Punjab or to any sovereign power whatsoever.

2. All property of the State of whatever description and wheresoever found shall be confiscated to the Honourable East India Company in part payment of the debt due by the State of Lahore to the British Government and of the expenses of the war.

3. The gem, the Koh-i-noor, which was taken from Shah Shuja-ul-mulk by Maharaja Ranjit Singh shall be surrendered by the Maharaja of Lahore to the Queen of England.

4. His Highness Dalip Singh shall receive from the Honourable East India Company for the support of himself, his relatives and the Servants of the State, a pension of not less than four and not exceeding five hundred thousand of the Company's rupees per annum.

5. His Highness Dalip Singh shall be treated with respect and honour. He shall retain the title Maharaja Dalip Singh Bahadur and he shall continue to receive during his life such proportion of the pension above-mentioned as may be allotted to him personally, provided he shall reside at such place as the Governor General of India may select.

The next day, Lord Dalhousie ratified the document, before writing to his superiors: "The Council of Regency and the Maharaja have signed the act of submission and surrendered the Koh-i-noor to the Queen of England; the British colours were hoisted on the Citadel of Lahore, and the Punjab, every inch of it, was proclaimed to be a portion of the British Empire in India . . .

"It is not every day that an officer of their Government adds four millions of subjects to the British Empire and places the historical jewel of the Mughal Emperors in the crown of his Sovereign. This I have done."

The government of the Punjab was entrusted to a committee of three members under the chairmanship of Sir Henry Lawrence, assisted by his younger brother John (the future viceroy of India) and Charles Mansel.

On 6 April 1849, Sir John Login, a forty-year-old physician who had been serving in India since 1832 and knew Sir Henry Lawrence, was appointed by the latter as tutor to the young Maharaja and governor of the citadel of Lahore.

In that capacity he was in charge of all that the citadel contained: the Koh-i-noor, the harem of the previous Maharajas, the political prisoners, among whom was Dewan Mulraj, the man responsible for the Second Anglo-Sikh War.

Login personally took the inventory of the toshakhana (jewel department) with the help of Misser Megh Raj.

Lady Login, who never saw the magnificent treasures contained in the Lahore Fort, got a description of them by one of her cousins who was serving in the Punjab at the time: "... I wish you could walk through that same toshakhana and see its wonders; the vast quantities of gold and silver; the jewels not to be valued, so many and so rich; the Koh-i-noor, far beyond what I had imagined; Ranjit's golden chair of state; silver pavilion; Shah Shuja's ditto; relics of the Prophet; kulgee (*pheasant's crest*) plume of the last Sikh Guru; sword of the Persian hero Rustam (taken from Shah Shuja); sword of Holkar, etc. . . and, perhaps above all, the immense collection of magnificent Cashmere shawls, rooms full of them, laid out on shelves and heaped up in bales—it is not to be described!

"And all this made over to Login *without* any list or public document of any sort . . ."

Misser Megh Raj was delighted to be unburdened of the Koh-i-noor. He confided to the new master of the place that the diamond had brought so much misfortune to his family that he never expected to be spared from its unlucky spell. His predecessor, Misser Beli Ram was imprisoned by Dhian Singh for refusing to send the Koh-i-noor to the Jagannath temple and executed by Hira Singh while six members of his family, including Misser Megh Raj, were kept in prison till the assassination of the young prime minister.

The Koh-i-noor was locked in a safe deposited in the toshakhana and protected round the clock by an armed guard. To show it to the handful who were allowed to admire it, Login placed the bracelet containing the diamond on a table covered with black velvet, the diamond alone appearing through a hole cut in the cloth, its brilliance enhanced by the blackness around it.

Meanwhile, the Marquis of Dalhousie had decided to send the Koh-i-noor to Queen Victoria, although he knew for certain that his initiative would displease the directors of the Company.

On 7 April 1849, he wrote to the Queen: "The Governor General has now the honour and gratification of announcing to Your Majesty that the War is at an end, and that the Punjab has been declared to be a portion of Your Majesty's Empire in India. In evidence whereof, and in token of the Maharaja's submission to Your Majesty, the Governor General, if his policy shall receive the sanction of the Government, will have the honour of transmitting to Your Majesty from Lahore the famous Jewel of the Mughal, the Koh-i-noor, the mountain of light."

However, as he had expected, the chairman of the East India Company, Sir Archibald Galloway, expressed his disapproval. "The more I reflect upon the subject", he confided to Sir John Hobhouse, the president of the board of control of the Company, "the more decided is my conviction that the Governor General has made a serious mistake in requiring the Koh-i-noor diamond to be surrendered to the Queen of England. There is not, I believe, a single instance in which the crown is recognised in any Indian treaty, or engagements; the administration of the territories of India being vested in the East India

Company, all treaties and engagements with native states are made in the name of the Company; and are ratified by the Governor General as their servant. The way, therefore, in which Lord Dalhousie has acted upon this occasion appears to me unconstitutional and irregular."

Fortunately for Dalhousie, Sir John Hobhouse was on his side: "I do not feel quite so sure as you seem to be in regard to the Koh-i-noor", he replied to Galloway. "If it is to be regarded as booty, it is clearly the Queen's and not the Company's; and I do not see how anything acquired by force of arms, or, in other words, by the conquest of the Punjab, can be considered in any other light than that of prize of war. It is a perversion of phrase to call the surrender of the sovereignty a treaty. The document signed by Dalip Singh and the Sirdars is only a written submission, giving up the throne and the state treasure with it."

The controversy, however, did not end there. In a bid to assert their authority over the Governor General, the directors of the Company decreed that should the Koh-i-noor be handed over to the Queen, it would be done through their intermediary. This decision went against Dalhousie's wishes. He felt that, with all due respect for royal dignity, the diamond ought to be presented to Queen Victoria as the tribute of a vanquished monarch and not as a present from her own subjects.

However, in spite of the Governor General's desire, the directors of the Company asked him by a letter dated 1 August 1849, to have the Koh-i-noor sent to them at the earliest possible, taking all the measures necessary for its security during its journey from Lahore to London.

Dalhousie was obviously quite irritated. But his friend John Hobhouse reassured him: "You need not have any anxiety about the mode of procedure in regard to the "Mountain of Light". I shall take care to carry out your views and see that it is delivered into the Queen's hands as a transfer from the late Maharaja of Lahore to Her Majesty."

The Governor General had to send the Koh-i-noor to England taking every possible precaution for its safety. After discussing the matter with his advisors, he opted for the sea route, provided the transport was made by the Royal Navy. He then requested Sir John Hobhouse to have the Admiralty send a frigate to Bombay to be placed under the orders of the Governor General. He also requested that no information should be given why the ship was required, to attract as little attention as possible to the movement of the Koh-i-noor.

On 7 December 1849, while HMS *Medea* that was to transport the diamond was making her way to India, the Marquis of Dalhousie entered Login's office in the Lahore Fort, to take official delivery of the Koh-i-noor.

He was accompanied by three members of the Government of the Punjab and the Secretary General of the Government of India, who countersigned the receipt given to Login. Once this was accomplished, the Governor General went to the latter's bedroom, put the bracelet in a small leather bag that had been made by his wife, and fixed it firmly around his waist, under his jacket, with a cord.

This is the official version as reported by none other that Login himself.

There is, however, another apocryphal though highly enjoyable version that has been told by John Lawrence's biographer. According to this anecdote, the Koh-i-noor lived the most comical adventure of its existence before being handed to Lord Dalhousie.

From the very outset, the Government of the Punjab was put in charge of the Koh-i-noor. Henry Lawrence and Charles Mansel decided to put it in the care of John Lawrence, as they considered him the most practical and businesslike of the three. This may have been true in the main, but not this time.

John Lawrence had no use for jewels, even though he was to be later covered with orders and medals for his services. Therefore, he could not appreciate the inestimable value of the diamond entrusted to him. Anyhow, he stuffed the box containing the Koh-i-noor in his waistcoat pocket and went about his business. In the evening he changed his suit for a dinner jacket and carelessly threw his waistcoat on a chair, forgetting about the diamond.

About six weeks later during a government meeting, Sir Henry Lawrence informed his colleagues that Lord Dalhousie had asked for the diamond, to send it to Queen Victoria.

"Send for it at once!" said John quietly to his brother.

"Why, you've got it!" exclaimed Sir Henry, barely able to conceal his panic.

Suddenly aware of the enormity of what he had done, John Lawrence was horrified. He nevertheless managed to hide his emotions and declare with Olympian calm: "Oh, yes, of course; I forgot about it." He then went on with the business of the meeting as if nothing had happened. A few minutes later, finding an opportunity to slip away, he returned to his private room. His heart pounding wildly, he asked his old Indian bearer if he had found a small box in his waistcoat pocket.

"Yes Sahib, I found it and put it in one of your boxes."

"Bring it here."

The old bearer went to a broken-down tin box placed on a table, took out a smaller box from it, and held it out to his master.

"Open it and look at what's inside."

The future viceroy of India let out a huge sigh of relief as the Koh-i-noor emerged from under the last fold of its protective covering.

The bearer, who seemed perfectly oblivious of the value

of the object he held in his hands, observed with astonishment: "There is nothing here, Sahib, but a bit of glass!"

Login had heard this anecdote: "To imagine for a moment", he remarked, "that the Koh-i-noor, set as an armlet, and enclosed in a box, could ever have found a resting place in any person's waistcoat pocket, however capacious, is taxing too much the credulity of the average individual, and has caused infinite amusement to the large number of officials aware of the ceremonial always observed in its transit, and the strong guard placed over it both in and out of the toshakhana.."

Whatever be the case, Lord Dalhousie himself took the Koh-i-noor from Lahore to Bombay, accompanied by his aide-de-camp, Captain Ramsay, and an escort of sepoys and British soldiers.

His wife had sewn the little leather pouch on a Cashmere belt lined with camel skin that her husband wore day and night. Two dogs, Baron and Banda, were chained to the Governor General's camp bed, and as far as we know, no one but his wife and Captain Ramsay knew of the secret. Only on one occasion did Dalhousie separate himself from the diamond. That was when he went to Dera Ghazi Khan. The road being infested with bandits, he put the diamond in a treasure chest and ordered his aide-de-camp to sit on it until he returned.

After the journey was over, he confessed to John Hobhouse: "I undertook the charge of it in a funk, and never was so happy in all my life as when I got it into the Treasury at Bombay . . ."

The *Medea* being late, extraordinary measures were taken to protect the Koh-i-noor until the ship's arrival. It was placed in a small iron chest which was double-locked and sealed. The key was given to Lieutenant-Colonel Mackeson, the liaison officer to the Governor General at the time of the last Anglo-Sikh War. The chest was then placed in an official despatch box, locked and sealed, and the keys were handed over to Captain Ramsay. Whereupon the despatch box was put in a safe deposit box at the Treasury, until the ship was ready to leave.

On 6 April 1850 the Koh-i-noor left the shores of Asia, never to come back again. So shrouded in mystery was its departure that even Captain Lockyer, the Captain of the *Medea,* was unaware of the precious cargo his ship carried.

The Koh-i-noor seemed to carry misfortune with it even on the journey. Before the ship reached Mauritius, cholera broke out on board, and two sailors died. When it approached the island, the inhabitants, fearing that the epidemic might spread, refused to supply it with food or fuel. They demanded the immediate departure of the ship and went to the extent of asking the governor of the island to sink it if it did not set sail immediately. But as Mauritius had been a British possession since 1814, Captain Lockyer refused to raise anchor till his demands were met.

This incident made the Marquis of Dalhousie smile. When he learnt about it through the papers, he remarked jokingly: "It would have been a pretty spot of work if Sir George Anderson (*the Governor*) had sent the Koh-i-noor to the bottom unawares."

A few days after it left Mauritius, the ship ran into further trouble. For twelve hours it was shaken by a terrible storm which caused the loss of two rowboats as well as of its railing.

At last, on 29 June 1850, the HMS *Medea* docked at a deserted quay in Portsmouth. A new era had begun for the Koh-i-noor.

On 3 July it was handed over to Queen Victoria by the chairman and vice-chairman of the East India Company at a private ceremony held in Buckingham Palace, at which Sir John Hobhouse was also present.

The Company was acting but as an intermediary, as Lord Dalhousie had wished. Sir Archibald Galloway made it clear in a short speech—approved in advance by Hobhouse—that the Koh-i-noor was "handed over" to the Queen, thus prudently avoiding the use of the term "offered".

On 19 April 1851 the Koh-i-noor was removed from its mount, so that a replica could be made for the British Museum. Its weight as calculated by Sebastian Garrard, the Queen's jeweller, was about 186 carats.

Two incidents that occurred within the space of a week cast some doubt on the assumption that the Koh-i-noor brought bad luck only to men.

On 19 May 1850, one William Hamilton, an Irishman who was visiting London, shot at Queen Victoria as she was going up Constitution Hill in a carriage. Though the pistol was loaded with blank cartridges, the episode caused immense panic.

A week later, on 27 May 1850, the Queen went to visit her aged uncle, the Duke of Cambridge, who was convalescing. As she was leaving Cambridge House, a retired officer by the name of Robert Pate stepped out of the crowd and hit her hard on the forehead with the brass handle of his walking stick. The hem of her cap dulled the impact to some extent but she still got a nasty bruise.

Spiteful tongues imputed these incidents to the bad luck attached to the diamond and held Dalhousie responsible. The latter, undaunted by this allegation, retorted by reminding them of the remarks of Shah Shuja about the Koh-i-noor: "Its value is good fortune, for whoever owns it is superior to his enemies."

Nonetheless, ill-fortune was warded off. It was claimed that the diamond brought bad luck only to men and perhaps to sovereigns. It is undoubtedly for this reason that Queen Victoria refused to have it set in the Crown of England.

The Great Exhibition of 1851 was held at the Crystal Palace, a building made of iron and glass that stood to the south of Hyde Park, between Kensington Drive and Rotten Row.

According to the *Magasin Pittoresque,* a French magazine of the period, "diamonds and jewels occupied the pride of place at the Great Exhibition. The most curious, the most diligent, those who wished to feast their eyes, flocked to see them. At some places one, at others two, four and even six policemen, are always busy asking the visitors to move on. Every time one hears 'Pass on, pass on, gentlemen, ladies', one can be sure that there is nothing in the wind, but diamond behind glass."

The Koh-i-noor was exhibited in a kind of glass bird cage, placed on a wooden column surmounted by a replica of the British Crown.

Among the jewels were a sapphire that once belonged to Philippe Egalité, the handle of Marshal Murat's sword, made of a single aquamarine; opals, topazes, rubies, carbuncles, and lastly, emeralds—remarkable either because of their rare colour, or the memory of the exceptional people who had owned them.

For the *Times,* however, the Koh-i-noor was decidedly the "Lion" of the exhibition. The diamond's aura of mystery was increased by the many obstacles to be overcome before reaching its cage. This aroused the curiosity of the visitors who clamoured every day in thousands to admire it.

". . . and yet, after all", added the *Times,* "the diamond does not satisfy. Either from the imperfect cutting or the difficulty of placing the lights advantageously, or the immovability of the stone itself, which should be made to revolve on its axis, few catch any of the brilliant rays that it reflects when viewed at a particular angle."

The *Magasin Pittoresque* observed in the same vein: "In

spite of the most laudable efforts made to have the diamond cast its light, neither gas lamps nor the sun have been able to make this mountain as luminous as a collection of well cut diamonds would be . . . The Indian diamond is very big but, in general, does not project any light. Its extraordinary proportions seem to have more value than the transparency, the brilliance and the nature of its light."

As for the *Illustrated London News,* it felt that the Koh-i-noor would lose much of its dimension were it to be cut by a European lapidary. "Its marketable value would, however, be increased. It would probably become, if properly treated, one of the finest diamonds in Europe."

In Calcutta, the Marquis of Dalhousie was following the coverage of the exhibition with a great deal of interest. "I see all sorts of sketches and pictures of the contents of the exhibition. If you can get me anything presenting well the Koh-i-noor in its cage, coloured, I shall be much obliged."

He too now began to find fault with the size of the diamond, even though in the past he had used the most glowing terms to entice Queen Victoria. "The Koh-i-noor", he commented, "is badly cut: it is rose, not brilliant cut, and of course won't sparkle like the latter. But it should not have been shown in a huge space, In the toshakhana at Lahore Dr. Login used to show it on a table covered with a black velvet cloth, the diamond alone appearing through a hole in the cloth, and relieved by the dark colour all around."

Queen Victoria and Prince Albert shared these opinions and thought that the brilliance of the diamond could be further enhanced if it were recut. They decided to call in the specialists for advice.

One of them, Sir David Brewster, a scientist who had devoted many years to the study of the polarization of light, was given permission to look at the Koh-i-noor under a microscope. Near the very centre of the diamond, he found three black specks scarcely visible to the eye, but which the microscope showed to be cavities surrounded with sectors of polarized light, and the same polarizing structure which indicates the existence of compressing and dilating forces. This virtually ruled out recutting the stone unless one was ready to accept a considerable loss of weight.

Other specialists consulted on the subject were in favour of recutting the diamond to enhance its brilliance. But they felt this could not be achieved without jeopardizing the size of the stone.

These reports were sent to Messrs. Garrard, the court jewellers, with the opinions of experienced lapidaries. Diamond cutting being then the preserve of the Dutch, Messrs. Coster, the famous Amsterdam diamond experts, were called in. They felt that the fears expressed by the English specialists were well-founded, but that the difficulties could be overcome with care and skill.

Garrard was thus given permission to proceed with the recutting of the diamond so as to convert it into a brilliant, oval shaped stone.

While two of Coster's best master cutters, Voorsanger and Fedder, left Amsterdam for London, a small steam engine was installed in London in Garrard's workshop, located at 25 Hay Market, to carry out the job.

On Thursday 16 July 1852, the Duke of Wellington, who was to die in less than two months at the age of eighty-three, rode from Hyde Park corner to Garrard's workshop on his old white horse. He had expressed the desire to inaugurate the work by personally recutting one of the facets of the Koh-i-noor.

An alloy of tin and lead was poured in a copper vessel and the mixture was allowed to cool till it acquired specific consistency. Then the Koh-i-noor was immersed in it in such a way that all its facets save the one to be recut were covered by the solder.

The old duke approached the lapidary's table, applied the exposed part of the diamond to a horizontal wheel and switched on the steam engine, making the wheel turn at a high speed. Thus the friction principle was used to recut the diamond.

The entire operation was completed in thirty-eight days, not without a certain amount of difficulty. It cost 8,000 pounds. The Koh-i-noor now weighed 108.93 carats, having lost 43 percent of its original weight. Many people were disappointed by this loss in weight, especially Prince Albert, even though he had recommended the recutting of the diamond. Experts who had not been consulted earlier observed on hindsight that the oval shape chosen by the Queen's advisors was bound to cause a maximum loss in weight and that the pear shape would have been better. By then the harm had already been done. The Koh-i-noor, however, lost none of its mystique.

Meanwhile, the last ruler of the Punjab was now in London. Dalip Singh, who had embraced Christianity under Login's influence, was permitted to travel to England. He arrived in London in June 1854, two months before his sixteenth birthday.

If Lady Login, the wife of Dalip Singh's tutor, is to be believed, he charmed Queen Victoria and Prince Albert. He was frequently invited to the court and the Queen took a particular interest in his education. She found him so handsome in his Sikh costume that she decided to have his full-length portrait painted by Winterhalter, the court painter. Dalip Singh would pose in one of the rooms of Buckingham Palace, converted into a studio. The young man was accompanied by either Login or Lady Login, and the Queen often came to observe the artist at work.

One day, while the painter was working on the details of the jewels worn by his model, Queen Victoria took Lady Login aside and asked her if the Maharaja ever mentioned the Koh-i-noor. "Does he seem to regret it, and would he like to see it again? Find out for me before the next sitting, and mind you let me know *exactly* what he says!"

Some time elapsed before Lady Login could find an opportunity to mention the subject to Dalip Singh. At last, one day before the scheduled sitting, as they were riding together in Richmond Park, she turned the conversation round to the Koh-i-noor and asked him if he was curious to see it in its new form.

"Yes, indeed I would", he affirmed emphatically "I would give a good deal to hold it again in my own hand."

This forthright answer startled Lady Login. Knowing how bitter her pupil was about the diamond, she wanted to know what had caused his sudden change of attitude.

"...I was but a child, an infant, when forced to surrender it by treaty; but now that I am a man, I should like to have it in my power to place it myself in her hand!"

The following day, while the Maharaja, standing on a platform, was posing for Winterhalter, the Queen entered the room, accompanied by her husband, and headed straight towards Lady Login. Delighted to hear of Dalip Singh's reaction, she briefly consulted Prince Albert and then sent a gentleman-in-waiting to fetch the diamond.

Half an hour later the door was opened to a group of Beefeaters from the Tower of London escorting the small casket containing the Koh-i-noor.

"Maharaja, I have something to show you!" said the Queen to Dalip Singh.

The latter immediately stepped down from the platform, moved towards the Queen, and found himself once more with the Koh-i-noor. Queen Victoria asked him if he thought it improved, and if he would have recognized it again.

Instead of replying, Dalip Singh walked with the diamond towards the window to examine its facets in daylight. While he was turning the diamond in his hand, as if unable to part with it again, a terrible thought suddenly crossed Lady Login's mind: what if in a moment of madness Dalip Singh threw the diamond out of the window?

Fortunately her fears proved to be baseless. The Maharaja slowly moved away from the window toward the Queen and, with a deferential bow, placed the famous stone in her hand.

"It is to me, Ma'am, the greatest pleasure thus to have the opportunity, as a loyal subject, of *myself* tendering to my Sovereign the Koh-i-noor!"

This tribute to the Queen would not stop him a few years later from claiming the diamond or, at least, the payment of a fair compensation for it.

Dalhousie was not amused by this incident. Suspecting that Login had egged on the Maharaja to make the demand, he wrote to a correspondent in London: "Login's talk about the Koh-i-noor being a present from Dalip Singh to the Queen is arrant humbug. He knew as well as I did, that it was nothing of the sort; and if I had been within a thousand miles of him he would not have dared to utter such a piece of trickery. Those beautiful eyes with which Dalip has taken captive the court, are his mother's eyes, those with which she captivated and controlled the old Lion of the Punjab. The officer who had charge of her from Lahore to Banaras told me this. He said that hers were splendid orbs."

The Queen had the Koh-i-noor mounted on a magnificent tiara where it was set in the midst of two thousand small diamonds. Five years later it was to adorn another one of her tiaras. In 1911 it was put on the crown of Queen Mary, who wore it at the coronation of her husband, George V. Finally, in 1937, the diamond was placed on the crown of Queen Elizabeth, the present Queen Mother of England.

Today the Koh-i-noor is kept with other precious objects

of the British Crown in a round display case in the basement of the "Jewel House" of the Tower of London. The display case is protected by a metallic bar and surrounded by two galleries. The first, near the glass, allows one a close but quick look at the royal treasures; the second, which is higher and further back, gives the visitors an opportunity to gaze at them for as long as they wish.

The Koh-i-noor continues nevertheless to give rise to both regret and envy in the countries it has crossed. In 1947 the Government of independent India demanded its return from the British government, claiming that in spite of the opinion expressed by Ranjit Singh's treasurer, the diamond belonged to the Jagannath idol. Another claim was made in 1953 at the time of Queen Elizabeth II's coronation.

But the real controversy was sparked off in 1976 when Zulfikar Ali Bhutto, then prime minister of Pakistan, wrote to his British counterpart James Callaghan, officially demanding the restoration of the diamond to Pakistan.

A few days later the Indian news agency, Samachar, reacted, declaring that the Koh-i-noor was of Indian origin and that India alone could have a legitimate claim to it. Samachar added that the simple fact that the English had taken the diamond from the Lahore treasury did not make it the property of Pakistan, "According to experts, the Koh-i-noor, discovered in a south Indian mine, has belonged successively to several Indian sovereigns. The last Indian sovereign to own it was Prince Dalip Singh, the heir to Ranjit Singh, who was dispossessed of it when the Punjab was annexed by the East India Company."

On 9 September, an influential Tehran newspaper, the *Keyhan,* added fuel to the fire by asserting that the diamond belonged in reality to Iran and that Britain ought to hand it back to that country.

The controversy was not going to spare the great-great-grandson of Lord Dalhousie who brought some humour to it by staking his claim to the diamond on the grounds that his illustrious ancestor had it in his possession for a little over a year.

All these efforts proved to be futile. Great Britain may have lost its Indian empire, but she is certainly not going to give up its greatest symbol.

At present the Koh-i-noor lies peacefully in its display case, far away from intrigues, assassinations, battles, fratricidal wars and lust. It only casts its brilliance on the millions of tourists who, for the most part, are unaware of its long history.

AFTERWORD: THE MYSTERY OF THE KOH-I-NOOR

In 1889 an English geologist and mineralogist, Valentine Ball, published a translation of Tavernier's *Six Voyages* with very detailed appendices on the origin of the Koh-i-noor. His commentaries helped revive a debate which began with the arrival of the controversial diamond in England, and continues with varying intensity even today. Of the two stones, Babur's diamond and the Great Mughal (or "Moghul", the name given to the diamond seen by Tavernier), which one was the Koh-i-noor?

Among those who have identified the Koh-i-noor with Babur's diamond, the most notable are the mineralogist Maskelyne and the nineteenth century London jeweller, Edwin Streeter. According to Maskelyne: "Babur gives its weight at about eight misqals. In another passage he estimates the misqal at 40 ratis, which would make its weight 320 ratis." After listing the varying weights of the rati at different times and places, he proceeds: "But the eight misqals of Babur afford a far more hopeful estimate of the weight of this diamond. This is a Persian weight, and seems to have been far less liable to variety of value at different times or places. The Persian misqal, or half dirhem, weighs 74.5 grain Troy, eight of these equal 596 grains, or 187.58 carats. The Koh-i-noor in the Exhibition of 1851 weighed 186 carats."

As for Edwin Streeter, he had, in his first book, *Precious Stones and Gems,* refuted all assumptions that the Koh-i-noor and Babur's diamond were identical. However, in a second book entitled *The Great Diamonds of the World, their History and their Romance,* he changed his mind: "All are agreed", he writes, "that Babur's diamond and the Koh-i-noor are identical and the Moghul's distinct."

In the opposite camp, we find the mineralogists James Tennant and Valentine Ball.

According to Tennant, the Koh-i-noor when brought to England "exhibited two cleavage planes, one of which had not been polished, and had distinctly been produced by fracture . . . No one can examine the authentic sketches and models of the "Koh-i-noor", without feeling a strong presumption that it must have been mutilated, after cutting . . . ."

Apart from the flaws similar to those observed by Tavernier in the Great Mughal, Tennant discovered others on the Koh-i-noor which made him deduce that the difference in weight of $82.\frac{1}{3}$ carats between the two stones was due to the losses incurred by the Koh-i-noor. (Tennant speaks of English carats.)

As for Valentine Ball, he writes: "We have now arrived at a stage when we can agree with those authorities who have maintained that Babur's diamond and the Moghul's were distinct; but with most, if not all of them, we must part company, as they maintain that the Moghul's diamond no longer exists, and that it was on Babur's diamond that Nadir Shah conferred the title Koh-i-noor in the year 1739 . . . The name was an eminently suitable one to apply to the Moghul's stone as it was when seen by Tavernier, though not equally applicable to it in its subsequent mutilated condition, in which it has been so confidently identified by some writers with Babur's diamond.

"The stone which now bears the title Koh-i-noor was taken by Nadir to Persia, and from thence we have rumours of its having been cleaved into several pieces, when or by whom is doubtful. Acceptance of these stories has been rendered difficult by some authors having attempted to assign names and weights to these pieces, the sum of the latter being greater than the total weight of the Moghul stone, as it was when seen by Tavernier. Thus the Orlov, the Great Moghul itself, and the Koh-i-noor have been spoken of as having formed parts of the same stone. This hypothesis is in opposition to everything connected with the histories of these stones which can be relied on; but as regards the possibility of the Koh-i-noor alone having been carved out of the Great Moghul's diamond, it is not argument—but is simply begging the whole question—to assert that the Koh-i-noor existed a hundred and twenty years before Borgio handled the Moghul's diamond. This Mr. Streeter has done, and in his accounts of these diamonds he several times repeats that all are agreed that Babur's diamond and the Koh-i-noor being identical is but rarely entertained; this, I venture to believe, was the sounder opinion than the one more recently advocated by him."

Ball concludes: "It is not the Moghul's diamond which, through failure of being historically traced, as some authors assert, has disappeared, but it is Babur's diamond of the history of which we are really left in doubt. The fixing of the weight of Babur's diamond at a figure identical, or nearly so, with that of the Koh-i-noor when brought to England, though used as a link in the chain, has, I think I have shown, effectively disposed of its claim to be identified with the Moghul's diamond in the first place, and secondly with the Koh-i-noor."

Ball thought on the other hand that the Darya-i-noor (River of Light), a flat stone which weighs 186 carats, that is now in the treasury of the Central Bank in Teheran, may very possibly be Babur's diamond. "I have in vain sought", he says, "for any well-authenticated fact which in the slightest degree controverts or even throws doubt upon that suggestion."

This suggestion is rejected by Ian Balfour, an eminent contemporary gemmologist, who asserts: "In the light of the examination of the contents of the Iranian Treasury undertaken in the 1960's, it has been conclusively proved that the Darya-i-noor constitutes the major portion of the Great Table diamond which Tavernier saw—and tried to buy—at Golconda. In all probability this diamond had been mined not long before his attempted purchase, thereby discounting it from having an earlier history, let alone one involving the Moghul Emperors. Furthermore, the descriptions of Babur's diamond as being valued at half the daily expense of the whole world and so forth, are surely inapplicable to the flat rectangular Darya-i-noor: one would think that a more appropriate metaphor would have been to describe it as the source of half the water needed for the world per day."

In April 1899, Henry Beveridge, the well-known scholar on India who translated Abul Fazl's *Akbar Nama,* shed some light on a hitherto unknown aspect of the problem, namely the voyage of Babur's diamond across Persia and the Deccan. In an article entitled *Babur's Diamond: was it the Koh-i-noor?* he wrote: "Mir Jumla, as a diamond merchant, can hardly have avoided hearing of Babur's diamond, and of its return to southern India. What more natural than that it should come into the market during the convulsions then occurring in southern India, and that Mir Jumla should purchase it or otherwise get possession of it, and then present it to Shah Jahan, or to his son? The fact that it was Babur's diamond, and a historical jewel of the Moghul family would make it all the more acceptable as a present."

He also confirms the existence of two diamonds, the first offered to Shah Jahan, and the second to Aurangzeb: "The diamond presented to Aurangzeb was an uncut one, and may very likely have been that which was afterwards cut by the Venetian. The other weighed, according to Khafi Khan, 216 sarkhs or ratis, while the author of the *Maasir-al-Umara* tells us that it weighed nine tanks, or 216 sarkhs."

This weight corresponds exactly to the estimate given by Shah Jahan in his letter to Abdullah Qutb Shah. However, far from setting store by this evaluation which would have put him among those belonging to the first camp, Beveridge attempts through a series of rather vague calculations to close the gap between the weights of Shah Jahan's and Babur's diamonds, finally reaching the figure of 300 ratis. This, in his view, "is not far short of the weight of Babur's diamond". (Babur had evaluated it at eight misqals of 40 ratis each, that is 320 ratis.) This figure is also close to the weight in ratis given to the diamond by Tavernier, even though according to Valentine Ball, Babur and Tavernier used ratis of different weights. This explains Beveridge's confusion, for although he was aware of the variations in Indian units of weight in different periods and at different places, he was unable to say with any certainty if Babur's diamond and the Koh-i-noor were one and the same.

We can see, therefore, that the origin of the Koh-i-noor is difficult to determine. But its aura of mystery only serves to enhance its value!

BIBLIOGRAPHY

MANUSCRIPT SOURCES

India Office Library, London

- *Treatise on precious metals*, in Persian: ms. or. 1717, Rieu's Catalogue III, 9956.
- *Manuscript of Khor Shah*, in Persian ms: or. 53.
- *Broughton Papers.*

NEWSPAPERS AND PERIODICALS

- *Asiatic Quarterly Review.*
- *Calcutta Monthly Journal.*
- *Calcutta Review.*
- *Illustrated London News.*
- *Le Magasin Pittoresque.*
- *The Times (London).*

PRINTED BOOKS

Abul-Fazl, *The Akbar Nama*, translated by H. Beveridge, 3 vol., New Delhi, 1989.

Alexander, Michael, *Delhi & Agra (A Traveller's Companion)*, London, 1987.

Aziz Abdul, *The Imperial Treasury of Indian Moghuls*, 1942.

Babur-Nama (Memoirs of Babur), translated by A.S. Beveridge, London, 1969.

Baird, J.G.A., Ed., *Private Letters of Lord Dalhousie*, London, 1910.

Balfour, Ian, *Famous Diamonds*, London, 1987.

Bence-Jones, Mark, *The Viceroys of India*, London, 1982.

Benson C. and Esher V., *Letters of Queen Victoria*, 1844-1853, London, 1906.

Bernier, Francois, *Travels in the Moghul Empire*, translated by Archibald Constable, London, 1914.

Bilgrami, S. A. A., *Landmarks of the Deccan*, New Delhi, 1948.

Bosworth-Smith, *Life of Lord Lawrence*, London, 1890.

Bouvier and Maynial, *Vie d'Aurangzeb*, Paris, 1983.

Cambridge History of India, vol. IV, New Delhi, 1987.

Chardin, Jean, *Voyage de Paris à Ispahan*, reprint, Paris, 1983.

Clot, André, *Soliman le Magnifique*, Paris, 1983.

Cotton, Julian James, *"General Avitabile"*, *Calcutta Review*, 1906.

Cuvillier, Fleury, *Notices Historiques sur le Général Allard*, Paris, 1836.

Dalhousie Login, E., *Lady Login's Recollections*, reprint, New Delhi, 1986.

Dayal, Maheshwar, *Rediscovering Delhi*, New Delhi, 1982.

Dowson, John, *History of India, as told by its own Historians*, London, 1867-1877.

Dunbar, Janet, *Golden Interlude (The Edens in India)*, Gloucester, 1985.

Eden, Emily, *Up the Country (Letters from India)*, London, 1984.

Edwards and Garrett, *Mughal Rule in India*, reprint, New Delhi, 1979.

Elphinstone, Mountstuart, *Account of the Kingdom of Caubul*, London, 1815.

Erskine, W., *Babur and Humayun*, 2 vol., London, 1854

Fainshawe, H.C., *Shah Jahan's Delhi*, New Delhi, 1979.

Fouchet, Maurice, *Notes sur l'Afghanistan*, Paris, 1931.

Fraser, James, *History of Nadir Shah*, London, 1742.

Frederic, Louis, *Akbar le Grand Moghol*, Paris, 1986.

———, *Dictionnaire de la Civilisation Indienne*, Paris, 1987.

———, *L'Inde de l'Islam,* Paris, 1989.

Gardner, Alexander, *Memoirs*, London, 1898.

Gardner, Brian, *The East India Company*, 1971.

Gascoigne, Bamber, *The Great Moghuls,* London, 1971.

Gemelli, Careri, *Voyage autour du Monde*, 6 vol., Paris, 1726.

Grenard, Fernand, *Babur, Fondateur de l'émpire des Indes*, Paris, 1930.

Griffin, Sir Lepel, *Ranjit Singh*, Oxford, 1890.

Gulbadan Begum, *Humayun Nama*, translation of A.S. Beveridge, reprint, New Delhi, 1989.

Hansen, Waldemar, *The Peacock Throne*, New Delhi, 1981.

Hanway, Jonas, *Revolutions in Persia,* London, 1762.

Hasrat, Bikramajit, *Life and Times of Ranjit Singh*, Hoshiarpur, 1977.

Hawkins, William, *Relation de la Cour du Moghol*, Paris, 1663.

Histoire de Thamas Kouli Khan, 2 vol., Amsterdam, *1740-1741.*

Howarth, Stephen, *The Koh-i-Noor Diamond*, London, 1986.

Hugel, Baron Charles, *Travels in Cashmere and the Punjab*, London, 1845.

Humieres, Robert d', *L'Ile et l'Empire de Grande-Bretagne*, Paris, 1904.

Hunter, Sir William Wilson, *The Marquis of Dalhousie,* London, 1899.

Irvine, William, *Later Mughals*, London, 1911.

———, *The Army of the Indian Moghuls,* London, 1903.

Ishwari Prasad, *The Life and Times of Humayun*, Allahabad, 1976.

Jacquemont, Victor, *Voyage dans l'Inde 1828-1831,* vol., III, Paris, 1843.

Jahangir (Emperor), *Tuzuk-i-Jahangiri*, London, 1909-1914.

Jauhar, *Tezkereh al Vakiat (Memoirs of Humayun)*, translated by Major Charles Stuart, 1832.

Kaul, H. K., *Historic Delhi* (An Anthology), New Delhi, 1985.

Kaye L. W., *History of the War in Afghanistan*, 2 vol. London, 1851

Khan, Raza Ali, *Hyderabad, A City in History*, Hyderabad, 1986.

Khosla, Ram Prasad, *Mughal Kingship and Nobility*, New Delhi, 1976.

King, C. W., *The Natural History of Precious Stones*, London, 1867.

Login, Lady, *Sir John Login and Duleep Singh*, reprint, New Delhi, 1986.

Lane-Poole, Stanley, *Mediaeval India under Mohammedan Rule*, reprint, New Delhi, 1990.

Latif, Syed Muhammad, *History of Lahore*, Lahore, 1892.

Loti, Pierre, *L'Inde sans les Anglais*, Paris, 1989.

Maasir-i-Alamgiri, translated by Sir Jadunath Sarkar, reprint, New Delhi, 1986.

Macrory, Patrick, *Kabul Catastrophe*,. Oxford, 1986.

Malik, Zahiruddin, *The Reign of Muhammad Shah*, Bombay, 1977.

Malleson, G.B., *History of Modern India*, reprint, Peshawar, 1984.

Muni, Lal, *Mini Mughals*, New Delhi, 1989.

Osborne, W.G., *The Court and Camp of Runjeet Singh*, London, 1840.

Princep, H. T., *Puissance des Sikhs dans le Penjab*, Paris, 1856.

Raychoudhary, S. C., *History of Modern India*, New Delhi, 1988.

Riazul Islam, *Indo-Persian Relations*, Teheran, 1957.

Rizvi, S. A. A., *The Wonder that was India*, vol. II, London, 1987.

Roe, Sir Thomas, *The Embassy of Sir Thomas Roe*, 2 vol., London, 1899.

Roux, Jean-Paul, *Babur*, Paris, 1986.

Sarkar, Sir Jadunath, *Anecdotes of Aurangzeb*, reprint, London, 1988.

———, *History of Aurangzeb,* 4 vol., 1912.

Sarkar, Jagdish Narayan, *The Life of Mir Jumla,* New Delhi, 1951.

Saksena, Banarsi Prasad, *History of Shah Jahan of Delhi,* Allahabad, 1958.

Scott, Jonathan, *History of the Dekkan,* 2 vol., Shrewsbury, 1794.

Sen, N. B., *History of the Koh-i-Noor,* New Delhi, 1953.

Sewell, Robert, *Forgotten Empire (Vijayanagar),* London, 1900.

Siddiqul, Abdul Majeed, *History of Golcunda,* Hyderabad, 1956.

Singh, Ganda, *Ahmad Shah Durrani,* Bombay, 1959.

Singh, Khushwant, *A History of the Sikhs,* 2 vol., New Delhi, 1963.

———, *Ranjit Singh, Maharaja of the Punjab,* New Delhi, 1985.

Sinha and Ray, *A History of India,* Calcutta, 1973.

Siyar-ul-Mutakherin, *A History of Muhammedan Power in India,* translated by John Briggs, London, 1832.

Smith, Vincent, *Akbar the Great Mogul,* reprint, New Delhi, 1988.

Spear, Percival, *A History of Delhi under the Later Mughuls,* reprint, New Delhi, 1988.

Streeter, Edwin E., *The Great Diamonds of the World,* London, 1896.

Sykes, Sir Percy, *A History of Afghanistan,* London, 1940.

Tavernier, Jean-Baptiste, *Travels in India,* reprint, New Delhi, 1977.

Trotter, L.I., *Life of Marquis Dalhousie,* London, 1899.

Weintraub, Stanley, *Victoria,* Paris, 1988.